DECLARATION OF INDEPENDENTS

SNOWBOARDING, SKATEBOARDING + MUSIC:

AN INTERSECTION OF CULTURES

DECLARATION OF INDEPENDENTS

BY THE EDITORS OF HECKLER MAGAZINE

JOHN BACCIGALUPPI, SONNY MAYUGBA, AND CHRIS CARNEL

CHRONICLE BOOKS

SAN FRANCISCO

Library of Congress Cataloging-in-Publication Data available.

ISBN 0-8118-2997-9

Printed in Hong Kong

Designed by John Baccigaluppi
Cover designed by David Carson
Letterpressed artwork that opens each chapter
by Cynthia Connolly

Distributed in Canada by Raincoast Books
9050 Shaughnessy Street
Vancouver, BC V6P 6E5

10 9 8 7 6 5 4 3 2 1

Chronicle Books LLC
85 Second Street
San Francisco, California 94105

www.chroniclebooks.com

HECKLER
SNO // SK8 // SND

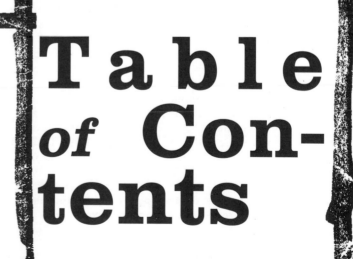

Table of Contents

Introduction: Skateboards Take You to Strange Places.

Surfing is the granddaddy of all board sports. Skateboarding was started by surfers when there were no waves. Some of the earliest snowboards had skateboards attached to them with foot straps. But this book is not about surfing for the simple reason that I, along with most of the rest of us, didn't grow up near the beach.

As we begin the next century, this country is certainly a very different place than it was at the turn of the last century. An industrial revolution followed by a technological revolution has turned a nation of farmers into a nation of worker bees. It has turned a nation of wide-open spaces into a country filled with cities, suburbs, mini-malls, and maxi-malls. With the exception of some parks and dwindling farmlands, the entire country is covered with concrete. It would seem that we've left a grim legacy for the next generation.

But a skateboard changes all that. It turns this concrete wasteland into an endless, constantly changing playground. Skaters look at things differently than other people. Where most people see an ugly strip mall, a skater sees a place of joy that will keep him or her happy and entertained for days and weeks on end. This different way of looking at things is why skaters evolve differently from the masses. As a group they are self-reliant, creative, and independent. I'm biased, but I think they're some of the best people on this planet.

Snowboarding started out in much the same way. Ignorant of each other's efforts, Jake Burton in Vermont, Mike Olsen in Seattle, and Tom Sims in Tahoe were trying to make their skateboards work in the snow along with their friends. Their only real motive was to have fun and to do something different in the winter. Out of this grew one of the biggest, most exploited, and misunderstood cultural movements of the end of the last century.

And lastly, over the past two decades independent music with "tags" like alternative, punk, and hip-hop completely changed the stale and conservative music industry. The common thread through all these genres was that creative artists were doing their own thing without regard for the mainstream. These artists pioneered the DIY ethic while creating what would eventually become, albeit in a watered-down version, the new mainstream.

Reflecting back on the last twenty years of skate/snow/music culture, **a common thread emerges. Independence. Do It Yourself. Creativity. Self-reliance. At its core is a purity that will never go away** for the true skater, boarder, or musician, no matter how overcommercialized and hyped-out things get—just like the original surfers who started the whole ball rolling.

This book reflects my own life to a large degree. I was a skater as a kid, and then a musician. I went on to a career recording records. After working in a high-priced professional studio making records that I would never have bought myself, I started my own basement studio so that my friends in punk rock bands could afford to record their music. The studio eventually moved out of the basement and into a large warehouse in a run-down neighborhood populated by the down-on-their-luck and those who preyed on them. Some of my more mainstream clients weren't too stoked at watching people smoke crack and get blow jobs, but the young bands I liked to work with loved the atmosphere and felt relaxed. We made a lot of good records at that studio with bands like Vomit Launch, 7 Seconds, Helen Keller Plaid, Knapsack, Brotha Lynch Hung, and Far. This is where I first met Sonny Mayugba, who became the force that would make *Heckler* an evolving reality. He was playing in a band called Drop Acid that was a side project for 7 Seconds vocalist Kevin Seconds. Sonny, who is a huge Metallica and Death Angel fan, was also playing in Phallucy, a popular local hard-rock band. Kevin recruited him to bring a little bit of a metal edge to the music. On drums was Abe Cunningham, who also played in Phallucy as well as in a newer, less popular, local band called the Deftones. Things have changed a bit since then.

When we first moved into the large studio, I thought it would be fun to build a quarterpipe skateboarding ramp and a basketball court into the high-ceilinged recording room. Ostensibly, this was to keep the musicians busy during the downtime, but I think I really just wanted to start skating again.

At some point just for fun (and with the hope that we would get free lift tickets) some friends—Matt Kennedy and Dave Sher—started *Heckler* magazine. The first issue was sixteen pages on the cheapest newsprint possible, and we gave it away to our friends and anyone else who wanted it. Many of those people later became our friends. Somehow it grew into a "real" magazine, and I now have a career in the publishing industry. Early on, Dave and Matt moved on and Sonny and Chris Carnel became part of *Heckler* because they too thought it would be fun. After three years of publishing, our newsprint "zine" had grown to over a hundred pages with full color and lots of advertisements. It went from a weekend hobby to a full-time job that didn't pay much and consumed our lives. We sold the magazine in 1996 to TransWorld Publications and they subsequently launched it onto the newsstand as a full color, oversized magazine, retaining us as the editors. The zine days were over, we had sold out. A year later TransWorld was bought by Times-Mirror, and they sold the magazine back to us. Since then we've shrunk the magazine down to a more economical size, traveled the world in search of places to ride, met some incredible people, and enjoyed some incredible experiences, all thanks to *Heckler*. We still work out of the same warehouse, the studio still supplies a stream of musicians hanging around the building, and the quarterpipe ramp is still there, even though it has been supplanted by several more ramps throughout the building. The three of us are partners and friends, and we still like to skate, snowboard, and play music with each other.

I'm sure I wouldn't be here if it wasn't for that first skateboard I bought when I was a kid.

This book is about those free thinking and doing people who paved the way so that today, anybody can go snowboarding (as long as they can afford it). Anybody can record and distribute their own CD. And any kid who can scrape a few bucks together for a used or new skateboard can turn their grim, urban reality into a paradise, a place for them to learn and grow up. And while some people may stop skating when they get older, they never really quit being skaters.

—*John Baccigaluppi*

Brian Plummer, skating down the street. Mural by Pheen. 8th & K Streets, Sacramento, California.

CHAPTER 1. IN THE BEGINNING

Chris Roach and Tucker Fransen on a good day at Boreal Ski Resort, California, in 1987.

In the Beginning

by Jake Burton

Starting Burton Snowboards back in '77, when the sport didn't even exist, was probably one of the stupidest things I've ever done in my life. But, that's what made it so right.

At the time, skiing was happening for a lot of people. *Skateboarder* mag was as thick as a phone book, and surfing was pretty strong. No one was asking for a new sport, yet here I was working seven days a week trying to make one happen.

Words can't describe how harsh the whole experience was. The boards were pretty much unrideable, no one was even remotely interested in selling the product, and the financial status of my company and the whole industry was a joke.

I'm often referred to as the "inventor of snowboarding." That couldn't be farther from the truth. But, from the first moment that I jumped on a Snurfer (age fourteen), I knew there was a sport there, and I've dedicated my life to making that happen.

My passion for the sport and my perseverance through the early days are the accomplishments that I am most proud of. Snowboarding would have happened and will continue to happen with me or without me, but I think I've helped make it a better sport. I was and still am dedicated, much in the same way people like Craig Kelly, Tony Alva, and Tom Burt are.

Opposite page: Jake in 1980 on an early Burton board.
Above: A New Zealand helicopter trip, 1998.
Left to right: Silk screening graphics on a board, 1981;
portraits, 1988 and 1998.

"This is T.A. calling you back. I'm down to do the interview.
I'm out streetskating right now. I'm skating and surfing every day.
I've got a new six–week–old son, Zephaniah Levi Alva. Life is good. Call me."

1995:   This is the message Tony Alva left on my machine the first time I called him. We later ended the phone-tag game and made arrangements as to where and when we would meet. A week later Chris Carnel and I were driving down the I5 in a rented dark-green Buick Skylark towards Santa Monica. Dogtown. The Memphis or maybe Nashville of modern skateboarding. Tony later called the car our "Narc-mobile" and he seemed comfortable driving it around the L.A. freeways while smoking a joint.

Chris and I spent two days skating and hanging out with Tony and his family. In case you didn't know, Tony Alva was once the most well known and highest ranked skateboarder in the world. I'm not sure where the title came from, but he was once dubbed "World Champion." In the mid-'70s when the urethane wheel was invented and skateboarding had its first big boom, Tony was the undisputed king. Back in the days when huge concrete skateparks were everywhere and *Skateboarder* magazine (*Thrasher* didn't yet exist) looked like the current issue of *TransWorld Skateboarding,* Tony and the rest of his crew pretty much dominated the skateboarding media. Santa Monica, a.k.a. "Dogtown," was at the forefront of progressive and aggressive skateboarding giving rise to skaters like Jay Adams, Stacy Peralta, Jim Muir, Bob Biniak, and Shogo Kubo. Much like San Francisco and Los Angeles today, skaters and the media made the pilgrimage to Santa Monica to seek knowledge. But this is not a story about the past. This is about the present. Tony was the first of the Dogtown skaters and now he's the last.

With the exception of Jay Adams, who moved to Hawaii and surfs every day, the rest of the Dogtown crew has quit skating. But not Tony. He skates and surfs every day and has done so for the last thirty-six years without fail. Tony is forty-three now, but he still skates like a motherfucker. His skating is all about speed, aggression, and style. Tony Alva is the Kurt Cobain of skating, just pure unadulterated soul and aggression. But instead of burning out, he grew up and matured, and he never quit skating.

We met Tony outside of his apartment in the Ocean Park (O.P. to the locals) district of Santa Monica. This is a quiet, older neighborhood overlooking the ocean just up the hill from the beach and downtown Santa Monica. After the usual greetings and settling in, we decided it was time to skate. Tony drove the Narc-mobile to a huge ditch in the Hollywood Hills called the Bronson Canyon Ditch. It was a big, fairly burly ditch with a downhill section that looked pretty fast. While Chris and I surveyed the scene, Tony took the kind of first run that only a local with years of skating under their belt can do: He took three or four big pushes on the shitty, hole-ridden service road that led up to the ditch, hit the crack on the top of the ditch, and pop-ollied into the ditch at high speed, landing halfway down the twelve-foot wall. Watching Tony skate was like watching a master bullfighter or gymnast. He's a natural with more style than most people will ever comprehend, let alone achieve. While not at the forefront of today's skating in terms of technical tricks, his aggressive, no-holds-barred skating still earns respect from anyone who watches him skate. T.A. can hold his own wherever he skates as we repeatedly witnessed over the next two days. —JB

T.A. pulls one of the first frontside airs in the Dogbowl, a classic shot by Glen E. Friedman, circa 1977.

The rest of these photos were shot in Santa Monica in 1995 except as noted.

Left: T.A. drops in at Bronson.

Right:
After our confrontation with "suit guy."
Note the vintage shirt from Skateboard,
a cheesy '70s movie that tried to capitalize
on skating's popularity at the time.
The photo is of Tony, who was a stuntman in
the movie, which starred Leif Garrett.
Chris had found the shirt in a thrift shop and
given it to Tony, who was stoked.

After skating Bronson, we left to skate a secret Santa Monica backyard pool a mile or so from Tony's apartment. As we were driving on the L.A. freeway system, more details of Tony's contributions to skating came out. Alva Skateboards is now in its fourth incarnation. Alva Skateboards was the first pro-owned skate company, even before Stacy Peralta teamed up with George Powell. Alva was the first company to manufacture skateboards out of high-quality plywood as they're still made today.

Before the Alva decks came out, skateboards were made out of big, heavy, solid pieces of hardwood and/or laminated fiberglass and even aluminum. Tony's signature pro model for Logan Earth Ski was a three-quarter-inch-thick piece of oak about twenty-six inches long and five-and-a-half inches wide with no nose and a glued-on slab of angled oak for the tail. His first model for Alva Skateboards was the precursor to today's skateboards. Soon after the Alva decks debuted, the other manufacturers followed suit.

If one's contribution to skating could be measured by how many young, talented riders they helped along with their careers, then Tony's contribution would be larger than most. Some of the riders he has sponsored include Christian Hosoi, Mark Gonzales, Eric Dressen, Adam McNatt, Ray Barbee, Ronnie Bertino, Steve Alba, Dave Duncan, Bill Danforth, and nearly three hundred other skaters, am and pro.

Circa 1975, all the skateboarding teams had matching jerseys and outfits and precise, technical, flatland-freestyle maneuvers were the norm, executed at slow speeds. Tony and the Dogtown crew showed up in their street clothes, skated fast and aggressively using the downhill ramps and banks for tricks, and dominated the contests. They pretty much changed the face of skateboarding at the time into what it is now. Reflecting on the competition scene back in those days, Tony talked about the Dogtown style: **"It's a low-center-of-gravity style based on surfing. Street-style surfing."**

We reached the pool and started to skate. Tony tore this place up as well. The tight bowl had burly coping that stuck out about three inches, but this didn't stop T.A. Tony rides only thirty-four- and thirty-six-inch long boards. He likes a larger board and says it rides smoother. When Tony skates these thirty-six-inch decks, they don't look like a long board because his skating is even larger.

The next day, we had planned on getting up early and shooting some surfing shots. But the surf was flat so we slept in. We ended up tooling around Santa Monica separately and hooked up later in the morning to shoot some streetskating shots downtown. Tony started streetskating before it was called streetskating. It was just skating. He skates street just like he skates banks and pools: full-on, fast, aggressive, and stylish. Riding the thirty-six-inch deck, he pulls bluntslides, shove-its, Smith grinds, board slides, nose slides, fast, fat ollies, and very tasty one-footed nose manual 360s. And of course he shoots the hills of the city at high speeds, dodging cars, running red lights and stop signs. "These are my streets," he says. "I know every crack of every sidewalk there is down here."

Tony in a backyard Santa Monica pool, as we pay homage to a famous vintage shot from Skateboarder *magazine in the '70s.*

I had remarked to Tony the previous night that he seems to have mellowed quite a bit from his bad-boy image of the early Dogtown days. He replied that he had just grown up and matured. But, **we found out that morning that the early Tony Alva was only put away inside and was channeled into his skating. The right situation would quickly bring it out.**

We were skating a bench in front of a trendy hair salon in downtown Santa Monica and Tony was doing high-speed board slides on it. Some older balding guy in a suit came up to us and in a very condescending and irritated voice asked Tony, "Can you go play somewhere else?"

"Fuck you! I'm not playing, this is my job. I was born and raised on these streets. I've got a fuck of a lot more right to be here than you do. I make as much money as you do doing what I like and I don't have to wear a fucking suit. Go back to the Valley, you fucking kook."

Then T.A. pulled the fastest, longest, and most aggro board slide he'd done yet and ended it with a power slide into the suit-guy's face.

"You call that play!" Tony screamed into the guy's face.

This just pissed off suit-guy even more and he went and sat down on the edge of the bench in an attempt to make Tony stop "playing." It didn't really work though, because Tony just kept skating the bench around the guy. After a few more minutes Tony had had enough and quit skating the bench.

"See you later Mr. Uptight!" he shouted at the suit-guy. "Have a nice day."

So, suit-guy was renamed Mr. Uptight as we left him to his job and went down to the beach to skate. Later we were talking about the incident and Tony elaborated on his views on life. "Defy authority," he said. "Don't let people tell you how to run your life. The world is a wide-open book, experience it. Your dharma is your purpose in life. You can't stray from that when you find it. Skateboarding is my dharma, the center of my universe. Go with your heart."

The rest of the day Tony continued to refine his dharma. Next we hit the Basic Bowl. This is another famous SoCal hot spot with a pool built for skating by the Street Rod clothing guys. The pool is a clover design, with ten-foot, seven-foot, and four-foot bowls all connected to each other. When we got there, there was a full-on session already in progress. Pool ripper Dave Reul lived at the Basic house, and he had the pool wired. Huge technical airs, aggro grinds, and lines that wouldn't stop. Also skating was Badlands legend Steve Alba, who still skates as full-on now as he did when he was a top-ranked pro. Like Reul, he had the pool wired with fat airs, endless lines and grinds, but he also had another trick called "Put a helmet on your infant son's head and then hold onto him while you carve the pool." Everybody seemed impressed, and Steve's son would start crying if he didn't get enough runs in. Needless to say, T.A. more than held his own, aggressively skating the pool. Besides the usual grinds and airs, he was pulling speed ollies over the hip and backside airs to disasters. It was one of the best skate sessions I've witnessed. After an hour or two, Tony found out from Alba that there was another empty pool on the way back to Tony's house. We decided to cut out early and go check it out before it got dark.

The pool was called the Champion Bowl and it was in a very sketchy part of Inglewood between the racetrack and the Coliseum. It was at a huge, deserted, abandoned motel and it felt like we were on the set of some weird movie about gangs roaming the Earth after a nuclear explosion killed most everybody off.

Chris was uneasy about his camera gear and I was just plain uncomfortable. Even Tony seemed a little off. "Let's just shoot the photos and get out of here," he said.

In the shallow end there was some gang graffiti with names and tally marks after each name. Most were between two and four. I was thinking that the numbers represented how many skaters each gangbanger had jacked. But the pool was ripping and T.A. wanted to skate. Pretty soon he was ripping too, and Chris got some of the best photos of the trip. After about thirty minutes, more skaters showed up and the vibe was much improved. Kevin "The Worm" Anderson was ripping the pool on a circa 1981 Alva deck with a one-inch nose and his buddy Scott was ripping just as hard on a new-school seven-inch-wide street deck. It was a meeting of the generations, coming together to enjoy the pool. Old, new, age, whatever.

Tony at the Champion Bowl.

Let's just skate. And we did.

"Your dharma is your purpose in life.
You can't stray from that when you find it.
Skateboarding is my dharma,
the center of my universe."

It was finally time to split, and shortly thereafter, Chris and I were back on the I5 headed north back home. It had been a fun two days and we were both stoked—stoked that we got to ride so many great spots with one of the living legends of skateboarding. But we were also stoked that we got to meet a very cool person. It is rare to meet people who are as balanced, focused, and at peace with themselves as Tony Alva is. T.A. may not be the big name or big industry that he and Alva Skateboards once were, but before the media discovered Dogtown in 1976, skating was underground and Tony skated every day. Nothing has changed. Tony's made his contribution to the sport and it's irreversible. He's seen the big money come and go and he seems very content with where he is. "You're wealthy if you have good health," Tony remarked at one point.

Not many people return to the underground or go back to their roots after a taste of the big time, but Tony never left. "Life is good if you're good to yourself," Tony went on to say. T.A. has been skating every day for twenty-seven years and shows no signs of slowing down. He seems happy, and that's something that many people search for and never find.

I suspect that Tony Alva will always be a wealthy man. May we all be so lucky.

Tony at the BFE pool in 1999.

IAN MacKAYE

Ian's a skateboarder and musician (first with Minor Threat and then Fugazi) and barely needs an introduction. Sonny and I were stoked to meet and talk with him before a Fugazi show at the Daily Grind skatepark in Sacramento in 1996. A lot has been written about how Ian's a legend and how much integrity he has. But he's also a skater, and like most skaters he's real people. —JB

ON SKATEBOARDING

I started skating when I was thirteen. We used to do this thing called dog-fighting where two people rode down a hill together and tried to knock each other off their skateboards. We also used to do catamarans—that's two people sitting on their boards facing each other and intertwining their legs. You steered by leaning back and forth.

The first time I saw a skateboarder was in some magazine, so me and my friend John Hargadon started skating along with my brother and a couple of other kids. Then there was this other kid I had met just before I went to California. He was this cool guy who had a BB gun. When I was out of town for nine months, something bad went down between him and my old friends, my close friends. So I came back and he was out basically beating their ass and stuff. I was getting my ass beaten by him too. As it turned out, he also skated and just because of the fact that we skated, we became friends. That was Henry Rollins.

So I knew Henry when we were eleven years old. Our friendship from the very beginning was like, "OK he has the BB gun, he had the Cheech and Chong records." He was a tough kid man. I would be hanging with my friend John and we'd see Henry coming up the street and Henry was after John so we would run, 'cause he was scary. But when we were skating, Henry and us, we became really close friends.

Then we formed a team, Team Sahara in 1976. I still have the T-shirts. Our colors were black and gold and we were all inner-city Washington, D.C., kids. Chevy Chase was a neighborhood up the street and kids up there were skating at the same time on their own ramps, and we met up with them. That's when we started jumping into pools. We had been building ramps for a while. At first, just one-shot deals with one sheet of plywood, then we got two. Then those kids were making ones with four. These ramps were only four feet wide so it was very scary. So we started getting really busy building ramps

and stealing a lot of plywood and that kind of stuff. We built our own little skatepark in an abandoned police station down in Georgetown called Cell Block 19 and we built all these different kinds of ramps. We discovered how to make curved ramps by wedging a board up against a brick wall and nailing it down to something heavy, and we'd see how many bricks we could get up the wall. That was a really cool little park.

Meanwhile up in Bethesda, which is a richer suburb, there was this skate shop called the "F & R Sunshine House" and they had their team. They were these suburban kids who were good skaters. We'd go to contests and there would be other teams from Ocean City and all these little sponsored teams and Team Sahara, which wasn't sponsored by anybody, just a bunch of city kids. But we were good. We had a good team, we had a couple of really good skaters, a couple of really good freestylers. Henry was a good freestyler. I wasn't that great of a skater; I never won contests. Maybe one time I won a slalom, but we were always out there and we had good presence and everyone was scared of us 'cause we were the city kids.

At the time, it was like, "D.C." Nobody could believe we skated there much less lived there. So what happened was Finnegan and Roberts (The "F & R" from the Sunshine House) actually came to us and said we want you to join our team and we're like "no way." I said, "If you want to sponsor us and give us discounts, we'll put F & R on our Team Sahara T-shirt. But we don't want to be on F & R, we're Team Sahara and that's it."

I kept on skating until I got into punk. It's funny, I felt punk and skating didn't have anything to do with each other. I was really into skating then I started getting into punk and I was like, "enough skating." And then the next thing I know, Tony Alva cuts his hair and Jay Adams cuts his hair and all these guys were going punk. Then I got back into it and skated a lot and I'll still ride at home now and then.

It kinda sucks; to me skating is a communal thing and I don't have any friends who skate at all. Most of my friends who did skate don't skate anymore or they moved away. If I go skating, I go by myself and it's kinda bleak. When you're by yourself, you stop and think "whatever," whereas when you're with a friend, you can talk about shit and take a break. It's a real communal thing and meditative, but for me, being alone, it sometimes makes me feel like I'm wasting my time.

There's a schoolyard in Washington that we used to drive by every day, and there was a perfect cement bank about four or five feet high, real mellow. But there was this grass field only three feet in front of it, so we were like "If they would only pave that shit that would be great!" About four years ago, I drove by and it was paved. I fucking pulled right over and got out and looked at it and I couldn't believe it. I went and got my board and came back with my dog. I got there and there were these two kids with their small boards and skinny wheels and I have my ten-inch-wide board, about thirty inches long, my big fat fuckin' '80s deck. I don't know if you've noticed, but on the cover of the Minor Threat single, "Salad Days," there's a picture with a skateboard in the corner and it has a Minor Threat sheep spray-painted on the grip tape. I still have that same skateboard.

So I get to the park and those two kids are skating and I'm like "Ah shit, somebody's already here," but I thought "Fuck that, I came all the way over here to skate." They're doing ollies and stuff and I don't ollie. I have this primitive version of the ollie before ollies were invented. It's this kick I used to do, but I do mostly slides and stuff like that. So these kids are staring at me and I flash back to '78 or '79 when me and Henry were skating this bank and this guy comes over and is like "Hey man, I'm a skateboarder," and he's like barefoot and doin' all these old-school tricks, and it's funny, 'cause I'm that guy now. These kids are

looking at me like "What the fuck is this guy's style? His board is so fat." I know how ruthless skaters can be, but I can give a fuck. Then they kind of whisper, "Hey, he's that guy in that band."

I try to be shameless in life. I think that's really the ticket. I know even hanging for a few seconds you feel that vibe and you get snaked. What a fucked-up feeling that is. I can remember, we used to go to the skatepark and these kids used to snake. It was a really dangerous approach cause you had to come off this hill before you could drop into the pool. They would come up behind you and snake in front and it was really fucked because they would slam you. They were these locals from Alexandria and they would do this shit and we would get into the push and the shove. We were bad guys too.

I love skating. I was a very moderate skater. I'm sad for the times in my life when I got caught up with other people and didn't keep going. There were some moments when I can remember doin' some incredible backside carves, totally edging along the coping and every time I'd do it, just hitting that same line and totally carving right out of the fucking pool. I would do that for an hour and somebody would say you're insane and I thought about it, but man it's so easy. Then I would think about it some more: "Man, how *did* I do that?" and psych myself out.

To this day, and I don't skate a lot now, I still will wake up in the morning, and during this little period of time between being dead asleep and actually getting up, while I'm lying in bed, I'll just dream about riding along the tiles of a pool. **I think skating was a really super-important part of my life, mostly because it gave me yet another extremely good opportunity to redefine the world that I lived in.** Most people, when they walk down the street, see the sidewalk and the street, they see a wall, and a hill up against a parking lot or something. But from my point of view, and all skaters' points of view, you see everything different, concrete is a whole different language to you. Even when I'm driving today it's like subliminal and I see a little hill, I think that looks pretty sweet. It just gave me an opportunity to redefine the world I lived in and that process of redefinition can actually parlay itself into any area of life.

Tony Alva & Ian in 2000
at the Arlington, Virginia, Vans Skatepark opening.

It's about reassessing what's given and making it work for you: that's what skating is all about. It's also making something out of nothing. You got a street and a skateboard—make something out of it. Go steal a bunch of traffic cones and slalom. We also had our own little company called DC Skates and we made boards, terrible boards though. My favorite board was the speedboard. It was narrow in the front and back with a wide belly so you could kneel in the middle. It had really wide trucks for maximum stability. We would have the trucks tight to keep them from wobbling with these four-inch-wide Sims wheels. We would downhill a lot, that was really fun. You'd have to do it late at night to avoid some really hairy accidents.

I remember reading that Alva interview in *Heckler.* He's an interesting guy. He was a really big hero to me and Henry and all the kids in D.C. I can remember when I met him back in 1980, he was a part of the insane total punk gang. Him and his brother Mark Alva, totally getting into these crazy fights. He was an HB [Huntington Beach] kid at the time. As a matter of fact, the first time I met Jay Adams I was playing in Minor Threat and we were playing at a place called Dancing Waters in San Pedro. I'm playing and there were all these kids in the front screaming, and I fall down and this one guy was screaming along with the song and I put the mic up to him and he just bites me on the arm. "Motherfucker!" BAM! I gave him a little crack, you know. That was Jay Adams. He was like "I fuckin' love you!" Jay Adams was insane.

ON MUSIC

Minor Threat broke up in 1983. It was time to stop, we didn't like each other enough. That's the thing. It's like a union, the four of us were working on something, and you're always going to have tension, but it's always a matter of the balance. When is it not worth the trouble or when is it not productive? We just didn't agree as a band about what to do with the band. Those guys wanted to get a manager, they wanted to consider signing contracts, and I just didn't want to do any of that stuff. They were also all really into U2 and were writing a lot of songs that sounded like U2. Keep in mind this was 1983, before U2 was really mega-mega, but it was a very bad sign. I was "Naw, I can't go there," and they were like, "Well, we have to go there." Actually, I have some really great practice tapes with about seven minutes of music and about eighty-three minutes of arguing. Fugazi doesn't argue that much 'cause we all have been in so many fucking bands that we know about it, we just know.

I didn't expect Dischord to be anything. I just wanted to cut my friends' records. Actually, I still do. It's weird I never thought it would be still going. I think about it when I'm driving, I do all the driving, the whole time, just thinking about all these different kinds of things. It's weird to be here. I was in Sacramento in '83 with Minor Threat and it was one of the weirdest shows of all time. I remember we were playing and I think 7 Seconds opened for us. We were having a problem because the P.A. guy was being a total fucking prick and treating us very poorly. It made me mad because we're headlining and we're the reason people came out to see the show, and we're the guys paying him, and he's treating us like a bunch of little assholes. He kept saying, "Dude, if you don't like it, you don't have to use the P.A."

So I was like OK, you're fucking with the wrong guy here. So right before we went on, I went up to him and told him, "Get your P.A. off the stage."

He was like, "What?"

"Get your P.A. off the stage. All night you've been threatening me about not using your P.A. I'm not going to even fucking touch your P.A. I don't want it anywhere near me."

He was like "Aw, come on, you gotta use a P.A."

"I'm not using the P.A., not going to happen." Then this big argument broke out and he's like "You have to use the P.A."

"I'm not going to use it, you're a fucking asshole and you've been threatening me so fuck you! Your P.A. is swill as far as I'm concerned." So I agreed to leave the actual stacks, but we covered them with curtains, and all the mics and the wires were off the stage, and I did the whole show with no P.A. I had to do the show with no mic. People were kind of bummed. I said to them, "There's no P.A. because the P.A. guy is a dick and he thinks he can threaten us, so here's the music. **I'll be singing, but you motherfuckers sing too.**"

"Fugazi" is a military slang word from the Vietnam era meaning "fucked up situation." I was reading a book called *Nam* by Mark Baker. It's a book of reflections of Vietnam veterans and at one point, this guy said everything was "Fugazi." I looked it up in the glossary and it said, "fucked up situation." It was right at the point when we were getting ready to do our first show and I was desperately trying to come up with a name, anything other than "Ian's New Band." It was really important for me and the band to not be "Ian's New Band." We all have an equal sharing part.

Minor Threat was a good band and I have no regrets about that band. I also have no regrets about breaking up. I knew right then and there that we could stay together and it would totally undermine the impact of the band. Some people tell me, "You should do another show." I'm thirty-three. If the four of us got on stage again, it would be a fucking joke. You don't want to fuck things up; don't let nostalgia fuck with the memories. Memories are awesome. Things that happened are important, but they're just there to be fucking thought about. They're not there to be re-created. They can't be re-created because the context is so completely different.

"Jay Adams was insane."
—*Ian MacKaye*

"Jay Adams for sure."
—*Mark Gonzales on who he would induct into the skateboarders' hall of fame.*

"You know who really rules is Jay Adams. He's a fucking freak from hell, totally fucking always on the run. He's just fucking cooler than fuck. That guy rules."
—*Duane Peters*

Jay Adams in Venice, California, 1988.

TERRY KIDWELL

BY MIKE CHANTRY AND CHRIS CARNEL
INTRODUCTION BY BOB KLEIN

When we think of the roots of snowboarding, who do we think about? Do you think of the guy from Finland that was snowboarding in 1932? Maybe. Do you think of Tom Sims and his red graphics and the connection to skateboarding? Probably. Do you think of Jake Burton? More than likely. Do you think of Chuck Barfoot and his perpetual struggle-just-to-make-ends-meet story? Maybe. It actually doesn't take much to think of any of these stories because the media has publicized them very well and they are really cute stories that give you a warm feeling inside.

How many of you wonder how the actual riding progressed? How many of you wonder who has pushed the sport further and faster than anyone? You probably think about one of the names above, or the obvious: Terje Haakonsen, Craig Kelly, Shaun Palmer. Those guys are great, and each has contributed to our sport in a huge way. There is a name, though, that should precede any other when we talk about roots, history, and contributions to the sport. Most people don't recognize the name anymore, and sadly, most don't appreciate or understand how Terry Kidwell has had a direct impact on their riding. Sure, you could say if it wasn't him, it would have been someone else, but no one has done what Terry has. He was the first real star of snowboarding. In the early to mid-'80s, Terry was Terje! He won every contest he entered, whether it was racing or freestyle. Terry helped make halfpipes what they are today by spending more time and energy digging the first renditions of pipes. The funny thing is that most people discount his riding abilities today because of his age, but just watch him ride! He can still podium with the best of 'em!

Terry had a hard time pushing his name as a star because he's a real modest guy, and he always thought there was someone out there who was equally talented or better. The reality is that there was no one better, with the exception of Allen Arnbrister, but he fell into the trouble trap and left the door wide open for Terry.

What sets Terry Kidwell apart from other "pioneers" is the fact that he always put riding first, and he never tried to capitalize financially. Terry just wanted to be the best, and he had a hell of a lot of fun doing it.

Above: Terry at Donner Ski Ranch in 1985.

Facing page: Terry at the Donner quarterpipe in 1985, with Bud Fawcett shooting in the foreground.

Upper right corner: Tom Sims and Terry at Mt. Baker in 1985.

The following interview was conducted between Terry, Mike Chantry, and Chris Carnel. Chantry has ridden with Kidwell for almost twenty years and has filmed all of Terry's classic groundbreaking footage. We conducted the interview amid Chantry's houseful of video cassettes. If they were all spliced together they would easily wrap twice around the Earth. Here's the finished splice.

CHRIS: WHO WAS THE FIRST ONE TO DISCOVER THE TAHOE CITY HALFPIPE?

Terry: I think Allen Arnbrister was the first to discover it.

MIKE: I PERSONALLY CAN'T REMEMBER WHO THE FIRST ONE WAS.

CHRIS: BUT IT HAD TO BE BUILT UP, RIGHT?

MIKE: YEAH, AND THEN ONCE SOMEBODY BAILED ON IT YOU'D BE LIKE, "SHIT!" AND SPEND THE WHOLE DAY FIXING IT (LAUGHING).

CHRIS: HOW DID YOU FIGURE OUT A HALFPIPE ON A SNOWBOARD?

Terry: I think just by skating, mostly in the summer. Well, actually we were out four-wheeling in the summer and we saw this ditch-like gully. We figured if we came back, once the snow was flying, we could probably snowboard in it.

MIKE: YOU GUYS WERE OUT THERE CARPETING IT ONE YEAR SO IF YOU BAILED YOU WOULDN'T HIT THE ROCKS (LAUGHING). THEY WOULD JUST EAT YOUR BOARD ALIVE.

CHRIS: DID YOU EVER THINK THE FOOTAGE THAT CHANTRY FILMED OF YOU THERE WOULD SIGNIFY THE BEGINNING OF FREESTYLE SNOWBOARDING? DID IT SEEM THAT SIGNIFICANT AT THE TIME?

Terry: No, not really, it was us just doing our thing day to day. We never expected it to be the beginning of the freestyle snow-boarding era or anything like that (laughs).

MIKE: YOU HAD NO CLUE YOU WERE GONNA BE THE GODFATHER OF FREESTYLE, HUH?

Terry: Back then it was just as far as a quarterpipe went trying to find something to hit like skateboarding. But you could do all the tricks you couldn't do on a skateboard 'cause it was a softer landing when you crashed. The progression curve was quicker compared to a skateboard where you knew it was gonna hurt when you slammed (laughs). Didn't really progress too much at skating because of just that.

CHRIS: WHO KIND OF INFLUENCED YOU AT THE TIME, ANY SKATEBOARDERS?

Terry: Yeah, pretty much Allen Arnbrister. I was best friends with him back then and he was one of the best skaters up here in Tahoe. All the local kids watched him and what he was doing. He was the best local snowboarder at the time too. I watched Allen and tried to learn from him in those days.

CHRIS: HOW DID YOU GUYS HOOK UP WITH TOM SIMS? I REMEMBER SEEING PHOTOS OF YOU GUYS ON WINTERSTICK BOARDS BEFORE THAT.

MIKE: TOM WOULD COME UP WITH HIS R&D [RESEARCH AND DEVELOPMENT] BOARDS: TWELVE BOARDS IN A BAG, A BOX ALL TAPED TOGETHER, AND A BUNCH OF BINDINGS. HE RAN INTO TERRY AND ALLEN AND GOT 'EM TO TRY BOARDS OUT. WINTERSTICK WAS GETTING A LITTLE SICK OF YOU GUYS RETURNING BOARDS FROM BREAKING SO MANY OF 'EM (EVERYONE LAUGHS).

Terry: Helped make 'em go bankrupt (laughing).

MIKE: EVERY WEEK OR TWO YOU WERE CALLING 'EM FOR A NEW ONE SO I JUST TOLD TOM ABOUT THESE GUYS AND A FEW OTHER LOCALS.

CHRIS: WHEN YOU WERE FILMING TERRY BACK THEN, WHAT WERE YOUR THOUGHTS ON THE SPORT? DID YOU TAKE IT THAT SERIOUS?

MIKE: I THOUGHT IT WAS SERIOUS ENOUGH TO QUIT SKIING. WHEN TOM SIMS FIRST CAME UP IN '77–'78 IT WAS THOSE FIRST FUNKY PLASTIC BOARDS. THE VIDEO FOOTAGE I DIDN'T START DOING TILL DECEMBER OF '84, RIGHT BEFORE THE LAST WORLD CHAMPIONSHIPS AT SODA. RIGHT BEFORE TOM SOLD 'EM OUT TO BRECKENRIDGE FOR A DOLLAR, GAVE AWAY THE NAME AND EVERYTHING; KINDA GAVE AWAY OUR SPORT (LAUGHING). HOOKED UP WITH SIMS AND THE REST IS HISTORY; TERRY GOT HIS FIRST SIGNATURE ROUNDTAIL AND THEN WENT THROUGH ALL THE OTHER COMPANIES. THE GOOD TIMES AND THE BAD TIMES KIND OF THING; LIKE A ROLLER-COASTER RIDE WASN'T IT?

CHRIS: WHAT DO YOU THINK ABOUT THE CURRENT STATE OF SNOWBOARDING RIGHT NOW? DO YOU THINK RIDERS ARE PROPELLED INTO A STAR STATUS TOO QUICKLY?

Terry: I think that the riders that have the superstar status today worked their way into it, whereas three or four years ago you were getting riders that were big and didn't have the ability to back it up. Today it's much tighter to build the superstar status as a snowboarder, the ones that do have that classification really can back it up by good riding. For a while there everybody was turning pro because the companies thought you had to have a pro model out to make it. It was like, who the hell's that? It finally weeded itself out to where the superstars really are at the top of our industry. It's not just marketing anymore.

MIKE: BACK WHEN CRAIG [KELLY] WAS ON TOP FROM MT. BAKER AND JOSE [FERNANDES] WAS BIG IN EUROPE, THEY HAD ALL THESE CLONE RIDERS FOLLOWING THEM AROUND. LIKE THE CRAIG KELLY CLONES. DID YOU SEE RIDERS EMULATING YOUR STYLE?

Terry: I don't know, I guess I really didn't notice.

MIKE: EVERYBODY HAD CRAIG'S STANCE AND EVERYTHING DOWN BUT I NEVER REALLY SAW THAT EMULATING GOING ON FOR YOU.

CHRIS: I KIND OF THINK IN A CERTAIN ASPECT THAT I SAW MAYBE MORE OF A SIMILARITY WITH PALMER.

MIKE: PALMER WASN'T A CLONE BY ANY MEANS BUT KINDA TOOK TERRY'S STYLE AND PUT POWER INTO IT. HE WAS GOING HUGE BACK THEN AT BRECK [BRECKENRIDGE, COLORADO]. TERRY'S RESPONSIBLE FOR HELPING ALL THESE RIDERS GET STARTED. YOU DIDN'T REALLY HAVE THE YOUNGER BOARDERS RIDING LIKE YOU, MAYBE A FEW BUT NOT TO THE EXTENT OF THE OTHER GUYS.

Terry: I think it might have to do with the fact that when I was at home it was a lot of my friends I'd snowboard with most of the time. They weren't top-notch pro riders but I had more fun riding with them even though their level of riding wasn't super high. I didn't really get caught up in the whole groupie thing that was happening.

MIKE: BUT BOARDING HADN'T REALLY TAKEN OFF THEN WHEN YOU WERE CREATING YOUR STYLE, THE LEGEND AND EVERYTHING. THEN CRAIG CAME ALONG AND THAT WAS LIKE THE FIRST SURGE OF SNOWBOARDING AND YOU COULD SEE IT. WHOEVER WAS LEADING THE PACK, IT WAS AN EMULATION OF THEIR STYLE. THEY NEVER DID THAT WITH YOU, WHICH IS COOL TOO; IT'S KINDA LIKE A TRIBUTE.

Terry: Yeah (laughing).

MIKE: I'M GLAD I GOT ALL THAT FOOTAGE; THE BEST AND WORST OF THE STARS IN THE BEGINNING. PRETTY CLASSIC. I'LL BE WORKING WITH THE HATCHETTS TO RELEASE A LOT OF IT; I'VE GOT ABOUT THIRTY-FIVE TAPES OF TERRY, ALLEN, PALMER. PLUS A LOT OF THE ROCK STARS OF THE INDUSTRY, LIKE JOEL [GOMEZ]. HAHAHAHHA. CHUCK BARFOOT AND ALL THE OLD BURTON GUYS. THE OLD FAMILY.

CHRIS: SO GIVE ME A RUNDOWN ON THE COMPANIES YOU RODE FOR.

Terry: First it was Sims, then it was still Sims even though Vision financially took over, then Apocalypse, and actually after that there was this company called Tran Snowboard out of Europe and I worked with them for about six months before going to Haz-Mat; that lasted for about four years. Now I guess I will be riding for myself (laughing).

CHRIS: WHAT YEARS DID YOU WIN THE WORLD CHAMPIONSHIPS?

Terry: '84 through '87.

CHRIS: WHAT WAS THE MOST MONEY YOU EVER MADE FROM SNOWBOARDING AND DID IT MARK A SPECIAL PLACE IN YOUR CAREER? (EVERYONE LAUGHS.)

Terry: A whole year's total or one day?

MIKE: BIGGEST PURSE YOU EVER WON?

Terry: I think it was like '86 and there was this contest up in Canada. I won the GS [giant slalom], I won the Slalom, and I won the Halfpipe; got about six hundred bucks (everyone laughs again).

CHRIS: WHO PUT THAT ON, KEN ACHENBACH?
MIKE: YEAH, ACHENBACH WAS RUNNING THE SUNSHINE VILLAGE STUFF.

Terry: I don't think I won more than five hundred bucks for anything in particular for any first place back then. I was snowboarding all the time and thought I would enter some contests. I just kinda took it in stride. Back then I don't think too many people had the opportunity to snowboard every day as far as having to work and make money. I used to just save up to snowboard all winter. Go to these contests, just get lucky, and do good at 'em. I guess at that point Tom Sims realized the importance of riders being used to better promote their product and picked up a bunch of us from Tahoe right away hoping that we would all take first places and be able to advertise and promote his boards.

Photos: Terry on a powder day at Mt. Rose, Nevada, 1996, and at home in 1998 with his new team shirt.

NORM SAYLER

I watched him kick Noah Salasnek off the mountain once, not caring who he was. But Norm's also a softy: "I remember when Rippey used to come up here with Carnel and they'd slide the handrails on the cabins. That caused me so much grief with all the Rippey wannabes trying to slide those rails." Of course he smiles as he tells the story.

With ski resorts continuing to consolidate, Donner Ski Ranch was one of the last independently owned resorts in the country. But in late 2000 Norm finally had to sell the ranch. And while its future as a place to ride is unclear as of this writing, the Donner vibe will live on in the memories of many. It's a small but super fun, low-key mountain where a lot of riders got their start. —JB

When we started coming up here we had to drive through downtown Roseville, downtown Loomis. You went right through the middle of every town up through Auburn. People complain about the drive now; well, many times it would take us six or seven hours to drive up from Sacramento. And when you got to Baxter, you put your chains on, you never even thought about it because we were going skiing. We didn't care what the weather was like. There was no snow or road report. When you got to Baxter if the road was closed, it was closed, and if it was open it was open. No hesitation, you just went for it. Now people complain if there's a flake of snow on the road. "Gosh, I'm not going to go up there." Back then, we respected the people who worked to get the road open for us. The snowplow operators, the California Highway Patrol, whoever it was who was out there. We went up and they said "You can't go up." We said, "Fine, we'll just sit down and wait." In those days, there were no studded tires, no 4WD, you either put chains on or you didn't go through. End of story.

When we used to ski here, there were no groomed runs. When we had snow that we couldn't ski, we would ride to the top of the T-Bar and sidestep all the way to the bottom. God forbid the son of a bitch who skied on our sidestepped snow before we got a chance.

In the early days of snowboarding,

Norm Sayler opened up Donner Ski Ranch to the sport when most of the other resorts had banned it. Although it wasn't a huge mountain, many of snowboarding's early pioneers cut their teeth at Donner because Norm gave them a place to ride. I met Norm after he banned *Heckler* from Donner due to some content in the mag. I went up to Donner to talk to him about censorship and freedom of speech. I got schooled, *Heckler* was no longer blackballed, and I've been friends with him ever since. Every spring, Norm opens up Donner for our annual Heckler party, and along with all of us and the kids, the legends come back: Dave Seaone, Mike and Tina Basich, Tom Burt, Jim Rippey, Mike Chantry, and more. They all pay their respects to Norm, a real hard-ass.

1995:
That old A-frame hut on the backside of Donner, that's the old Sierra Club hut. They used to call this mountain Signal Peak. They had a rope tow that they built in 1935. If you look at the Who's Who of skiing in California, they all started with the Sierra Club. Lang's Crossing by Nyack, there used to be a rope tow there. Yuba Gap, there was a rope tow there. I started skiing at Donner Ski Ranch in 1949 when there was nothing here but a T-bar and a couple of rope tows. In 1955 I helped to build the first chairlift. My wife and I took over as managers in 1958. Now my family owns the ranch. We started with nothing. My wife and I started with $233 to our name. We were lift ops just like all these people who are coming up now, standing out in the cold doing the jobs. I said, "Hey, I gotta live, I might as well live up here." I got lucky and was able to put some stuff together and buy the place.

Above left: Norm in 2000 at The Ranch. Above: The Fifth Annual Heckler Day party, 1998. Left to right: Amy Comeaux, Danielle Bostick, Mike Basich, unidentified, Edgar Rivera, Bryce Kanights, Dave Seaone, unidentified, Randy Katen, unidentified, Tucker Fransen, Don Bostick, Paula Wickstrom and Norm Sayler.

Lance Mountain is a legendary early member of the Bones Brigade. He skated all terrain: vert, pools, ditches, street, and was an early handrail rider. He's now married, and his son, Lance Jr., skates. He also founded his own skate company called The Firm.

LANCE MOUNTAIN

BY RON CAMERON

So how's everything going, Lance? Are you happy?

Yeah. It's going great.

What would be a perfect happy day from start to finish? What would be your dream day?

To me, having every day be a little bit different is what I enjoy. I really can't stand having the same day over and over. Some days I really want to go skating and be on a tour, some days I wanna do artwork, some days I wanna shoot pictures of people, and some days I just want to hang out with people. I like variety. I can't stand the same thing, it really drives me down.

Do you still find time enough to skate a lot?

It goes on and off. I've been skating a lot lately. There have been times when I haven't skated. I've owned the business for almost five years now, and for the first year and a half I could not skateboard. I couldn't find the time. It was so new to me that I was overwhelmed, and at that time skateboards turned into floppy disks. I didn't even know how to skate. I was like tripping out—like why am I in skateboarding if I can't do it anymore? I just didn't have the time, you know? But now, yeah, I make the time. There's times when I wish I only skated. I wish I was only a pro again. But if I was ever pro again, I'd be like I wouldn't know what to do. Get up at five and maybe go skate. I'd die of boredom!

How long have you been pro?

I turned pro for Variflex in 1981. It might have been the beginning of '82. I was an amateur for them for two years. My friends and I built a halfpipe, a vert ramp, in 1978. These guys were like four years older than me. They built it with a flat bottom, which was way ahead of its time. No ramps had flat bottoms. We rode skateparks too. We were fairly good and they wanted us to ride for the parks. So I was watching my friend, and he was like, "No, don't ride for anybody." So I never did, but then he was like fading out a little bit more, and I was like—I'll get some free stuff! You know? At that time I was like a local dude on Variflex, so when all the pros would come through, they'd sometimes flow me stuff cause I was one of the local guys that was fairly good at the park. Steve Olsen and Pat Brown came and skated and they were really stylish and rad. They said some things about me and I was like—whooo, kinda stoked, ya know? I guess Pat said something to Steve Olsen, and Steve Olsen said something, but I overheard it. You know, I was a little kid, and I was like, whoa, those dudes think I'm like cool, or a good skater, and have good style. So I was like whoa, getting big-headed or whatever from just a compliment.

Somebody that you thought was good thought you were good.

And then this guy asked me to ride for Variflex and at that time I was like, "No, I'm not going to ride for anybody." Then a year later I went to this amateur series and I won. Then I really wanted to ride for somebody. That was when Stevie Caballero and Scott Foss came down, and I was like, "If I'm going to ride for anyone I'm going to ride for those dudes." But they didn't like me 'cause I was a halfpipe dude; I couldn't skate right. So I followed them around, they thought I was lame.

So you were a "Varibot"? Were you ever called that when you were on there?

Oh, yeah. So I ended up going to this other contest and my board got stolen. Steve Hirsch let me ride his board. It was weird because at that contest Potatohead asked me if I wanted to ride for Indy, and I said I would. At the same time, Variflex asked me again, and I'm like, "OK, I'll ride for you guys next year. At the time, they were the guys that were inventing all the tricks. At that time, I still liked the guys that skated like Steve Olson and Duane Peters. Stylish guys. So it was kind of a strange thing, 'cause I was in the middle. I was on Variflex, and Steve Alba blew his nose at me 'cause I was on Variflex. All of a sudden I was uncool, 'cause I was on Variflex. It was cool 'cause I remember Duane and those guys were like, "Ah, he's alright, out of all of them, he's alright!" I heard them say stuff like that, and I was like, "Whoa, that's kinda cool!" But yeah, they hated Variflex guys. They'd spit on us. Actually, Eddie Elguera won this Upland contest, and they were spitting and booing at him and stuff, and he just basically left skateboarding at the top, being number one.

You always seemed like one of the later pros who were different than the rest of those guys.

That's what was rad about Variflex. When I turned amateur, they took us all on a U.S. tour and turned me pro at the end of it. I don't think any amateur ever got to go on tour before. At the end of the tour, all the pros that were pro quit. That's when I got a board, when everyone else left.

I got in a car accident and my whole life was in turmoil. Right after that I broke my collarbone. I was young, and I was really trippin' out. I didn't even dig being pro. We were only getting sixteen dollars a month. There was no use in being a pro. There were only eleven pros going to the contests, and I would get last place 'cause I'd goof off. I didn't even take it serious.

How about a little later on, when you and Neil and GSD and those guys started getting pictures streetskating and stuff, like dorky streetskating. You guys were at the forefront of street style, which changed skateboarding. What was it like back then—or had you guys always skated like that—doing streetplants and stuff like that?

When I started skateboarding, it was basically street style. The first contest we went to, we got to see a Cadillac Classic contest. Then we went to see the Freeformer contest in 1977 in the sports arena. Basically, those contests back then were street-style contests. They'd have launch ramps, people gorilla-gripping off them, riding up them and trying to do 360s and come down. So when we started skating we were doing handstands down our hill, putting a piece of board against bricks and trying to roll off it. So when I first started skating, there wasn't really vert at all, and then the Dogtown thing came in, and the magazines started showing pools and skateparks. So I kinda followed the skateboard scene all the way through. It was different than the guy that started skateboarding when ramps were already up. All they saw were ramps. I see a lot of guys nowadays, they only focus on one thing. They think it makes them excel at it, but I don't see it that way. We were high-jumping, the first contest I entered was high-jump. I don't know if I would follow it if skateboarding changed into something totally different. But it's kinda done that. If it went back to high-jumping and that's all they did and that's all that was in the magazines...I don't know, I'd probably still do it.

THERE NEEDS TO BE VARIETY, AND A LOT OF PEOPLE ONLY DO ONE KIND OF SKATING.

Well, I'm not saying anything about them. At the time that you're talking about with Neil and stuff, we were really skating the skateparks a lot, and John Lucero and Richard Armijo got kicked out of the skatepark. They'd hang out at the fence and watch us all day because they got kicked out; banned from the park. So at that time, Neil and I and Lester and all the crew were learning how to do slide 'n' rolls like really long and as far as we could in the pools and stuff, and we'd look out and John would be doing 'em on the curb out front. Stuff like that. So we'd go skate with him a little bit out front, and we'd try to make little street contests out in the parking lot. No one ever entered; it got banned. We were just messing around. That whole crew at the time was just having fun, you know?

IT SEEMED LIKE IT OPENED UP A LOT OF DOORS FOR SKATEBOARDING. I WAS FROM SACRAMENTO, AND IT LET THE AVERAGE KID HAVE FUN SKATEBOARDING AND THINK THAT HE MIGHT BE ABLE TO GET IN MAGAZINES SOMEDAY JUST DOING WHAT HE SEES IN THE MAGAZINE. ALL THE SKATEPARKS WERE CLOSING DOWN EVERYWHERE, SO IT WAS A GOOD THING.

Here's how the coverage would happen: We'd do this stuff, and the media would seize that, and they wanted to "make it happen," you know? Like they always do. So lots of times we got taken places, like, "Hey, do something." And we'd be like, "This is retarded! There's nothing to do here!" So we'd be stupid, like yeah, do something here, so we'd just hang on something, you know what I mean? That's where a lot of it came from. A lot of it was that mofo just enjoyed being around us, being dumb. So he'd always try to take us to the worst stuff and watch—and make us be stupider each time 'cause there was like nothing to do. And then people like Mark Gonzales and that type, they actually went out and started doing it. I remember this dude, he'd come to our ramp and skate. He always came at the time when we weren't skating the ramp. This guy would come early and skate by himself. I'd look out the window and he'd be looking up to see if I was looking at him. One day I took him to the bus stop and dropped him off, and he got out of the car, and just ollied up the curb, like ollied off the thing, rolled, ollied again. And I was all...what is going on? What is that? And it was Mark [Gonzales], but he wasn't "Mark" back then.

Left: Lance in the pipe at Calgary, 2000.

Above: A 1987 Bones Brigade strategy session with Steve Caballero, Lance, and Stacy Peralta.

YEAH, HE WAS JUST A KID. BACK THEN *THRASHER* HAD SEQUENCES OF RODNEY MULLEN, AND SEQUENCES OF YOU GUYS DORKING AROUND. THEN YOU JUST PUT IT TOGETHER, AND IT SEEMED LIKE IT STARTED A WHOLE NEW KIND OF SKATEBOARDING. SO I WAS ALWAYS WONDERING IF IT WAS INTENTIONAL, OR IF THE MEDIA PUSHED IT AND IT JUST BECAME THAT. THAT WAS THE ONLY WAY I COULD SEE SKATEBOARDING BACK THEN WAS THROUGH THE MAGAZINES.

Yeah, the magazines gotta come out. The magazines got so many photos. Every issue you gotta pump it up, pump it up. You get bored of the same stuff. You're looking for something new. Sometimes it's too serious, sometimes there actually is a little scene going on, and you actually want to push it—you know how it is. Now it's like rails, rails, rails....

I KNOW, WHAT'S NEXT?!

Every kid thinks handrails is what's happening. It's just that, you gotta get photos of something....Then it gets really overdone. It's the same thing, I think the dorking was really overdone. It was all because they needed photos, and they'd be like, Lance will dork around for something, and it made us be even more stupid, because we were like, "What are they [magazine photographers] doing?!"

SO WHEN THE STREET-STYLE CONTESTS HAPPENED, AND THEY STARTED GETTING WAY OUT OF HAND IN THE LATE '80S, WERE YOU GUYS JUST SICK OF IT OR WERE YOU STILL HAVING FUN? WHEN DID IT GO TOO FAR AND GET BORING?

Well, it was weird because around that time the next step was the jump ramps/streetplant thing, and it really pushed things. It really helped skating 'cause everyone could do it, you know? To me, streetplants were the same thing as breakdancing. This little circle, you came out and you'd do it, then the next guy comes in and one ups—it was just so funny!

IT ALMOST HAD NOTHING TO DO WITH SKATEBOARDING.

No, I don't think so. But it came from dorking around, then it got pushed, and it turned into this whole thing and blew up. That was a time that really bugged me in skateboarding. Vert was calculated "not as popular." Like, "Oh we got to push mini-ramps to the street guys more." When it's calculated, which it always is, but when you know about it, it's kind of weird. We had to go on a U.S. tour with a jump ramp on the roof of the car, and it's like—I couldn't even do it, you know? I couldn't even jump ramp right. You want to do a good job. You don't want to show up and be an idiot, so you try to do a good job, and you end up just getting hurt. It hurt my back, it hurt my ankles. I couldn't do it right, I was embarrassed at every demo. I liked skateboarding so I tried to do my best. I never felt I was in the position where a lot of these dudes are that are so good: that they can just hide out, and by word of mouth people say, "He's so good." I just don't feel that way. I feel like you have to do your best and excel at it.

IF YOU'RE GOING TO BE A PROFESSIONAL, IT'S A JOB.

It's a hard line. I mean, I think it's all progression. The whole jump ramp thing taught people to skate a certain way, and skateparks taught us how to skate a certain way. It was all progression right? And then it got really crazy, like real small little flippy things, freestyle and stuff. That just progressed to be what it is now, you know? And it's not just going to stay there either. That was a weird time, you know?

A LOT OF PEOPLE WERE REALLY AWKWARD ABOUT THAT TIME. TOTALLY READY TO GIVE UP SKATEBOARDING, AND GETTING MAD AT IT AND STUFF. WHICH I NEVER ACCEPTED BECAUSE I ALWAYS JUST THOUGHT SKATEBOARDING WAS FUN. AS SOON AS YOU'RE PISSED AT IT, YOU'RE LOOKING AT IT WRONG. YOU NEED TO IGNORE THE PART THAT'S MAKING YOU PISSED.

That was a weird time, 'cause there was a whole vibe going on, like... if you couldn't flip your board and land on a curb, you didn't know how to skateboard. Get out of skateboarding, get away, you have nothing to do with skateboarding, this is the only real skateboarding. That whole vibe was put out by a few people, and a lot of skaters didn't really care or think about it, but they were being used to promote that. It really cut down on the skate market. All my friends quit skateboarding. They quit buying skate-boards, and it made a smaller marketplace of skaters who are only going to buy that type of board, and the dudes that are doing that are going to be the heroes, so it's like they own the whole market. I don't think it's calculated, I just think that's just what happens.

I THINK IT'S KIND OF SAD NOW, THAT EVER SINCE I STARTED SKATING IN THE LATE '70S AND UP UNTIL THE EARLY '90S, THERE HAS ALWAYS BEEN REPRESENTATION OF THREE OR FOUR OR FIVE KINDS OF SKATEBOARDING. NOW IT SEEMS LIKE IT'S PRETTY MUCH ONE. I FEEL SORRY FOR KIDS NOWADAYS WHO ARE GROWING UP NOT KNOWING ABOUT OTHER TYPES OF SKATING. YET AT THE SAME TIME IT IS JUST SKATEBOARDING.

It's all business, which is what it comes down to. And now that people see that, they are going to capitalize on that.

CAPITALIZE ON WHAT?

Well, right now it is going to be cool to do everything, it is going to be more open. You're going to see it advertised, you're going to see it pushed, you're going to see somebody try to make money off it. The money side is what really drives what people see. And the reason they didn't, is because there was no money to be driven out of that before. Now, you see longboards all over the place because that market's there again. People advertise it again.

WHERE WOULD YOU LIKE TO SEE SKATEBOARDING GO?

That one's too quick! Just wherever it goes. Wherever skateboarding goes that's fine. It's going to go where it wants to go. I just want to be involved with it. You know, it will be a whole crew, a crew of companies claiming they put it there, when it's already there. But it goes where it wants to go. I personally want to be there, and that's about it.

Above: One-footed invert at the Ashland, Oregon Skatepark, 2000.

BONNIE & JIM ZELLERS

Jim and Bonnie Zellers are a constant in the world of snowboarding. They are consistently aware of what's going on in their immediate environment whether they're exploring steep secret slopes two miles from their house in the Lake Tahoe–Donner section of Truckee, California, or sleeping on a peak somewhere in Nepal. They're a team that explores and rides mountainous regions all over the world. When they're not watching after their young child, Dylan, they are hiking or finding powder to ride weeks after a storm. It's fair to assume the Zellers family has spiritual connections with the mountains that everyone else is lacking. —CC

Above: Bonnie, Dylan, and Jim Zellers.
Right: Jim riding Mt. Nun, Alaska, 1994.
Opposite: Bonnie riding Donner Ski Ranch, 1996.
Page 35:
The Zellers with pioneering snowboard
magazine publisher, Tom Hsieh, 1997,
and Jim riding near Juneau, Alaska, 1994.

I'M ASSUMING, JIM, THAT YOU HAD A HEAD START FROM THE REST OF THE WORLD ON SNOWBOARDING?

Jim: I got my first board pretty early on. My younger brother Joel (who now lives in Idaho) and I were snowboarding at Alpine Meadows in 1978.

DID YOU HAVE A WINTERSTICK THEN?

Jim: No, I had a Sims Lonnie Toft.

THE YELLOW BOARD WITH A SKATE DECK AND RUBBER STRAPS?

Jim: Yeah (laughing) I still have it. That year, we had a pass to ski at Alpine Meadows and then the following year we started hiking Mt. Rose.

SO THEY ALLOWED YOU TO RIDE A SNOWBOARD AT ALPINE THEN? HOW?

Jim: No, we would hike "The Promised Land" right next to the road for some good powder. No one went over there at the time so it was easy to board there. We never got kicked out.

SO YOU WERE RIDING BACKCOUNTRY BEFORE ANY OF THE RESORTS WERE LETTING SNOWBOARDS ON?

Jim: Until Slide Mountain [now the Mt. Rose resort] opened up. That's when we hooked up with Avalanche [Snowboards] and started snowboarding all the time. Then we started scheduling our classes around it. That was the year Bonnie started riding. What year was that, Bonnie?

Bonnie: I think it was '85. I graduated [from college] in '86.

I REMEMBER SEEING YOU GUYS AT MT. ROSE AROUND THAT YEAR RIDING AND DOING SHUTTLE RUNS, AND THERE WAS A GIRL WHO WAS JUST LEARNING—IT HAD TO BE BONNIE.

Jim: Oh yeah, we were doing laps there (reflecting). Oh that's right! I think I remember...another group was doing car shuttles.

Bonnie: Do you remember what year that was?

IT HAD TO BE 1986. I HAD AN AVALANCHE AERO BOARD WITH THE THREE SKEGS. IT HAD A SWALLOWTAIL AND A POINTED NOSE. THE NEXT YEAR THEY WENT FINLESS, BUT I REMEMBER MY FINS COMING OUT IN THE ICE. CHRIS SANDERS AT AVALANCHE TOLD ME, "LEAVE 'EM OUT, IT'S THE WAVE OF THE FUTURE" (LAUGHING).

Bonnie: Boards were so funky back then and way harder to ride.

Jim: Oh yeah, and I think how quickly people learn today. It took me weeks to learn riding hardpack, with no highback binding type of support. Riding powder was easy.

Bonnie: Yeah, just Fastex buckle bindings (laughing).

Jim: Tom Burt and me were like, "This is stupid." So we got a fat Wiffle-ball bat and we cut it in half, so your heel sits on part of it. And we used it as a highback. At the time we thought it worked groovy (laughing). It was ridiculous. Maybe that's why we still ride hardboots.

How did you guys [Jim, Bonnie, and Tom Burt] all hook up and start doing expeditions together?

Jim: The three of us were in a climbing class and we all really liked rock climbing. Just climbed more and more and all my heroes were climbers and big mountaineers. So it was really boring to climb and walk down. So we were like shit, let's just climb and snowboard down. The turning point was after going through the whole contest stage at like Slide Mountain and the World Championships at Soda Springs. We competed in the halfpipe had a good time and everything. Then it came down to the World's in 1988 at Breckenridge. Me, Tom, and Damian Sanders were on the Avalanche team. We competed in the halfpipe and Damian was the only one who made the top sixteen—he made it to second place. That was the year Bert Lamar [former pro rider who started Lamar Snowboards] rolled out, hit the fence, and said a photographer on the deck got in his way. He was sponsored by Swatch, who was sponsoring the event, and that day when they announced the winnings, Damian was in fifth and Lamar was in second. It was Paul Alden, the evil Reagan dude, who was behind all of it, just sort of lurking in the back and we knew it. The next day was the mogul competition. Me, Tom, and Damian all made it into the top sixteen and there were 125 entrees.

And we were psyched, 'cause we were the smallest company (Avalanche Snowboards). Then we made it into the top eight the next rotation. So there were only five other people. We were stoked, we had been kinda training for the moguls and that was a fun thing for us to do at the time. Then we were gonna go into the next rotation and they came up to us and said, "Jim you're out. Tom and Damian, you have to go again and requalify for the top eight." Now this was a pretty straightforward deal where five people at the bottom of the run hold up cards and say who wins. We were rotating in and all of the sudden they said you're out and you have to go again. So that's the night the whole team dressed in black at the awards ceremony.

Tom and I went and xeroxed off these big pictures of Paul Alden on a flyer and put a circle with a line through his face saying, "Wanted out!" And hung 'em everywhere on these black balloons. All I could think was, "This is fucked!" That was the last competition I entered. The next year we started hiking and I figured if I'm gonna make it with this I'm not going through

contests. That was the year we did a Juicy Fruit commercial, which gave us a lot of money to be able to float for a while and what we did at the time was that we got a mailing list of photographers from *Powder* magazine and wrote them all letters saying, "We are cruising around and we will hook up with you if you're into it." And when we got to their respected area we shot photos with them, and then all of a sudden just started shooting for the hell of it. It worked and we started going on backcountry trips where someone would do a story on it. It just sort of evolved. There were always peaks like Mt. McKinley and Everest that we wanted to do and only a few were feasible for descent on a snowboard. Our goals in climbing were to do the big mountains and stuff. We quickly learned that it wasn't that easy, so we just stuck to the smaller ones. Bonnie and I used to spend tons of time in Yosemite climbing.

So Bonnie, you started riding around 1985?

Bonnie: Somewhere around there. It was pretty much through riding with Jim and Tom that I started snowboarding and hooked up with Avalanche Snowboards. I did the World Cup in Breckenridge, Colorado, back then and got frustrated, so I adapted my desires for rock climbing into hiking and snowboarding different peaks. I took the classes they taught at UNR [University of Reno, Nevada], which had a big influence on my life. It was **the way they taught climbing from a historical perspective that taught me a lot about snowboarding in the mountains and such.**

Jim: They're great guys that always kept me from taking life so seriously, living the typical American lifestyle.

Bonnie: You were the all-American kid who went four-wheeling and played baseball. The all-American right-winger who chewed tobacco (laughing).

When did you guys get married?

Bonnie: We were married at Sugar Bowl in 1993. It was a lot of fun.

I've seen articles in magazines of you doing expeditions with other women. Do you usually ride and do expeditions with Jim or do you ride with a lot of female friends?

Bonnie: I've done some peaks with women friends of mine and I always like riding and traveling with Jim. I've done things with other people but you have to go with people you trust when you're doing difficult hikes in the mountains, people you can rely on. I can always rely on Tom Burt;

he's a good strong partner. I like riding with Tom Hsieh [a good friend of theirs from San Francisco who used to publish the first snowboarding magazine called *International Snowboard* throughout the 1980s]. He's a great rider and a great person. It seems if the snow conditions are good and the weather is good I get really stoked on snowboarding in general.

Where's one of the most hairiest places you've ever ridden, besides maybe Alaska?

Bonnie: I would have to say Chamonix, France, 'cause it's so accessible and you can get yourself into trouble really fast. There's a lot of rocks, a lot of cliffs, a lot of ice, a lot of crevasses. And in Alaska, there is the potential for getting in an avalanche or falling into a crevasse. It's so overwhelming there; you can get crushed in a heartbeat (laughing).

Jim, tell me about the peak called Pumori you did in Nepal.

Jim: Yeah, it was just really high and also really steep.

How long did it take you to get to that destination?

Jim: The whole trip was six weeks but we probably did it all in five. It's ten days into base camp, another ten or twelve days to the summit and another week out of there. But the snow just isn't that great up there. It's too hit and miss. I probably won't do it again, but it was cool to snowboard up that high. It was like twenty-three-five [23,500 feet].

It must be insanely hard to hike there.

Jim: (Shaking his head) Yeah. I'm sure you've hiked counting your steps. There you hike and you're counting your breaths.

Tell me about the mountain you hiked where it later collapsed?

Jim: That was Mt. Cook in New Zealand. That was a weird deal. This Kiwi and me went to do it and a TV crew came along. It's a hard technical peak with a couloir that ends in a cliff. Then there's traversing over exposed rock on a snow bridge that's as wide as this room (twenty feet) and tilted up. **Then you follow a three-thousand-foot bridge that ends in a big jungled ice fall,** you gotta be careful of that—don't fall up high, 'cause it's all pretty steep—45 degrees minimum pitch and steeper. So it took about a month for us to get the right weather to do it. It worked out good. Then five days after we left the top of the peak just collapsed, it avalanched and the mountain is now thirty feet shorter. It wasn't a normal occurrence either, it just happened.

HAD YOU EXPERIENCED ANY AVALANCHES FIRSTHAND BEFORE?

Jim: I was with Tom Hsieh once and we were hiking this chute across from Taos in New Mexico and this snow was steep and sounding hollow. We were running from tree to tree hiking up it. Then when we finally reached the top and dropped in, I kept pulling out of it [riding off to the side of the fall line] for some reason. And sure enough the third time I pulled out it slid right by me. Tom was below and pulled out also. It was pretty major, slid the whole way and had a huge deposition zone. It snapped trees off that were this big in diameter (motions with his hands about ten inches). **It's amazing how powerless you are** in an avalanche, even if it's small. I was in one at Sugar Bowl, just a little sloughier under the main chair there and it pulled me into a gully and buried me up to my waist.

DO YOU ALWAYS WEAR A PIEPS [AVALANCHE BEACON] AND A SHOVEL?

Jim: Yeah, Bonnie and I do because we like to hang out together and would like to continue to do so. And I'm not an advocate for everyone wearing a Pieps and shovel, but I would like to keep the backcountry open everywhere. I'm definitely not a crusader to save the world, at least not the people in it. But if you were to ask me, "Shouldn't everyone wear Pieps and shovels?" Well, just the people I like should. I just see so many people being so aggressive about being safe. Why would you care if anyone else is being reckless with themselves?

Bonnie: Yeah, but then you become responsible, there are certain situations that you can't walk away from. If someone gets caught in an avalanche, you see them and you're involved, you can't just leave them, even though they were stupid in the first place. I'm gonna have to deal with them 'cause I'm there.

Jim: Yeah. I guess you're right, that's a good point. I just figure they're on their own.

Bonnie: Darwinism?

Jim: In a way (laughing).

"There are a few constants in snowboarding. It has no purpose as a transportation function to it. It has no competitive function to it. It's kind of hard to play a game of basketball without competing, but you can go snowboarding without competing. What it comes down to is, it is fun and it comes down to just carving powder; those are constants. That's why it came to be, it will always be like that. The waves come and go but everyone comes back to this freeride thing. Just riding the mountain and using the natural terrain."

—Jim Zellers

TOM BURT
BY JIM ZELLERS & CHRIS CARNEL

Tom Burt is a snowboarder whose professional riding spans nearly two decades. He's a resourceful thinker and pioneer who has claimed various first descents on many major peaks around the globe. Like many people who value personal and financial security at the top of their list, Burt could have played it safe and stuck to his job of teaching high school algebra. He could have lived the plush life in the suburbs. He could have....No "could haves" here, Tom Burt is a contender. Tom reminisced from his home in Kings Beach, California, on Lake Tahoe's North Shore about his early days. During the interview, Tom and his longtime friend Jim Zellers loudly squabbled over early friendships and priceless memories. —CC

Above: Tom Burt and Jim Zellers with their vintage boards at Donner Ski Ranch in 1998.
Left: Valdez, Alaska, 1995.
Opposite: Tom in 1998 with his quiver.

Jim: I remember you had a mattress under the stairwell.

Tom: No, I had a mattress in the kitchen 'cause there were two bedrooms and two guys living there. I slept where the kitchen table should have been. I only got paid a hundred bucks a month, that's all I could afford (laughing).

Jim: Yeah, teachers don't get paid enough.

Tom: Not really. That was 1987 and I had to make a decision between snowboarding and teaching. Up to that date I had made seventy-five bucks from placing third in the World Championships at Breckenridge (laughing). I remember telling my parents I wanted to be a professional snowboarder.

Jim: Yeah, I remember they kinda freaked (laughing).

WHEN WAS THE FIRST TIME YOU EVER WENT RIDING?

Tom: At Mt. Rose with Eric Arnbrister, Jim's roommate. No relation to [early free-style pioneer] Allen Arnbrister. We both had plastic Sims boards and I also had a homemade wood board.

THE PLASTIC YELLOW SIMS BOARD WITH THE SKATE DECK ON TOP; RUBBER STRAPS FOR BINDINGS?

Tom: Yeah.

DID THOSE RIDE GOOD IN POWDER?

Jim: Actually the nose always folded.

Tom: Well, then I modified it.

WERE YOU RIDING THE FIRST PROTOTYPES WHEN AVALANCHE [SNOWBOARDS] STARTED OUT?

Tom: Not the first. They were out for a year before we ever met Chris and Bev [Sanders, who started Avalanche]. Shaun Palmer had been riding for 'em and had just switched to Sims. We met all those guys up at Slide Mountain [Mt. Rose ski area near Tahoe]. It was 1985.

Jim: That was Tom's first big score.

Tom: Yup, I took third place behind Terry Kidwell and Bob Klein.

TELL ME ABOUT YOUR NEPAL TRIP THAT YOU GUYS DID IN 1995, WHEN YOU GUYS CLIMBED PUMORI [A TWENTY-THREE-THOUSAND-FOOT PEAK VERY CLOSE TO EVEREST].

Tom: We talked about going over there for a long time. We always wanted to go to the Himalayas. We always thought about McKinley too.

WHAT WERE SOME OF THE FIRST PEAKS YOU GUYS CLIMBED THAT REQUIRED TOTAL MOUNTAINEERING SKILLS?

Tom: As far as glacier travel, the Ruth Glacier [in Alaska] in '89. That was our first serious mountaineering trip. Back then we were green, but we wanted to learn (laughing).

Jim: We pretty much tied ropes to ourselves (laughing).

Tom: We knew a lot of rope technique from rock climbing and stuff so we were comfortable with that whole thing, but up until that trip we had never ice climbed before. We learned to ice climb on that trip. A lot of learning there. Where else have we been? Pico de Orizaba, in Mexico. Well Jim missed that one.

Jim: Oh, yeah.

Tom: Lost Bonnie [Zellers, Jim's wife] at 16,000 feet. That was an 18,000 foot peak.

OUT OF MEXICO CITY OR SOMETHING?

Tom: Well, it's south of Mexico City a couple of hours. From the top you look down right on the Gulf of Mexico.

WOW. HOW LONG DID IT TAKE YOU TO CLIMB THAT?

Tom: Well that's kind of a weird thing 'cause you drive to about elevation fourteen thousand and you go from there. We just spent like a few days doing it. You acclimate for a day then you just kinda go for it. The way the mountain is kinda set up, you're not really acclimated. You go up and basically hurt your body as long as you can and if you make it to the top you're lucky. Out of the six of us that went, two of us—myself and this other guy—made it to the top and the other four people got hurt too much by altitude.

HOW DO YOU USUALLY ACCLIMATE TO THINGS LIKE THAT?

Tom: Once you get above twelve—thousand feet you've gotta start acclimatizing; depends on the person. You start to really feel it at that range. Then once you get above sixteen thousand it's the threshold; it really slows me down. That's when I take a step back and really acclimatize. What else have we done together?

Jim: Well the U and the V Notch are two really cool things in the southern Sierras; they're really steep too. We went there when we really didn't know what to expect from our snowboards at all; we were still on these pretty flimsy boards with not much running edge. We wanted to check these things out and I mean they're pretty substantial, they're ice climbs in the summertime. Those were two big ones that were really scary at the time. We repelled in on that one. It was kinda gripping but at the same time you were in complete control. I'd love to go back soon.

Tom: It's actually one of the only glaciers in California, it's down near Big Pine. Around elevation fourteen thousand.

Jim: We did some stuff in Chamonix, France.

Tom: Yeah. We basically did seven couloirs which weren't done too much at that time. Now they're almost casual, things have up-stepped in France.

Jim: People do them all the time and for us to go back and do them all the time we'd still be really concentrating.

Tom: France was a good warm-up for Mt. McKinley.

Jim: We just wanted to do all these descents. So we just picked 'em out and said we're just gonna hang here for a month.

Tom: We were lucky with the stuff we got to do, the conditions were really good. We did about ten descents on that trip.

Jim: We waited out a lot of bad weather too.

I made a return visit to his cabin in Kings Beach to talk to Tom while he was doing home improvements. He tells me he's a fourth-generation Tahoe native who has conquered seventy-two-degree snow spines on a once-in-a-lifetime snowpack in Tahoe's backcountry. He rode chutes and couloirs in Jackson Hole, Wyoming, and Canada. He did local resort riding at Alpine Meadows in Lake Tahoe. Each April, Tom heads off to Alaska to work on his movie segments, searching and riding deep into the unridden mountain ranges of the Chugach and the Chilkat. He also guides for helicopter operations as well. But what does he encounter when things go awry?

CAN YOU RECALL ANY HAIRY SITUATIONS FROM ALASKA HAVING FREQUENTED THERE OVER THE YEARS?

I did one descent some years ago that was pretty scary for me because there was a lot of blue and black ice underneath the snow and you could see it. The slope was steep and you were really exposed over the top section. You'd come out over rocks and there were all these really steep snow runnels. In all the runnels there was ice. So, you're making turns on these spines of snow but there's ice right there so it kinda makes it really, really hairy. You're kinda on the edge the whole time (laughing). Then once I made it past the cliff exposure, it got to where there was even more blue ice exposure, hanging tracks and shit. There was potential exposure to death the whole time. It wasn't like you were ever really in a safe zone. This was pretty rare and challenging. I was pretty scared just dropping in. We had looked at the slope like a day before, and pretty much part of it was not doable. We knew that this one line could easily avalanche. We thought the conditions were kinda weird. The first day was too warm anyway; we didn't do it. Then we looked a couple days later and it got cold so we went out there and checked it out. We were like, "I don't think we're going to be able to do it at all." It was fucking like potential death—the ice and everything! And I was skiing with Doug Coombs who's a really good extreme skier. Then we both looked at each other and I said, "I don't think we can do this." We looked at it again from the helicopter and then I finally said, "I want to do it!"

Through the middle of the descent I had to stop twice because of sloughs. The sloughs weren't very big but because of the ice danger I didn't want to get smacked and lose control. So my heart was pumping. Coombs skis a lot up there; he's a guide. He skis a lot of steep shit and he's like, "That's the first time I've been scared all season." It was pretty funny. We got out of the helicopter and Doug pulls out this helmet. A lot of people skied in helmets that year. I'm like, what the hell is the helmet for? That's the first time I've ever seen him wear a helmet. So, that was a good Alaska time I fondly remember.

WHO WOULD YOU SAY IS ONE OF YOUR INFLUENCES FOR RIDING "EXTREME" (USING THIS WORD IN THE CONTEXT IT WAS REALLY MEANT FOR) TERRAIN?

Well, that's a tough one. In snowboarding, I don't know. The only guy I can think of is Jim Zellers of course. Now there's a lot of really fun people who do a lot of really outrageous stuff. But in the past, there wasn't really anyone to look up to in the snowboarding industry. When I first started, guys like Terry Kidwell, Bob Klein, Keith Kimmel; guys like that were my influences in snowboarding. But as far as extreme stuff, Scott Schmidt who's from the ski world. I've always been a skier; I really liked his stuff. There were a lot of really good local skiers around here. Guys like Steve McKinney, a speed skier who did a lot of stuff around here. I mean there was a lot of great skiers here in Tahoe. I had a lot of influences from the ski world growing up here. So it was a lot more just local guys who I grew up with around here.

Tell me about teaching avalanche safety courses.

I don't teach the courses but I give seminars and things like that. If it gets through to just one person you feel as though you've done something. Just even giving people tips. But, I've only taken one course in avalanche safety. There's really a lot of basic things that you learn that you can predict about the snow. Most of it is just digging in the snow and being around it. Just through years and years of being out there I've learned how to be pretty safe.

Lastly, I know snowboarders who buy new cars, new boats, and live in two-story, mega-complex housing. You fix your own cars, do your own remodeling, and keep life pretty simple.

All that stuff, to me, is more headache. I guess it all boils down to where you come from, how you are raised. When I was growing up we didn't have a huge house, but we had a lot of family interaction. That part of the family nowadays is almost gone. The family unit today diminishes because mom, dad, and sister live so far apart in a home that they never see each other. **In America right now it's almost like an expected thing to be wealthy, independent, and an individual. In other parts of the world people are living in shitholes but they have their family.**

Left: Tom, Valdez, Alaska, 1995.
Right: Donner Ski Ranch, 1987.

DUANE PETERS

BY CURTIS FRANKLIN

Duane Peters is one of the reasons why the public at large hates skateboarders. He helped usher in the snotty, punk-rock style, aggression, and attitude to a sport that was bound up in nut-hugging Op shorts and bound for an Olympic future to a soundtrack of Fleetwood Mac or the Eagles. Since then, it seems natural to assume that if you skate, you are a punk. Without covering all the tricks Duane has invented (many) or reviewing his checkered past, I'm going to say that Duane still skates (rips, actually) and is still a punk (he sings in the U.S. Bombs). Some things never change.

ON SKATING

I'm still skating whether I make anything or not. You know what I mean? That is what it's about for me.

ON SNOWBOARDING

I would feel like a traitor just to even think about snowboarding, you know what I mean? There's so many queers in Huntington that just turn me off. It's just so fucked down there. It's like growing my hair out and saying, "It used to be punk." Those are lines you don't cross. I don't fucking lick my own cum when I blow on a chick's stomach, right? There are certain lines you just don't cross and I started thinking maybe this is one of those lines.

ON HEROES

If you don't have heroes you're fucked, man. I've got tons of heroes: Olsen, Alva. None of those other fuckers. Just mainly them. The only guy that is still skating from that time that's a good friend is Salba. You know who really rules though is Jay Adams. I think that he is the only guy left who is really down for his shit. He's a fucking freak from hell, totally fucking always on the run. He's got baggage everywhere he goes. He's just fucking cooler than fuck. That guy rules. Every time he calls he's got a new story. I really relate with that.

*Left: Duane with his band, the U.S. Bombs.
Opposite: Laying back at the Santa Rosa, California, skatepark in 1995 and Kelly Belmar's pool, 1996.*

ON THE 7-ELEVEN INCIDENT

RICKY WINDSOR: TELL US ABOUT 7-ELEVEN. THEY WERE ON FUCKING *CRIME ALERT*. CHECK THIS SHIT OUT. WE WERE WATCHING TV AND ON *CRIME ALERT* THEY SHOWED THESE GUYS, ALL PUNK ROCK WEARING AFROS.

Yeah, big Ronald McDonald wigs.

THEY PULL UP TO A 7-ELEVEN AND STEAL A BUNCH OF BEER. TWO WORKERS JUMP ONTO THE BACK OF THEIR TRUCK, JUST TOTALLY HANGING OFF THE BACK.

McCorkendale threw the case back at the worker. We ran out 'cause they were on to us. We had done the same thing the night before, but we were so drunk that we didn't realize that this was the same store! We forgot that we had already burned them. I jump into the driver's seat while McCorkendale and the 7-Eleven worker are doing the whole cowboy box out in the back of the truck. The guy was hanging out of the back of the truck totally scraping his knees. McCorkendale is trying to kick his hands off the truck while we were going about seventy miles per hour. Finally the guy just rolls off the back of the truck. Meanwhile, I'm paranoid 'cause I don't know that any of this was going on, I just want to get out of the driver's seat 'cause I had just got a DUI. So I find a cul-de-sac. McCorkendale's all, "Did you see that shit?" and I go, "What? You gotta be fucking kidding me, where's No Style and [Pat, Tales Of Terror Vocalist] Stratford?"

We left them back at the 7-Eleven!

KRISTIAN JAMIESON

BY JOEY WASHBURN

I first met Kris Jamieson when he came to Sacramento to work with pioneer snowboard clothing-maker Randy Schaffner and I at Randy's company, 916 Clothing. It was 1993 and the best winter of my life. I totally admired Kris's abilities because he was pushing the limit every time he rode, riding with a super-fluid style. He was a pro snowboarder when there were few and is an undersung hero of our sport. We spoke at dinner one night about snowboarding's early professionalism.

His roots in the sport and business of snowboarding run deep. He hails from the Northwest, home to some of the world's best riders. Jaymo rode for initiatory snowboard company Mervin Manufacturing and became good friends with company founders and snowboard pioneers Mike Olsen and Pete Saari.

He just loves to talk to anybody, anytime, pretty much about anything: "Try as hard as you can to be yourself, not somebody else," were the words of wisdom that I remember. These will stick in my head for a long time to come.

LET'S START FROM THE BEGINNING. WHAT IS THE HISTORY OF SNOWBOARDING WITH YOU?

I was born and lived in Hawaii for the first fourteen years of my life. Then I moved to Oregon. I had just gotten into skateboarding. I actually got my first skateboard when I was twelve. It was a G & S Dennis Martinez Flying Aces model. I really liked to skateboard, but I wasn't very good. I had just started; I was doing kickturns and riding ditches. We had moved to Oregon and I was far away from the beach. Coming from Hawaii, I didn't think that I was going to be able to surf or hang out at the beach, so my parents and I took up skiing. Anyway, we went skiing a couple of times, so it was just a hobby. Then in *Powder* magazine I saw an issue that had snowboarding and they had like Burton...No! No! Wait, it was a skate shop in town called Oregon Skates. It was a roller skate/skateboard shop. This was back when roller skates used to be cool. Anyway, they had a Burton Backhill or Performer or something and all of us were like "Yeah man, we gotta try that!" So we all pitched in and bought a Burton Performer. We went hiking these hills together, all taking turns riding the same board, odd as it seems. If you've ever ridden an old snowboard, boy, it ain't exactly snowboarding like we know it today! So let me set it up in a little chronological order for you.

Squaw Valley, 1993.

1987—Summer

I was up at Mt. Hood riding my Sims 1700 Ultimate and the Gnu Team at the time—Mike Ranquet, Dan Donnelly, Carter Turk, Suzi Riggins, Amy Howat, Matt Cummins, Mike Olsen, and Peter Saari—saw me riding. So Mike Olsen got on the chair with me and said "Wow, you ride good." I said, "Oh thanks," and Mike said, "I build these boards called Gnu, would you like to try 'em?" I said "Sure, I'll try one." He gave me a board that day. We ended up all riding around together all summer long. Then one of those guys took a picture of me on a Gnu and that picture ended up being the cover of *International Snowboard Magazine* in November of '87. I think it might have been the first color issue. I was pretty jazzed.

1988—Fall

Tried college, no go. It is kinda funny because through high school I had this weird growth period where I wasn't very strong or coordinated. I would trip and I wanted to be a good skateboarder and would crash and break my arms and snowboarding wasn't coming along very easy. Just as I graduated high school things were starting to come along and I just couldn't go to college. So I moved to Bend, Oregon. Mike Ranquet and I lived in Craig Kelly's living room. Back then Craig was the only professional snowboarder.

1988—Summer

We made *The Gnu Meal*, the greatest snowboard film of all time. If you have not seen *The Gnu Meal* you haven't seen snowboarding. We made the movie at Blackcomb Resort, Canada. Carter Turk was doing double backflips. The funny thing about this story is Matt Cummins and I were riding up the T-bar, we had been asking all the locals where the best place to ride was and they all would just say the same thing: "Up on the glacier." No one knew about the windlip. So Matt Cummins and I were riding up the T-bar and we looked over the back and saw the windlip. The whole movie ended up being filmed at the Blackcomb windlip.

1991—Winter

Gnu and Windline, the distributor for Gnu, started going wacky and I was bummed. The boards started going downhill and there was nothing I could do about it. That's when Hot Snowboards ruled, especially the race boards. In 1990, no one was building. That was during the Terry Kidwell, Sims banana-freestyle-board era, where everyone was building these freestyle boards in the shape of bananas. They were so slippery they just stunk. So I couldn't even ride freestyle boards. I just bagged it and started riding hardboots and race boards. Hot made these race boards that were so good that I used to freestyle, freeride, or whatever you want to call it because you could go bigger, you could go faster, and people used to wonder "How do you go so high?" I would say because you get going faster. Look at that board you're riding, you're riding these sloppy boots, weak bindings, and a board that is shaped like a banana. Look at what I am riding, I am riding a board with a camber and sidecut—of course I am going to be able to go bigger and faster. This is when racing got so popular because the halfpipe was a joke to watch because the boards were so weak. In 1991, they had this huge race at Squaw Valley, it was Slalom, GS [Giant Slalom], and Halfpipe. "The Vision Pro in the Snow." I won the Slalom and the GS and I don't remember what I got in the Halfpipe but I ended up second overall. Jason Ford got first overall. Everybody used to race, that's the silly thing. Shaun Palmer, Andy Hetzel, everyone raced and everyone did freestyle. Palmer was a damn good racer.

1992—Winter

Mike Olsen calls me up and tells me he broke free from Windline. We are starting a new company called Lib Tech. (For those who don't know "Lib" stands for Liberace.) He sends me this board with a skeleton on it. It was the coolest graphics. He would build me these giant 185 downhill boards with pictures of John Travolta from the cover of *Saturday Night Fever* on them. They hauled butt. **Everybody was still riding these super-cheesy freestyle boards that you couldn't land anything on.** Then Lib Tech comes out with the Matt Cummins Pro model. Pretty much the first freestyle board that worked.

Matt and I were at the U.S. Open and I didn't do very well and we were sitting in the hotel room and decided that we were going to start our own snowboard company. We came up with a name: Joyride. We went with the name and got graphics done up by my friend Sean Donnel. We got investors together and started Joyride. After about six months we decided we were not businessmen and sold the company for two thousand bucks. So we bagged that and stayed with Lib Tech, which was the smartest thing we could have done because Lib Tech is the greatest company. 1992 was also the debut of Fishpaw. Joey Boisineau started making mitts in my garage. The name was put on with a paint pen. That was the beginning of Fishpaw and everyone knows about Fishpaw now. Up until 1992 nobody really knew why they were snowboarding. There were no "pro" snowboarders. Then people were just starting to promote themselves, and I just couldn't do it. So I started going to school and now I teach third-, fourth-, and fifth-grade kids.

2000

A little while ago, someone asked me, "How have you been?" There is, of course, the standard American answer of, "Great, and you?" I never give that answer. My answers have always varied from the truth to some wisecrack. This time in particular, I responded, "I am exactly the same...only better at it."

Ambiguous? Maybe, maybe not.

Growing up as a Northwest shredder has been the greatest thing to ever happen in my life. In passing thirty years of age, I feel like I have only just begun, and still feel the deep-rooted motivation I have always worried about losing. I don't think it will ever go away. I will skate and ride forever.

If it was not for the Northwest and the uncompromising pursuit of happiness through non-financial means, I don't know where I would be. Snowboarding, skateboarding, and surfing can all be achieved in the Northwest. You don't need money. Here in the land of trees and rain, you only need a smile and a committed style. You don't even need to be good as long as your style is yours alone and not copied from a magazine or a video. The Northwest has developed an anti-style style; our style is fashionless. Our style is "action" speaking for words and gimmicks.

When I look at Mervin, my friends, and my world...I just laugh. Why do people like us? When it comes down to it we really just focus on the now, the moment. We certainly have never made plans to be "down" with a certain crew. Heck no. Mervin's moments have been plenty, and paid for in cash. Luck? Maybe. Business skill? No way! I believe it was because founders Mike Olsen and Pete Saari surrounded themselves with the things and people they cared about most. They made sure that each moment was special. So that when you stacked all those moments on top of one another, your whole life is suddenly a collection of wonderful moments. That is the Northwest style.

CANAL BOARDING

Modesto, California, is home to some of the most DIY boarders we ever met. Burton rider Jason Cochram, his friend Lance Kimball, and the boys in the band Grandaddy all partake in a sport ESPN has yet to exploit: canal boarding.

• Take one piece of half-inch thick plywood and cut it into a teardrop shape about eighteen-inches wide and two-and-a-half feet long.

• Next, go to Modesto where the irrigation canals that run through the town pass over a seven-foot manmade waterfall every mile or so to keep the current moving.

• Now tie a rope to the concrete wall above the waterfall, wade out into the roaring water along the slippery, algae-covered bottom.

• Lastly, kinda just place the board on the water and jump on while holding the rope. Now you're riding. Should you fall, you need to run downstream, taking huge, sure-footed steps into deeper water or you'll be dragged along the jagged rock bottom.

Sound easy? It is, as long as you don't mind being covered in bloody scabs the first day or two while you learn how to get onto the board. Punk as fuck if you ask me; like a ghetto-ass version of the North Shore. —JB

Lance Kimball, makin' it look easy.

RANDY KATEN & THE N-MEN

Skateboarding is all about being creative, breaking rules, and finding your own path. I learned this at an early age as a junior member of the NorCal skate rats called the N-Men. Being an N-Men meant exercising your creativity by figuring out where to skate before there were any skateparks, breaking rules by draining your neighbor's pool while they were on vacation so you could skate it, and finding your own path as you either ran from the police or talked your way out of going downtown when all your friends had gotten away and left you standing in the bottom of the pool with your skate.

Most people sit in their suburban house on their off-white couch and call this juvenile delinquency. I look back on it years later, and to me it's inspiring. Inspiring in that most of my "criminal" skate friends are still creative, productive, and happy (except for the one or two in jail). It's inspiring that a few of them still skate, like Randy Katen, forty-one, father of two children, small business owner, and a Boy Scout troop leader. And it's inspiring that skating is bigger than ever and still embodies these ideals. If you skate you already know how I feel; it's ingrained deep in your bones. If you don't then all I can say

is parents, please let your children grow up to be skaters. You'll be glad you did, because skaters are some of the best people on Earth.

It can be hard to get by and be a good person in today's society, but skateboarding is the cheapest way I know of to teach individuality, self-reliance, grace under pressure, and confidence. Any popularity or media coverage aside, to me this is the legacy of the N-Men and skateboarding. —JB

Skatin' Katen at the Strawberry Bowl in 1999 at 41 years old. For the record, here's to Doug Jones, Danny Grady, John O'Shei, Tim Kelly, Gary Cross, Steve-O, Dean Randall, Frank Camp, Marty Radan, Sam Cunningham, Rick Winsor, and Curtis Franklin.

Throughout the late '80s and early '90s an American snowboarder by the name of Craig Kelly was taking first place at every major halfpipe contest in the U.S. Having grown up in the small town of Mt. Vernon, Washington, near the U.S.–Canadian border, Craig could see Mt. Baker, one of the best ski resorts in all of North America, from his house. This is where the seed for his unique and smooth style was planted. The days spent learning Mt. Baker's lines were internally logged and years later the creation of a snowboarding legend and guru came to life. He eventually became the second snowboarder ever to have a signature pro model. —CC

All photos at the Three Sisters, British Columbia, 1997.

Craig: I snowboarded up there [Mt. Baker] for four years without seeing much outside influence. Then, in 1985, Tom Sims, Terry Kidwell, Bob Klein, Joel Gomez, Scott Clum, and Keith Kimmel came to town for the Mt. Baker Banked Slalom contest. I just remember seeing Kidwell do this stylish method air over a big roller next to the halfpipe and couldn't believe it was real! An air like that; so fast and so smooth. The next year, on the way to the '86 World Championships in Breckenridge, Colorado, I stopped in Lake Tahoe for about four days to pick up some new boards and ride with Terry and Shaun [Palmer]. I ended up staying at Mike Chantry's house and also met and hung out with Bud Fawcett. Kidwell had this prototype called a "roundtail" that was a massive twelve inches wide. It was the new board he was riding at Mt. Baker.

CHRIS: WERE YOU RIDING FOR SIMS SNOWBOARDS THEN?

Yes, and that thing was the hardest board to ride I had ever been on in my life. Rocker bottom, no sidecut, but it was a good experience. Rode Donner Summit with Terry Kidwell and Damian Sanders.

PRIOR TO ALL OF THIS WHAT RIDING INFLUENCES DID YOU HAVE BACK IN THOSE DAYS?

I didn't really have any back then. All I had were pictures in the Burton brochures. There was an old one that had Jake Burton doing a frontside air out of this quarterpipe, and I tried to emulate that by doing frontside airs for a long time. I had that picture on my Pee Chee folder during high school actually (laughing). Then once Terry Kidwell came to town he was definitely my hero. I still think of his style when I do a method. I think everyone always has their first influences on their methods. Like Chris Roach, his has always been from [Shaun] Palmer. And I know Palmer's was from Kidwell; and Kidwell was kinda the beginning of it all in the '80s. You could definitely say that Terry's my hero.

HOW DID YOU SWITCH SPONSORSHIPS FROM SIMS TO BURTON SNOWBOARDS?

Well, Sims started licensing out their product to Vision. Vision Street Wear they were called in the day, and the guy who ran that, Brad Dorfmann, just didn't give a shit at all about snowboarding products—where it was going or the progression of it. And Jake [Burton] totally did. I had this run at Stratton [Vermont] in the U.S. Open in Slalom and I did really well, ended up winning the race after the first run. Jake just came up to me and said, "I just wanted to say nice run, congratulations, how's Tom [Sims] treating you over there?" You know he was just being cool, he wasn't trying to be like, "I'll do what it takes, I'll steal ya!" but it was more like if you ever need a place to come [for sponsorship]. Then when I got pissed off at Sims a couple of years later I just said to Jake, "I'd like to ride for you guys." That's when I rode the blank board. Then Burton had the crate that said "Mystery Air" with a picture of a snow plumer with somebody going through the air; but there was no snowboarder in it (laughing). I was in the middle of trying to break out of a contractual agreement with Sims and going through some legal battles. It all worked out; then later that year they did an ad with me that said, "Free at last!" with me doing a method with the same plumer of snow flyin' through the air.

I REMEMBER THAT SHOT OF THE WHOLE BURTON TEAM [KEITH WALLACE, JEFF BRUSHIE, NOAH BRANDON, JASON FORD, AND CRAIG] WITH YOU GUYS ALL STANDING ON A CAT AND JASON FORD DOING THIS RAD FRONTSIDE AIR OVER EVERYONE'S HEAD. IT WAS JUST SUPER COOL, MAN. IT KINDA SIGNIFIED A REAL TEAM IN SNOWBOARDING.

(Reflecting) **We were a great team; it was killer.**

Craig suddenly faded from the contest circuit in the early nineties. He was only randomly seen freeriding powder in print media and hardly ever in person at a event or contest again. It was almost as if he went into hiding. His former teammates went on to ride for other companies, but he was still hanging tough with his own board model and doing lots of R&D [research and development] with Burton on the newest designs and developments. His new stomping grounds became synonymous with the snowcat operation called "Island Lake Lodge" outside Fernie, British Columbia, Canada. Having experienced quite a bit of contest traveling to places like Europe, Japan, and even Russia in the earlier part of his career on Burton's team, he was ready for something new to expand his world scope. In the late nineties, Craig filmed for Warren Miller Productions somewhat frequently and had an epic segment in the IMAX documentary movie Extreme, *in which he descended some intense, never before ridden mountains in Alaska. He went off the beaten path on trips to places like Iran and Greenland for magazine travel stories. A spiritual change was slowly coming about.*

HOW DID YOU MAKE THE TRANSITION FROM BEING THE NUMBER ONE HALFPIPE RIDER IN THE WORLD ON THE CONTEST CIRCUIT TO WHERE YOU ARE NOW TRAVELING THE GLOBE, FREERIDING IN THE BEST SNOW?

About the same time when I was really doing well, the first snowboard videos came out. I was involved in doing *Smooth Groove* and Burton's video *Chill*. After doing those I realized it's way more fun, challenging, and stimulating to go out and film. Plus you always get to ride powder, of which Mt. Baker's always been my thing because it's a total powder mountain. What I was gonna do that first year is just hit three major contests like the World Cup events and film the rest of the year. Then I started filming and it was so much fun I just totally blew off all the contests. But the last year I competed I didn't really dominate. I won the Mt. Baker banked slalom contest and I won the last contest of the year, this big P.S.T.A. [Professional Snow Tour of America] contest. There were like twelve contests I entered that year and then I just realized: This is not really that great, what am I doing this for?

HOW DID IT TURN OUT THAT YOU GOT TO RIDE THE MOUNTAINS IN IRAN?

The idea of that trip came from a guy named Jack Turner who managed Big Bear Ski Area. It took a long time for their government to let us go there. But once it happened, culturally and experience-wise it was the funnest trip I've ever done. It was insane! I've actually gotten to enjoy going to Japan again because for the first couple of years I was with the Burton team and went only to do the contests. It was bumming me out. I went there with my friend from home, Jeff Fulton, and his girlfriend about seven years ago to just ride and hang out. It was relaxing and the snow was really good. In fact, we got the best snow of that whole year. It snowed like ten feet in a week!

SO NOWADAYS DO YOU MOSTLY JUST RIDE WHEN IT'S POWDER AND DO YOUR ERRANDS WHEN THE SNOW IS SHITTY?

Yeah. I used to ride in the rain, especially in Washington, because as you know it's famous for it. I'd ride every day, even when it was pouring. I'm not that hardcore anymore. I just sleep in and drink coffee now and show up late for my appointments (laughing).

DO YOU RIDE HALFPIPE OR ANYTHING LIKE THAT ANYMORE?

If one's in front of me, I'll ride it, but I probably wouldn't hike it (laughing). I love the feeling of it (pauses). Actually, I think I ride as good now as I ever did in the pipe. I just don't progress anymore though; I'm not into learning new tricks. I don't care about progression at all, actually; I'm into my freeriding and accessing a lot of new terrain with my snowmobile. I just wanna have fun and sometimes progression is part of that.

An Inkling of Foresight

by Norman & Chris Carnel

Mid-1940s, Squaw Valley:

A not-so-average couple park their vehicle on Highway 89 (approximately where 7-Eleven and the entrance to Squaw is today). They hike through desolate forest (what is now Squaw Valley Road), strip off their clothes, and cross the bone-chilling Squaw Creek. The couple dry off, re-dress, and put on skins (snowshoes) to hike the rest of the basin. In their minds, they foresee and want to create something. So they scout out terrain for potential chairlifts and lodges (things that you and I take for granted every day). Before sunset, they would finally ski down. We are looking back to that day.

The snow was caked thick on the incline. Mr. Wayne Paulsen takes his run and Mrs. Paulsen watches. Mr. Paulsen cuts to loosen the snow of potential sluff.

"I sat there and sat there. I thought about waiting 'til spring, 'til the snow melted!" Bravely, she decides to traverse this run, and then carefully drops in and works her way down the steeps as husband Wayne watches her descent.

"Wow, Gladys," Mr. Paulsen says. "It took you twenty-two kickturns to come down that face!"

And so the infamous KT-22 run at Squaw Valley got its name.

In 1959 my late Uncle Norman photographed Squaw, one year before the Winter Olympics were held there. I then reshot the same photo in 2000.

—CC

The first group of snowboarders to ride Squaw Valley, April 1988.
Backline: Chris Roach, Monty Roach, Bonnie Leary, Bill Olsen,
Chris Sanders, Tina Basich, Heather, Gil, Tom Hsieh,
unidentified, Edgar Rivera.
Frontline: Tucker Fransen, Paula Wickstrom, Rich Abbot,
Crystal Aldana, Bev Sanders, Don and Danielle Bostick,
Kyle Franklin, unidentified.

CHAPTER 2. THE MELTING POT

Jim Rippey takes a streetskating move to the snow at Donner Ski Ranch in 1992.

The Melting Pot

by Don Bostick & Andrew Hutchison

In this section, I have the honor of introducing a few adventurous souls that have successfully crossed over to the winter wonderland of snowboarding, having first established their roots in skateboarding. As a group, they have had a profound effect on the direction and path that so many have followed. They have successfully incorporated their skating skills to snowboarding, showing the rest of us a fresh and different approach to riding. Be it jibbing, bonking, riding handrails, riding switch, or just plain ass going big, these guys rip in both mediums and they rip it up with tons of style. Having known this crew and having watched them progress over the years, I'd like to say thanks for the inspiration and thanks for the good vibes. "Skate on, my children; board on, my friends; for he that does both, will have the most fun in the end." —DB

Which is better? Waking up at 6 A.M. for a powder day or skating until the sun rises? Brand new wheels and bearings or a freshly waxed board? Sliding a log or grinding a ledge? Exploring a city for the first time or dropping into those trees you never noticed? Catching your edge or getting wheel bite? Tony Hawk or Terje Haakonsen? Mark Gonzales or Shaun Palmer? Riding pipe in July or skating while it's snowing? Frostbite or road rash? Slashing a windlip or carving the deep end of a pool? Falling on ice or slamming on concrete? Building a mini-ramp in your backyard or a kicker at the pass? Taking your friends to your powder stash or to your secret spot? Any way you look at it, skateboarding and snowboarding complement each other in so many amazing ways. Doing both allows you to explore the whole world around you, from the most desolate mountains to the most crowded urban environments. Skateboarding makes you a better snowboarder and snowboarding makes you a better skateboarder. Tricks cross over between the two mediums. Something you've always wanted to do on your skateboard is possible on your snowboard and vice versa. Regardless of how much you compare and contrast, when it comes down to it, skateboarding and snowboarding fulfill the same needs. —AH

Professional skateboarder Noah Salasnek turned professional snowboarder, 1992. H-Street was one of the biggest "new-school" skate companies at the time.

"I don't think being able to ride a one-and-a-half-foot funbox should make you pro. I feel that being an all-terrain vehicle is really the way to go."
—Brian Patch, pro skater

SHAUN PALMER

leather L-shaped couch is in the center of the room where Palmer takes calls on his cordless during the few days a year he's actually home. On his left hand, he toys with a fifteen-thousand dollar four-ring set that reads P-A-L-M, gold and diamonds. "They're real!" he assures me. Everything he has, he earned. No trust fund. No rich parents. No lottery ticket. But life for Shaun was not always this blessed.

Palmer was born in San Diego on November 14, 1968. Shaun's father left him when he was born. He grew up in Escondido with his uncle who raced motocross in nearby Carlsbad. At age five, he moved to South Lake Tahoe to live with his mom and grandmother. South Lake Tahoe became a stomping ground for young Palmer. "At first I grew up BMXing, then I moved on into selling drugs, and went through high school selling dope, coke, mushrooms. I was a high school dropout."

NO ONE ELSE EVEN COMES CLOSE

Broken homes, broken records, broken boards, broken windows, broken promises, broken hearts, broken noses—Shaun's broken 'em all.

In 1983 at age fifteen, he, with Terry Kidwell and a handful of friends, was one of the only snowboarders in NorCal. Tom Sims, founder of the snowboard company bearing his name, saw talent, and Shaun earned the world's third-ever pro model, after Kidwell and Craig Kelly. He became famous for his outrageous style, showing up to snowy contests in a vintage Cadillac, as opposed to the newest 4x4. He was known to arrive at a halfpipe contest, down a bottle of Jack Daniels, and then proceed to put shame in everyone's game. Despite bouts with sponsors, his family, and his wrecking of rental cars, Shaun emerged stronger than ever. Being professional in four sports simultaneously—snowboarding, motocross, mountain biking, and BMX—is a feat that had never been accomplished before Shaun. He has been on the cover of the world's largest newspaper, *USA Today,* as well as in *Details* magazine, back to back with a feature on basketball great Michael Jordan. He also runs a snowboard company bearing his name. **There is no lack of focus in Shaun Palmer.**

Down a windy West Lake Tahoe road, I was anxious to see Shaun's house, which is a behemoth beauty that lies hidden among Tahoe's pines. Stained wood, a three-level deck, and a full-length glass tower facing the nation's deepest natural lake. Inside, is a TV modified with Cadillac fins for a box. Every one of Shaun's pro boards lay on the floor, including the first board he made in eighth grade out of plywood and bicycle tire tubes for bindings. On his fireplace sits the Palmer mountain bike he raced in the World Championships. Next to his dining table is a stationary bike facing the lake. The classic

Opposite page: Palmer at home in Rubicon Bay, Lake Tahoe, California, 1998. To his right, the first board he ever made in eighth grade. To his left, his signature mountain bike. Below that, Shaun at the second world championships, Soda Springs, California, 1985.

This page: At left, skating the vert ramp at the Nevada State Fair, 1987. Below, one foot out in the Squaw Valley pipe, 1993. Bottom, Tahoe in 1996.

"The new school/old school is just a bunch of bullshit.
Fuck, half the time I never even went to school.
I might as well be a goddamn bus driver.
I'll drive you all to school, motherfuckers!"
—Shaun Palmer, 1994

At the dawn of his teen years, Shaun discovered snowboarding on Spooner Summit between Carson, Nevada, and South Lake Tahoe. "At first I was in love with boarding just for fun," Shaun says. "My friends told me to go up to the summit one day and try it. So I went up there and we hiked to the top of the hill with three buddies. We were getting it and I hiked back up twice as much as the other guys. But, from that day on, I just... I fell in love with it. Next thing you know I'm flying to Vermont for a contest two year later at age fifteen."

By seventeen, Shaun had begun to define the snowboarder-as-a-rock-star lifestyle. His hair was long and dyed or bleached, he drove a vintage Cadillac, would have a shot (or two) of whiskey before doing a winning run in a contest. Legends of mad drinking binges, taking a shit in a girl's bathroom sink at a party, and rolling vans at seventy mph and walking away unscathed. The irony is that they all were true.

As snowboarding really started to grow in the early '90s, Shaun was a rock star and life was pretty good. He had a pro model on Sims, a huge travel budget, owned a humble house in South Lake Tahoe, and was one of the world's most famous snowboarders. But his past was not far behind.

When Shaun was twenty-one, his father contacted him. "He just popped up when I was twenty-one and decided he wanted to actually meet me. I said, 'Wow, that's fucking great! A little late though, buddy.' He showed up, like we're friends. But I wouldn't even really consider him my father or nothing 'cause I don't have time for it. Obviously, why would I make time for him when he couldn't make twenty years for me? Sure, he had problems back then, but I don't care. If he wants to bail out on me when I'm born, he should bail on me the rest of my life." All the elements building in his life created an inextinguishable drive to win, and by 1990, he was the halfpipe champion of the world.

In 1995, after a long career with Sims, Shaun broke off and started his own snowboard company bearing his name. He assembled a monster team including Andy Hetzel and Temple Cummins. But snowboarding alone could not hold Shaun's interest.

Shaun, along with K2 skiers Brad Holmes, Bob Klein, and Dan Pozniak, started a punk band called Fungus. Shaun dyed his hair clown red and shaved the top of his head, making a "bozo" hairdo. He was the lead singer and they were a show to see: "Those were some good years. We just got together, bought a bunch of equipment and started jammin'. **Kinda took away time from snowboarding 'cause I was so drunk the whole time and didn't want to go out in the cold. Fungus was fun days."**

Left:
Tahoe, 1987.
Below:
Saas–Fee,
Switzerland,
1994.
Right:
Brad Holmes
and Palmer in Fungus.

On January 10, 1998, Shaun qualified pro at a main event of Supercross, a tough feat. He even mounted the actual bike he raced on the stairwell of his house. As well, Palmer attacked mountain biking. "I just started and I was fuckin' immediately good. I started doing all these races, beating all these pros, and then I turned pro." He took the mountain bike world by storm, and in usual cocky Palmer style, he blew a lot of guys out of the water and stole their thunder. "When I first came into it, I blew it out. I was like the Elvis mountain biker." The industry took notice. In a mere three years, Shaun appeared on seventeen different magazine covers. Specialized, the world's foremost mountain bike manufacturer, signed Palmer to a sweet endorsement deal that included a high-tech, high-priced signature bike.

And in his spare time, if you can call it that, Shaun went to Santa Barbara to a BMX race, where he nearly beat a long-seated champ, but came up a still-impressive second. The next day, they turned him pro.

Being a competitive spirit is something that Shaun brings on himself, but the coolest thing about him is that he is an individual with a great personality: "I have to perform for the American public eye. But, I bring more pressure on myself than I think most people do, so it's hard on me just because of my personality, of wanting to be the best at whatever I do."

So with all this great success in multiple sports, I asked Shaun if he had to resign himself to one sport, which would he choose? He replied, "I'd choose fishing. I know it's relaxing and mellow. I'd turn to pro bass fishing." Palmer. PalmDaddy. Mini Shred. Cadillac Kid. Pizalm. He has been called many names, not all of them nice. But the one thing that he will always be called is a champion. —SM

Clockwise from bottom: Squaw Valley Vision Pro Giant Slalom, 1990. Shooting at Sand Mountain, Nevada, 1988. Portraits, 1993 and 1998.

YUKON CORNELIUS
AND....FROM SEATTLE
SAGE
WITH
FRI NOV
12
FLOSS & MONKIS
9:00 -ALL AGES - $5. 21 & OVER / $6. OVER 21
The **CATTLE CLUB**
7042 FOLSOM BLVD. (Between 65th & Howe)-SACTO (916)454-CLUB

"The band was called Yukon Cornelius. It lasted about five years. We actually got kinda good. I still got a flyer at my house. It says: 'Headlining: Yukon Cornelius.' That was kinda cool. But anyway, I did that for a while, and then one day I went snowboarding and I just saw music being kinda a dead end, just the way that we were going. We would be playing clubs at twelve o'clock at night, leave at one in the morning, and deal with all the drunk dudes. The whole band would be fucked up. The whole band would be wasted on weed, acid, whatever, and we would end up driving home. It just seemed to be a dead end, ya know. It just didn't seem like we were getting anywhere with it. I mean, the music was good and we could have done something with it. But, as a person, I didn't want to become an addict of some sort. So I slowly got away from that, snowboarded a little more, skated a little more."

—Kevin Jones,
pro snowboarder, on playing music

TODD RICHARDS

As much as anyone, Todd Richards represents the connection between skateboarding and snowboarding. Best known for consistently taking first place at snowboarding halfpipe events, most people didn't know he could rip a vert ramp. Instead of pigeonholing him as a "snowboarder," we wanted to talk to him about skateboarding. —CC

Growing up in Paxton, Massachusetts, becoming a skateboarder in 1984 with my Suregrip board was quite an experience. There was one "punk rock kid" in town (I wasn't into music then, I was just like a misfit) who had a vert ramp that I couldn't skate. I just pumped the transitions. **One kid brought back a *Thrasher* from his trip to California** and that was our only access to equipment, through mail-order places like Skates on Haight. I thought skateboarding was cool, fell into it, and kept skating when everyone else who sessioned that ramp had quit.

I always looked up to East Coast legends Fred Smith and Tom Putnam, both of whom were doing inverts and lien to tails at one particular contest that I attended with friends. We were in awe! I'll never forget those days, we could only kickturn at the time. Within the next two

summers I built my own ramp and learned to skate better. It was typical old style; eight-foot tranny, a foot of vert and sixteen feet wide with a channel. I never skated street though because it wasn't really happening back then, but I skated a pool in Cambridge that had a six-foot tranny with a kink to vert. We would just go in there and carve around and pump the transition. Fred Smith and those guys would roll in off the diving board and rip the shit out of it! I've never been really good at pools anyway, I've been a back-and-forth vert guy my whole life pretty much (laughing).

Once I started to get a little older my parents started to trust the people that I hung out with, so we'd go on road trips and stuff to these obscure East Coast ramps made out of particle board with funky kinked BMX transitions; just really weird. We would do some

pretty strange road trips like from Massachusetts to Pennsylvania or to Connecticut...or down to Virginia Beach, Virginia, and skate Trashmore...like once every three weeks. It was on a regular basis for me and my friends to drive like twelve hours. The East Coast went from having nothing to skate to all of a sudden in one year (when skating got popular) having like five rad parks.

Getting to travel with snowboarding is rad. I bring my skateboard a lot and when I'm at home I regularly ride the park here where I live in Boulder, Colorado. Tim Payne did a rad job of building it. It has a steel vert ramp, a steel mini-ramp, a cement street course with a bunch of steel quarterpipes, and some obstacles. It kind of sucks to think that all of the eighteen years that I lived in Massachusetts there wasn't one skateboard shop.

"*I'm always glad to be snowboarding.*"

—*Nate Mendel of the Foo Fighters and Sunny Day Real Estate*

JOHN CARDIEL & THE BROTHA' LYNCH HUNG

I had known Kevin Mann a.k.a. the gangsta rapper known as "The Brotha' Lynch Hung" for many years, as I'd worked with him recording his first couple of albums. When I found out that John Cardiel, Thrasher's "Skater of the Year" in 1993, was a big fan of Lynch, I thought it would be a good idea for them to meet.

The resulting conversation was a meeting of similar minds from dissimilar circumstances coming together and discovering that they had a lot in common. Lynch was in the middle of working on his new CD, and his whole posse was present and took part in the discussion, especially Max Kunitz, a.k.a. "Sicx" and Lynch's half-brother. When the talking wound down, John started skating on the five-foot quarterpipe at the studio (also the Heckler offices). Lynch and his crew were familiar with skating from ESPN and video games and were stoked to see the real thing. John did an invert and Sicx yelled, "That's the sickest move!" When he pulled a big FS ollie to disaster, hitting the ceiling in the process, Lynch yelled, "That was fucking tight!" The boundaries of artist, athlete, and audience had been blurred and crossed, and were no longer meaningful. —JB

JOHN CARDIEL: AT LEAST YOU GUYS AREN'T IN JAIL.

Sicx: Not to sound clichéd, but the music saved us. We had our crazy times, bangin' and stuff, but we had our talent. We didn't need to do that stuff.

Above: John, Tall Can, 1st Degree, Lynch, Beta, D–Dub, and Sicx, 1998. Right: The Heckler quarterpipe, 1998.

I THINK YOUR SHIT'S SO SICK, MAN.

Lynch: The thing is a lot of rappers are coming out the same all the time. It's fucking up rap. People aren't buying as much rap these days as they used to. So my objective is to come up with some new stuff. A lot of my stuff is rapping, pausing, singing, but it's like funk stuff. It's not going to be your average gangsta rap album. Rap is going to have do something else. Like bringing in a live band. That's my goal, to maybe play in a live band later on. Playing the piano in a live band, I think that's the shit.

Sicx: Yeah, because it's real.

SO, DO YOU GUYS LIKE SKATEBOARDING?

Lynch: Yep. I really like to watch skateboarding.

I ALWAYS THINK THAT SKATEBOARDING AND RAP ARE A LOT ALIKE.

Sicx: Yeah, it's the underground shit.

PEOPLE LIVING THEIR LIVES AND TRYING TO GIVE A LITTLE BIT OF THEMSELVES AWAY.

Lynch: I want to snowboard hella bad. I never heard too much about it until I started buying *Heckler* magazines.

Sicx: I like skateboarding, BMXing, stuff like that. It's always cool to watch that shit on ESPN.

YOU GUYS SEEN THOSE X-GAMES AT ALL?

Lynch: Yeah, extreme we be on that shit. We've got the game of it for PlayStation. I like reading about skateboarders and them talking about what they've been through. It's not real different then what I've gone through.

Sicx: I just recently found out all the shit you guys go through. All that commercial and underground shit.

YEAH, THEY ALWAYS TRY AND BLOW OUT THE HYPED SHIT. IT'S KIND OF FUCKED UP BECAUSE PEOPLE OUT THERE ARE JUST TRYING TO SKATE AND KEEP IT REAL AND HAVE FUN, AND BIG COMPANIES ARE FUCKING IT UP.

Lynch: What do you do about it? You guys ever have conflicts like the West Coast/East Coast thing?

YEAH, WE ALL TRY AND GET ALONG. I GO OUT TO THE EAST COAST AND HANG WITH MY FRIENDS, SKATE, AND DRINK BEERS. WE DON'T REALLY TRIP ON ALL THE STUFF. WE SKATE. THAT'S WHAT WE DO.

Lynch: So do you guys have distribution?

YEAH, I WORK FOR A COMPANY CALLED DELUXE DISTRIBUTION AND THEY HAVE SKATEBOARDS DISTRIBUTED ALL OVER THE WORLD.

Sicx: That's tight.

John: I love it.

Lynch: Is skateboarding different from the '80s to now?

YEAH, EVERY DAY PEOPLE DO NEW SHIT.

Lynch: Yeah, people always doing shit. We used to be into stuff like that, like breakdancing and stuff, but we got too old and drank too much beer. You know how it is banging your whole body up. Growing up watching all the skateboarding stuff, I always thought it was so technical. Now reading all the interviews and stuff I find out it's just regular shit. I like reading other people's views and opinions.

Below: John boardslides a picnic table as skater Wade Speyer
and ex-pro skater, current actor, Jason Lee take notes.

YEAH, SKATEBOARDING IS KIND OF UNDERGROUND IN A SENSE. SKATEBOARDING IS BANNED IN MOST CITIES IN AMERICA.

Lynch: Why is that?

BECAUSE THEY THINK WE DESTROY EVERYTHING. THEY LOOK AT IT LIKE IT'S DIFFERENT AND THEY DON'T DO IT.

Lynch: That's what I mean! They're always tripping on the shit we do. What do they trip on that you guys do?

YOU KNOW, JUST THE PAINT OFF THE RAILS. STUFF LIKE STAIRCASES.

Lynch: The underground is going to have to fight all the time to keep their shit going. Have you been making money with skating?

WE MAKE DECENT MONEY.

Lynch: A lot of endorsements?

YEAH. YOU'VE JUST GOT TO PROMOTE YOURSELF AND IT JUST GETS KIND OF HARD. IF YOU PROMOTE YOURSELF AND GET ALL BIG, PEOPLE WILL LOOK AT YOU AS KIND OF BEING DIFFERENT.

Lynch: You guys actually make a living at it?

YEAH, IT'S HARD BUT YOU CAN DO IT. IT'S TOUGH, THOUGH. IT'S EASY TO GET HURT. I JUST CRACKED MY FUCKING HEAD OPEN THE OTHER DAY AND MY NECK HURTS. I'VE BEEN TRYING TO GET SOME ACUPUNCTURE GOING.

Lynch: Say, for instance, you keep doing the same ramp-style stuff—do people get tired of the same old stale shit?

YEAH, THINGS GET STALE AND SHIT, YOU'VE GOT TO KEEP UP WITH IT. I'M SURE IT'S THE SAME WAY IN RAP. I KNOW FROM MY POINT OF VIEW SEEING YOU AND SICX RAP IS THE SICKEST SHIT, I WOULD LOVE IT ALWAYS. THAT'S WHAT I LIKE. MAYBE OTHER SKATERS CAN SEE IT TOO. SHIT, I LIKE HIS STYLE, HE DOES THE SICKEST SHIT.

Lynch: See now if we could get that attitude in rap. Does music affect your performance? Do you guys listen to music when you skate?

YEAH, MOSTLY HEAVY METAL BECAUSE IT GETS YOU HYPED. I JUST LIKE CRAZY SHIT. DEMENTED SHIT.

Lynch: You will always hear that on my albums. You will always hear crazy shit. On this album I'm really trying to do my breakthrough album. Sick shit. Like medieval.

Sicx: It's fucked up. Because a lot of shit we've being doing for a long time people are doing now and getting away with it.

Lynch: Me and Sicx have been recording this stuff for years and we were sending it to Priority [Records] and they would always tell us it was too hard for them. Nowadays everyone is picking it up. It's just a trip. I think we were ahead of our time.

Left: Squaw Valley, halfpipe, 1997.
Below: Burnside, Portland, Oregon, 1992.

I SEE WHAT YOU'RE SAYING. YOU DON'T WANT TO FUCK UP WHAT YOU'VE GOT SO YOU BALANCE IT OUT TO KEEP IT GOING.

Lynch: We're comfortable with our shit and would never do something just because someone told us to do it. You will always hear the sick shit in whatever we do.

MIKE RANQUET

It was April 15, 1995, as I sat inside the Aldersheim Lodge thirty miles north of Juneau, Alaska. The power was supplied by generator, the phone was similar to a CB radio, and the water was pumped from a well. Downstairs there was a room with a few bunk beds, a pool table, and a couch in the center of which was a guy named Mike Ranquet. Ranquet wasn't saying much but was belting out tunes on his steel-string acoustic guitar. Zeppelin, Metallica, Randy Rhoads, and various blues riffs resonated from the instrument. —CC

"Almost ten years ago to this day I was skating the Del Mar Keyhole [one of the most famous skateparks of the 1970s] and checking out one of the big pro contests," said Mike. "Man, I was just a kid!" He then went sporadically into an Ozzy riff.

It was only the second time I had ever met him and he was pretty cool. The next day the helicopters arrived and Mike was on the first flight out. I was here shooting for *Snowboarder* magazine and I felt like a little kid in front of the line to Space Mountain at Disneyworld. Somehow things got miscalculated and I never got to go out that day. Until later.

One heli came back to the lodge with Ranquet aboard and could take us for three solid runs across the water channels to the seldom-ridden Chilkat mountain range. Ranquet was just back from a close encounter with suffocation by an avalanche; he was literally buried to his waist.

Cinematographer Artie Kreihbill got it on film and claimed, **"No worries, Mike, I was ready to dig you out."** Mike was quiet and by the time my heli arrived about an hour later he had made the decision in his mind to take another trip out to the wilderness.

After a scenic ride over the southeastern Alaskan water inlets, we were dropped off for some of the best riding of any snowboarder's lifetime at the top of this beautiful peak called Mt. Nun. I watched as Ranquet dropped into some steep-as-shit chutes. He kept looking over his shoulders, but he hung in there. Talk about getting back on the horse and riding when you're thrown off: He got back on and threw the horse down. Quite a jump from the keyhole at Del Mar to an impressive and controlled snowboarder.

An impressive guitar player as well.

Left: Mike cuts out just in time,
Juneau, Alaska, 2000.
Above: West Seattle Bowl, 2000.
Right: Mike playing guitar as
Matty Goodman, Temple Cummins,
and Andy Hetzel watch, Alaska, 1995.

SIMON WOODSTOCK:
THE FIRST (AND ONLY?) SNOWBOARD KICKFLIP

At the height of the snow/skate crossover era in 1993, small wheels ruled the day and the kickflip was the trick to learn. Simon Woodstock is an amazing skater and athlete but is more well known for his sense of humor. One day out of the blue, he called **Heckler** *photographer Matt Kennedy to shoot this sequence.*

Left to right: Simon, Mike Ranquet, and Noah Salasnek.

Pro snowboarder and founder of Lamar snowboards, Bert Lamar.

CHRIS ROACH
BY MICHAEL ORION DAY

In a world of prima-donna rock star fashion, mainstream media, and product-endorsing glory hounds, few people set the standard with their snowboarding alone. It goes unsaid that Chris Roach has always been part of the upper echelon of that elite group. Attacking any line with authority, Chris displays dominance on the mountain.

Chris is one of the pioneers of skate-influenced snowboarding. Coming from Grass Valley, California, he was respected for his style, fluidity, aggressiveness, and his reputation for drinking and getting crazy. When he started riding at Donner Ski Ranch, it seemed like he was the second coming of Shaun Palmer. In the late '80s and early '90s, no one was blasting methods the way Palmer and Terry Kidwell were. Chris Roach was the first to touch on their greatness. As his riding progressed, he developed a signature Roach style; his style became the epitome of NorCal style, smooth and aggressive riding. Roach's style forged the foundation that was necessary for today's top contenders. Roach became a huge influence on the riding style of many heavy hitters like Mike and Tina Basich, John Cardiel, Noah Salasnek, and Dave Seoane.

Left to Right:
The Church Ramp, Nevada City,
California, 1991.
Squaw Valley, 1987.
Chris executing the trick he
invented: the Grasser,
Squaw Valley, 1996.
Yuba City, California,
Skatepark, 1999.

TELL ME ABOUT YOUR FIRST YEAR AS A PRO.

My first year pro was 1988 in the California Series. That was the funnest times, traveling around NorCal, all friends competing.

TELL ME ABOUT YOUR FIRST SPONSOR.

We went out to the World Championship at Breckenridge in 1987. I broke my board in the pipe and Tom Sims gave me a Kidwell. I was hooked up from then on.

HOW MUCH LONGER DO YOU SEE YOURSELF SNOWBOARDING ON A PROFESSIONAL LEVEL?

I don't know how much longer I'll be pro. I don't ever want to stop riding.

DO YOU THINK KIDS TODAY SHOULD KNOW THEIR ROOTS?

I think that the kids should know who the all-time rulers are: Shaun Palmer and Terry Kidwell.

HAVE YOU ESTABLISHED ANY MANEUVERS?

I haven't established any moves, but everyone from Grass Valley did backside airs the same so we'd call it a "grasser." Then we started throwing 'em to fakie, called it a "grasser revert."

WHAT ARE YOUR FEARS?

Avalanches are my biggest fear—that shit is gnarly.

WHAT MOTIVATES YOU IN LIFE, WHAT DRIVES YOU?

Adrenaline, having fun, progressing, my family, and friends.

DO YOU HAVE ANY REGRETS IN LIFE?

I don't have any big regrets. I guess every time I get myself in shitty positions.

DO YOU HAVE ANY ADVICE FOR THE KIDS?

Get pants that fit, tighten your stance, set up your board backseat, go fast, and go big.

NOAH SALASNEK
BY ISRAEL VALENZUELA

Noah Salasnek is one of snowboarding's superheroes. Originally from the Bay Area, he adapted his skateboarding roots to snowboarding to create a style that continues to feed the progression of riders today. Going from skating for Powell to the legendary H-Street team, Noah had his first video part in Mack Dawg's first shred film, Hocus Pocus. As Mack Dawg moved further into making snowboard films, Noah was always one of the featured riders. Subsequently, Mack Dawg's popular films with Noah's sick riding helped each other's budding careers. Noah recalls, "It wasn't like 'let's get Noah on my program,' it was more like we both just kind of started together. He was filming with Super-8 and all kinds of low budget stuff that was really creative and together we both got stoked on making movies. Fortunately, there was a market and they did well."

Mack Dawg, the largest snowboarding filmmaker, had one rival: Mike Hatchett's Standard Films. Noah eventually hooked up with Standard and became a mainstay in Hatchett's TB (Totally Board) series. Dawg focused on freestyle and Hatchett on all-mountain riding, and since Noah was a master of both, it was sensible that he became a snowboarding movie star.

He was on the Sims super team, alongside one of his idols, Shaun Palmer. Noah had one of the best-selling signature boards ever. Like most great athletes, his talent spills over to other sports such as motocross, biking, racing go-carts, BMX, and of course skateboarding: "It is very good to be able to do many different things. Motocrossing and skating, biking and racing go-carts are all ways to keep it diverse. As much as I love snowboarding, I don't think it's the only thing I ever want to do. Everything in my life is somewhat relative to snowboarding balance-wise. Skating is the best, and I find that I'm still progressing and am very stoked to be able to do it all." Noah is the type of athlete that will never stop, not even for age. His effect is marked in history and will be noted forever. "I gather up my experiences, like riding in Alaska, and even just jumping or whatever, and as a whole, I feel like a much stronger rider. I've learned so much by going to Alaska and it all transfers back into the next season. I feel like I progress every year."

Jaws dropped and movie houses ooooohhed and aahhhhhed at the premiere of Salas riding the big mountains of Alaska. The following is an excerpt of an interview done by fellow rider and longtime Heckler contributor, Israel James Valenzuela.

WHAT PROMPTED YOU TO TAKE UP SNOWBOARDING?

I'd always go ski with A.V. [Aaron Vincent], and he was always boarding. So, that fed my curiosity. I actually made a snowboard in wood shop my senior year shortly after getting stoked in boarding. But, the first time I went, I hated it so much that I put the board away after half the day. I had no control and was trying to steer it like a skateboard. It just did not work with me that first time. I stuck it out and just became completely stoked on it.

WHEN DID YOU START COMPETING WITH SKATING?

I started competing when I was eighteen. I did some of the regionals and did well, so I got stoked and kept advancing and actually got to the amateur finals further down. I never directly planned on going pro in skating. Obviously, it is a dream when you start as a grom and look around at your heroes.

HOW DID ALASKA CHANGE THE WAY YOU LOOKED AT RIDING MOUNTAINS?

Alaska was a turning point for me. I went up there for a contest, and I looked at the mountains and thought, "What am I going to do here? I don't wanna compete. I have nothing to show here." I just wanted to ride down. They fly you up in the heli, and you didn't get any warm-ups. I seriously took the easiest line down. I didn't even care what anyone thought. I was more concerned with living. It was that gnarly. There was so much untapped terrain that it seemed stupid to participate. Then I got hooked up with the Hatchetts and have gone back there ever since. Every spring, I go there; it is the most amazing terrain, without a doubt.

Left: Valdez, Alaska, 1996.
Above: Northstar vert ramp, 1999.
Right: Squaw halfpipe, 1993.

ALASKA HAS NOT ONLY CHANGED YOUR RIDING, BUT HOW HAS ALASKA ITSELF CHANGED?

Alaska helps you define your riding in every way. Negotiating steeps, sluff management, and having confidence in what you're doing on the mountain. Every year it takes me a good week to get in the state of mind that you need to be in when you ride there. It's always spooky. I've always loved AK, because it's coastal, which usually means it's stable. I've been going for years and never had any real bad experiences. Back in the day [early '90s], we didn't even have guides. **We were just barging at will and getting very lucky.**

THE DANGER CAN BE OUT OF HAND.

Yeah, right off the bat, it can be hair-trigger fractures, a guide will cut something and the whole face will go. When you're trying to get footage, it gets so gnarly. You're already in dangerous places, but the pressure to get footage makes you put yourself in some *really* dangerous positions. The footage doesn't always come easy.

HOW DO FEEL WHEN YOU RETURN FROM A TRIP LIKE THAT, WHERE THERE HAVE BEEN A LOT OF CLOSE CALLS, BUT YOU COME BACK UNHARMED?

Every time I come back from AK, I walk in my house, and it's all quiet and peaceful. It's crazy to think about what you just went through. Your brain is still going a hundred-thousand miles an hour and you realize that you just did the craziest stuff, and now you're just kicking it. It's high stress even on down days up there. You go through so many emotional highs and lows once you get on the hill there. It's so amazing that nothing matters. Everything is so big.

LOOKING BACK AT THE YEARS, WOULD YOU HAVE EVER THOUGHT THAT YOUR LIFE WOULD BE WHAT IT IS?

Hell no! I never would of thought that any of this would've come together the way it did. Everything I have is from doing what I've done since I was kid. I have had an incredible life so far, and I am thankful for it every day.

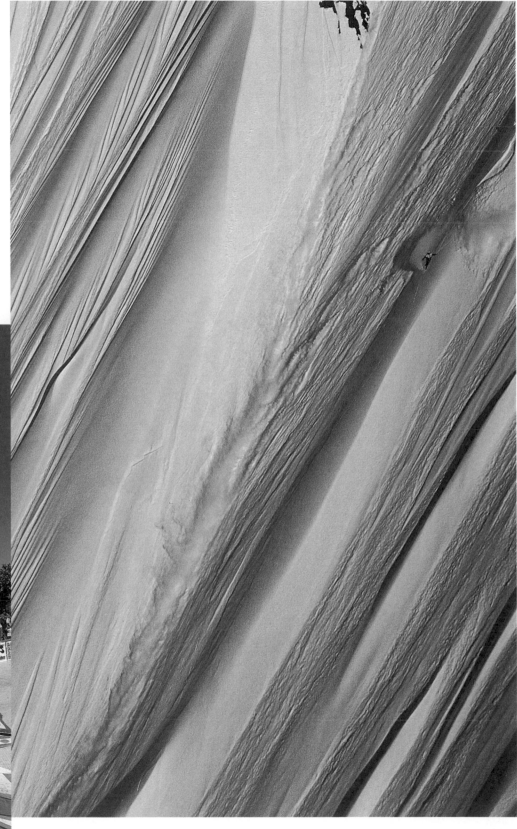

Opposite page and above: Valdez, Alaska, 1996.
Left: Taking fourth place at the Back to the City Streetstyle Contest, San Francisco, 1991.

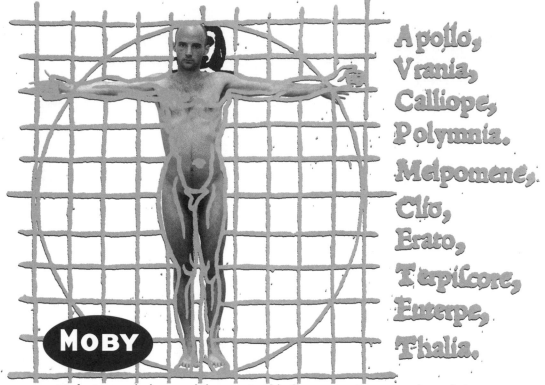

Apollo, Vrania, Calliope, Polymnia, Melpomene, Clio, Erato, Terpsicore, Euterpe, Thalia.

MOBY

Moby's music is a melting pot of influences. From punk rock to raves, he's created his own unique sound, and has always easily crossed boundaries. In 1998, he was not an obvious choice for a snow/skate magazine, which is exactly why we wanted to talk with him. —JB

It's about being comfortable with unconventional mores and standards, which is a difficult thing to do. Once you start defining things for yourself, you realize where you stopped. This woman I was dating, we were talking about that and it's like sexual mores are an interesting thing because most people do approach their life, be it sexually, work-related, inter-person, in very conventional ways. The moment you start to question that, you realize there's a lot of stuff that's up for grabs. Not necessarily rejecting convention or rejecting conventional morality, but at least making it more subjective. And saying, **"OK, well, why did people do this? Why do people have these standards and practices, why not invent things on our own?"** After a while you end up in a very lonely place. If you're reinventing your whole life and all your standards, you realize that you have nothing in common with anyone else. I'm not saying I've gotten to that point but it's quite possible, or you end up like Theodore Kaczynski (laughter).

People's basis for intolerance is very arbitrary. I can understand being intolerant to someone if they're raping school kids. There's a justifiable reason. They're imposing their will on someone else, but a lot of the foundation for most people's intolerance just doesn't make sense to me. Someone chooses to be gay, someone chooses to take drugs, someone chooses to cut their hair funny. It doesn't impact anyone else's life at all. Most people when they think of compassion and tolerance think of it towards the disenfranchised person, "Oh, we should be compassionate towards those poor homeless people." But what about compassion or tolerance towards the jerk who cuts you off when you're driving? What about extending compassion to the difficult people? That's the most necessary.

Homophobia is something that for the life of me I don't understand. I just don't get it. What basis can people have for being homophobic? I like Christ an awful lot and I especially don't understand Christian homophobia, Christian judgmentalism. Christ stressed nonjudgmentalism so much. I think they mention homosexuality three times in the Bible as maybe not the best thing to do, but there are an awful lot of things that get mentioned way more. Christ never mentions homosexuality. Paul says it's a bad thing. But it's funny, in the Old Testament where they mention homosexuality they also say that you're not supposed to have sex with a woman while she's menstruating or for a week after she menstruates. If a man has an emission of semen in the night, he's supposed to sacrifice a pigeon and bring it to the priest. These are very selective interpretations of what you're supposed to pay attention to. And like things you're supposed to eat and not eat and very interesting laws that made a lot of sense if you're trying to have this ragtag bunch of people survive in the middle of the desert away from modern hygiene. Sure, maybe homosexuality is not such a good idea if you need every person you can get.

One of my goals is to sit down with Ralph Reed [the head of the Christian Coalition] and just have a half-hour conversation, just to ask him questions. Where does the word Christian enter in to it? Christ so specifically says don't judge other people and work out your own salvation before you start to consider the sins of other people. I don't understand how they can justify such hateful, judgmental thought and action. And life is such a big messy ambiguous thing. I'm wary of any sort of fundamentalist, that makes me real nervous. Especially people that try and limit the parameters of existence. With the essays I'm just sharing my opinion and trying to create a dialogue, I don't want people to believe what I believe but rather just set up conditions for dialogue. This is what I believe. Pick and choose, and maybe I'm completely wrong. It's quite possible. I've been wrong so many times in my life and I'm certainly not saying that I'm right now.

Whether it's "extreme" sports or whether it's experiencing different things, thinking different things, whatever. It's like you just kind of test yourself and see what you're like in different circumstances and different contexts to sometimes figure out who you are. I think most people define themselves by their convention, by their routine. So you take yourself and put yourself in Laos for six months picking land mines out of the rice paddies and see what you're like in that situation and then you develop a broader understanding of who you are, hopefully.

We had been bouncing around the idea of a tasteful nude portrait in the magazine, and while we were talking to Moby, he seemed like he might go for it. "Sure," he said with no hesitation at all.

TUCKER FRANSEN

The seed for Tucker Fransen's foray into the second generation of freestyle snowboarding came from the ramps and pools of his home in the foothills of Grass Valley, California. With local friends John Cardiel, Chris and Monty Roach, Toad and Chris Senn, they would skate all summer. Then in the winter they would drive an hour into the Sierras, where Tucker would school his friends applying what he had learned on the cement and masonite transition to the snow. —CC

Left: Skate-influenced frontside handplant in the June Mountain pipe, 1993.
Above: Skating Emile Janicot and Chris Senn's backyard pool, 1994.

I first met Bob Burnquist at Slam City Jam in Vancouver, Canada, in 1996. It was his first pro contest. He was an unknown skater from Brazil, but that soon changed when he won the vert contest against the best in the business. He fit right in with the pros like he had been skating with everyone for years. He left quite an impression on me as well. Since that time I have been fortunate to watch Bob over the years at all the contests. He has established himself as one of the premier skaters of all time. Although he has come so far in such a short time, he remains a guy who just enjoys doing what he loves best: skating, traveling, and being able to support himself as well as his sister and his mom.

He has also taken up surfing and snowboarding. I had the chance to ride with him at Donner Ski Ranch and Homewood in Tahoe. He takes his boarding seriously. I remember at Homewood that 32 Boots had sent us several pairs of boots, and Bob and his sister happen to wear the same size. Well, it turned out that the pair Bob had wouldn't fit in his bindings, it being a powder day and all, so Bob made his own sister switch boots with him so he could go riding. Meanwhile, she had to figure out something for herself.

On the chairlift headed up to the top, Bob's friend, Taro (also from Brazil) dropped a glove. I figured since he'd never been here before, we'd help him retrieve it. Instead Bob says, **"Hey, he dropped it, it's his problem. I'm getting some powder!"**

Later that day, he entered the USASA (United States Amateur Snowboarding Association) Slalom event and took home a bronze medal on his first run through the course ever. Bob became one of the best skaters in history and was the first to do the one-footed Smith grind, a trick of the utmost difficulty. His talent is overflowing, superceded only by his passion for life and easygoing demeanor.

BOB BURNQUIST
BY DON BOSTICK

Sunday, May 3, 1998, in Vancouver, Canada

BOB, WHAT'S IT BEEN LIKE SINCE YOU WERE ANNOUNCED SKATER OF THE YEAR BY *THRASHER* MAGAZINE? HAS LIFE CHANGED?

I've started to notice that at contests—a lot of kids come up to me, they're really stoked and congratulate me for it, asking me for autographs. It's been really rad! I haven't really changed myself, it just makes me want to go skate more, have some fun, and hang out with the kids.

I KNOW THAT JAKE PHELPS AT *THRASHER* HAS PLAYED A BIG PART IN HELPING YOU OUT. DID YOU SKATE WITH JAKE MUCH?

Oh yeah, Jake always has the Hellride sessions, which is on Fridays after work from four to five o'clock on his ramp. I'm always there, I go into Real, I go into *Thrasher*. I love hanging out with Jake. He's got a lot of history in skateboarding. I love hearing what he has to say.

WHEN YOU WERE A LITTLE KID IN BRAZIL, DO YOU REMEMBER HEARING ABOUT TONY ALVA? I KNOW HE USED TO GET DOWN THERE.

I heard stories about him through Bruno at Charger [skate distributor]; he used to hang out with Tony. But the only pros I remember coming down were Tony Hawk, Lance Mountain, and Christian Hosoi.

YOU WON SLAM CITY JAM THE FIRST TIME YOU CAME HERE, AND SINCE THEN YOU HAVE RACKED UP AN IMPRESSIVE CONTEST RECORD. YOU WON THE HARD ROCK FINALS LAST YEAR, BEATING TONY HAWK. WHAT WAS THAT LIKE?

I remember just having a great day at the Hard Rock. The whole week was fun. I was down there with my friends in southern California just having a good time surfing and skating. I have a bunch of friends from Brazil that live there, so I try to go down there as much as possible. All my friends were there at the contest. I was just stoked to be there and skate with everyone. The ramp was good and I remember just being comfortable and not nervous that day. It didn't really sink in until a couple days later when I was thinking and looking at the trophies, "That just made my life right there." Not the fact of beating Tony Hawk, but being out there skating, actually doing good. I mean it was awesome.

HAVE YOU SKATED WITH TONY MUCH BESIDES CONTESTS?

I skated with him once before at Birdhouse. We got there and he didn't know we were there. He was just going off by himself with no one else around. I mean, that right there tells you a lot about someone. He's out there by himself just pushing it. We skated for like an hour or two. It's rare, it just doesn't happen that much. Then, at the MTV contest we had a little session: no pressure, it's **awesome. I wish I could skate with him more.**

TONY'S BEEN AT IT FOR A LONG TIME. WHERE DO YOU SEE YOURSELF IN, SAY, TEN YEARS?

I don't know. I mean, I respect Tony for how long he's been doing it and for how long he's been enduring it all. When I look at myself in the future, and seeing that Tony just turned thirty, I see myself thirty years old and skating like he is or just being on my board, healthy.

BOB, HOW LONG HAVE YOU BEEN SNOWBOARDING?

It's been probably two years, two seasons now that I've been going a lot. I did it for the first time about '93 with my cousin in Colorado. We just went out and hiked up this little hill and went down. It was pretty fun.

WHAT KIND OF BOARD WERE YOU ON?

I can't remember the first one, it was a pretty big board and I couldn't turn it and I was starting to get mad at it, I couldn't make it turn. I thought it was like skateboarding, but I just had to get the hang of it.

HOW LONG DID IT TAKE YOU TO GET JAMMING?

Took me like a couple rides to go down and get the turns down and then we went to the resort and then we had more time going down so I got on it pretty quick. It was pretty easy to get if you have the balance.

I'VE SEEN YOU AT DONNER A FEW TIMES. HAVE YOU BEEN ABLE TO GO MORE?

Yeah, I try to go as much as I can. Whenever I'm home, Rebecca [his sister] is always into going boarding. We try to go up every weekend. It's just fun. I go up there and hang out, boarding's rad! I try to take as many people as I can.

PRO SNOWBOARDERS RESPECT PRO SKATERS. WHAT PRO SNOWBOARDERS DO YOU RESPECT?

Well, I haven't really ridden with that many. I've just seen them in magazines. I don't know that many names, but at Board Aid in Switzerland I hung out with Bobby Meeks. He was there and he was ripping up the pipe and going really high. I didn't get to see Terje, but I hear he's really good. I've only seen footage of him. Cara-Beth Burnside, she's an awesome snowboarder as well. She's rad to watch. Todd Richards too. At MTV Sports, I got to know those guys. Jim Rippey, now they're all popping up in my head, Trevor Andrews, the Canadian. I'm stoked to get to go to all these places and meet these guys. **They're doing the same thing that I am—just snowboarding and it's rad to see and just hang out with all those people.**

Previous spread, left to right: Santa Rosa handrail, 1998. Verbier, Switzerland, 1997. Japan Air at Max Schaaf's vert ramp, 1998. Above: Santa Rosa skatepark, 1998.

PUNK IS PUNK: THE STAN EVANS STORY

BY JIMMY CLARKE

Most skiers kinda suck. But once in a while you run into one or two who are cool as fuck, and you just have to overlook that two-plank handicap and ride with them a bit to see what they got going on. This guy definitely fits the bill. While we were at Bredger Bowl we met this guy on skis, and there wasn't much else you could say other than he ripped. I was there to shoot some snowboarding photos and he was showing us some killer shit when we saw this snow fence from the lift. The light was killer and it looked super cool. I wanted to check it out, but when we got there there was no ramp up on the back and nowhere to get speed but a really little hill. So, being the optimists that we were, we proceeded to build this kicker while Stan (the skier) smoothed out a runway. He was devising a plan to skate-pull and sling-shot the snowboarder up to speed to clear the fence. A great idea, but after an hour and no luck getting anyone on a snowboard up to speed to clear the fence (an act that required Stan to hike it about fifteen times, as well as skating hard to pull the snowboarder down the hill) we were about to give up. Suddenly Stan says, "Fuck it, I'm gonna do it." **I was a bit skeptical, but what the hell, there's film in the camera.**

Stan hiked up, pushed off, and came at it with speed. He lost speed on the little turn in the runway but went for it anyway totally crucifying himself on the fence. Once we figured out he was OK and managed to untangle all those poles and shit from the fence, we all just about died laughing. I figured it was time to move on, but Stan's like, "Fuck that, I'm doing it again." So he hikes up again, and I'm

thinking nothing but Kodachrome courage all the way. This time he hits it with speed and totally clears it solid. So that is why I'm sending you a picture of a skier. Stan is a cool guy, he rips, punk is punk, and determination will get you there. I love a happy ending.

Never quit.

METALLICA

Metallica created a sound that decades later, has had a profound effect on music. When they started, most bands were playing friendly rock, with a few playing punk, but not both. Metallica took rock and punk and sped them up to create the sound known as "thrash metal," a hybrid aggressive music, a dangerous sound. They shunned the norm by not wearing the then-popular spandex pants, thick makeup, and cheesy puffy hair. Metallica played fast, raw, and hard and wore T-shirts, ripped jeans, and long hair. They've sold over fifty million records. They were the first of their kind, and their effect will be felt for decades to come.

The first time I heard Metallica was in 1984. I was fourteen, dating a chubby punk-rock girl, dealing weed, playing guitar, and skipping freshman classes from my South Sacramento high school. One day she handed me a Walkman with a blank TDK tape in it and said, "Hey, you're a rocker, check these guys out; they're hair farmers, but they're pretty good. You'll probably like 'em." I took it home, put the Sony audio plugs in my ears and heard "Fight Fire with Fire," the opening song on Metallica's sophomore full-length Ride the Lightning. *I was blown away. My life changed. —SM*

James Hetfield: The main goal of starting Metallica was to not have to work regular jobs. We'd get together after work and just bash it out in the garage. It was an escape and a release. We'd play all the songs with our fucking bosses' faces in our minds. We thought maybe one day we can play some gigs and not have to work. That was the first step. We were pissed off. We hated quite a few things. One thing was L.A.; we hated it. We didn't like the club scene, we didn't like the music that was coming out of there. We didn't like what was popular there. A lot of the bands were fluff and no substance. Lars had introduced me to Motorhead. Lars was into heavier stuff and he had a record collection from Hell.

I would sit and record his stuff to cassette for hours. When we first started playing clubs, we started playing cover tunes. Tons of these obscure bands that people had never heard of in America. So we'd play these songs that all the people thought were ours. We had to tell them they weren't. We just started writing songs that were similar to that: a little more aggressive, and we liked a lot of punk stuff. We didn't think that punk had as much musical talent though. We'd play these L.A. clubs and just look out at the crowd and get pissed off. They were having hair contests over at the bar. Instead of getting into our music, they were seeing whose hair was taller. It made us play faster and angrier.

All that stuff really helped develop our style. There were a lot of clubs that wouldn't let us play. They thought we were a punk band. I recall at the Troubadour some security guard throwing chairs at us and calling us punks. It was like, "Who gives a fuck who we are, we're here to play some heavy music."

People didn't understand us, they didn't get it. Sometimes we were too young to play some places. Playing little Huntington Beach clubs, just getting our tapes out, we sort of tried to mix punk and metal.

In high school, I was sort of lost. I didn't fit in with all the groups. I'd come to school with my Scorpions T-shirt and my punk glasses on, all the kids would be like, "You can't hang out with us."

It was just like, "Fuck all of you." It was kind of crazy. Nowadays everything is pretty much well accepted. Back then people were constantly labeling people. It was pretty ridiculous. But there were a lot of bands back then like Suicidal Tendencies, who were sort of hard-core, skate punk type of stuff. It was all aggressive music and whoever played it didn't matter. When we first moved up to San Francisco, there was so much more acceptance for music. There were actually people who finally came to the shows to hear us play. We ran into our first fans up there. Punk and metal went hand in hand.

There has been some pretty horrible shit that's happened, but that stuff makes you stronger. We are absolutely happier on this tour [supporting the album *Load*] than we have ever been. This last studio project really got the brotherhood together a lot more. Just growing up a little more and understanding each other better. I think we've got our home life a little more together. We're not such frantic road dogs anymore. It's still fun as fuck, man.

I will respect anyone who does shit their own way. Someone who really hasn't bent over for anyone else. We've heard "sell-out" forever. People have always said Metallica sold out since *Kill 'Em All*. It's like what is this? We're entertainers, writing the type of music we like to play. We're getting a lot of that shit today. If you don't like what we're doing, then fuck off. Just hop off the bus.

I was always into skating as a kid, and I got back into it on tour. Always bored as fuck after sound check. Zorlac thought it would look great to have "Metallica" on a deck, so me and Kirk got some boards from them. Actually the other day, (Burton Pro Snowboarder) Craig Kelly brought his old Zorlac board to the show to have me sign it.

Falling off the coping into the pool was the last skating I did before I got these pins and bolts in my arm. That's when I decided that Metallica was a little too important to go this wild sometimes. We had to cancel *Saturday Night Live* and a studio project. I felt I let the guys down. Even though I'm out there doing what the fuck I want to do, I had some responsibilities to the band, you're a family. When you let everyone else down it's not a good feeling. So now I'm into safer things like riding motorcycles and snowboarding.

"It's the adrenaline rush that I get. I love the feeling of learning a new trick or riding really well. Like with snowboarding, there's a lot of girls that are doing it and that's cool because it's easier to work on new stuff when you see other girls at your level. But basically I do 'em because of the amp; it's the best high I could get. I live for that kind of thing. I just go crazy if I don't skate or snowboard. I turn into a freak; people are like, 'What's wrong with you?!' I can just go skate or snowboard and have a good day and just be so stoked and just be like skipping around all day 'cause I'm just so high…that nothing matters."

—Cara-Beth Burnside

Professional skateboarder & snowboarder
15 years skating, 10 years snowboarding
4th place in the first-ever snowboarding Olympic event.

*Good friends Jeff Toland (left) and Noah Salasnek (right)
represent two different facets of professional board riders.*

CHAPTER 3.$

PASSION OR PROFESSION

Passion or Profession?

by David "I May Suck, but I'm Still a Pro" Sypniewski

Rumor has it that the guidance counselors in high school suggest that students pursue a career in which they may have an interest. I never actually met any of my high school guidance counselors; I was a little busy wasting my time "thrashing." Later, when most of my ex-classmates were at various universities learning how to be professionals in corporate America, I was busy shredding.

My interest had grown into a way of life, not into a job. But then one day, a company decided to pay me to live the way I lived and gave me free boards to do it on. I became a professional snowboarder. After a few years, my father asked me when I was going to stop messing around and come back to Indiana and learn a trade. I guess in his mind a valid "paid professional" isn't someone who gets seven hundred dollars a month to go sledding—this was even after I explained how some professional snowboarders make over six figures.

The free money train crashed a few years back, so I did what so many others had to do: I got a job. But all the jobs I've taken have revolved around my lifestyle.

That's the story of my pro career, which is also the introduction to this chapter. This chapter deals with passion and professionalism, which is a blurry subject. To me, if you are passionate and your life revolves around your activities, then you are already a pro. If you're getting paid, but you'd walk away if the money stopped coming in, then you're a jock.

Opposite: Dave's sledding towards a corporate career.
Left: Portraits from an interview Dave did with
Willie Nelson for Heckler *in 1998.*

PERSPECTIVES ON PROFESSIONALISM

Professional snowboarding has more diversity than most sports. And though many of the responsibilities and duties of being pro are the same for all riders, snowboarders have differing attitudes and ideas on professionalism. One man's meat is another man's poison. I thought it would be fun and interesting to ask ten renowned pros the same set of questions and hear their perspectives on professionalism. The older riders gave some history while the younger guns shed some light on the future. The following are a few excerpts that look into the mind of a pro.—SM

MIKE BASICH
Along with sister Tina, Mike has been pro for many years. He is a do-it-yourselfer who will stop at nothing to support his riding habit. Mike currently lives Salt Lake City, Utah.

MARCUS EGGE
Marcus is an all-mountain rider who is not afraid to drop monster cliffs. He currently resides in Bend, Oregon, and fancies himself a fly fisherman.

TEMPLE CUMMINS
If the encyclopedia listed "Northwest-style snow-boarding," Temple's photo would be there. Representing the soulful side of the sport, he lives in Gig Harbor, Washington, in a house he built himself.

JIM ZELLERS
Jim is one of the pioneers of backcountry snowboarding. He is very rarely in the limelight, and he rides well over one hundred days every year and currently resides in Lake Tahoe, California.

ANDREW CRAWFORD
One of the top pros at the turn of the century, Andrew goes from filming in the seclusion of exotic locales to standing on the podium in the biggest contests. He lives in Salt Lake City, Utah.

TOM BURT
A high-school teacher turned pro snowboarder, Tom Burt is known for dissecting gnarly lines on huge mountains. He lives in Lake Tahoe, California, where he occasionally surfs the lake.

MORGAN LAFONTE
One of snowboarding history's top female contenders, Morgan Lafonte dominated the contest circuit. She helped take snowboarding to the mainstream by being featured in a Mountain Dew commercial and in a spot on NBC's news magazine *Dateline.* Originally from Colorado, she now lives in Lake Tahoe, California.

LANCE PITMAN
A man of few words, Lance represents snowboarding's feisty spirit. He was born and still lives in Jackson Hole, Wyoming.

FROM THE TIME THAT YOU FIRST STARTED SNOWBOARDING TO NOW, BEING PRO, IS IT EVERYTHING YOU THOUGHT IT WOULD BE?

Basich: Heck no, when I first started snowboarding in '85 it was very different, even as a pro, than it is today. I didn't join the pro division 'til '91, I figured it would be a fun way to travel the world for a couple years. Growing up I never thought I would be a pro athlete. Snowboarding has changed forever from back in the day, some good some bad. But the reason I started my first day is still why I snowboard today, the fun and adrenaline of it. It's the heart of the sport and always will be. There are some bigger obstacles in the way from the industry and media but underneath if you search hard enough you'll find the heart of it like it was your first day.

Egge: No and yes. When I first started, nothing mattered except riding and getting better at riding. My gear was hoopty, I had a tough time getting to the hill, and I really didn't know what a pro was for a year. I then met or said hi to J.D. Platt, Kurt Heine, Robbie Morrow, and Kris Jamieson. These guys were really, really good. I would see them at the mountain or doing contests that I would attend. I always thought being a pro would be the best job in the world. This dream started to turn into a goal after I was exposed to other pros like Jeff Brushie, Craig Kelly, Terry Kidwell, and a heap of others. I would read about the world travels and endless days of riding pow and hitting kickers. What a life. And it is. But what I didn't realize was that all of these people had worked incredibly hard to obtain this life and once they "made it," the work only increased. To sum it up, I feel that I have the best job in the world and I wouldn't change a thing. But I know now that being a pro isn't just riding every day, it's working hard at a lot of different things to help the people that are helping you live your dream.

Zellers: I didn't think it would be anything. To start off with, it was just something to do. There was no sport to speak of so I didn't have any expectations. It just sort of ended up how it was. As far as being a professional snowboarder, being what I thought it would be, **it wasn't really a job application at the time.** There was really nothing to think about in the future, it was more of just what do you do every day—ride and develop the gear.

WHAT DOES IT MEAN TO BE A PRO SNOWBOARDER?

Basich: A lot of people say I'm lucky for what I do for a living. Sure, maybe that's true. I get to travel the world and not have a nine-to-five job. But when I go to work, my worries are not about giving a report to my boss or something. I worry about making it through the day without breaking a bone or getting stuck in an avalanche (knock, knock). Your body takes a beating. You're never home. Lots of lag time at the airports. You're in the cold all the time. Sometimes I wish I was a pro surfer. But I think it's worth the risk.

Blaise Rosenthal noseblunts in South Lake Tahoe, 1999.

Crawford: To me what it means to be a pro snowboarder is that I'm no different than a lot of other people, it's just that I've been snowboarding a long time and I get paid to do it. And the way I try to look at it is as being a role model because when I was a kid I had people that I looked up to, and to me that was the coolest thing in the world: seeing someone do something so incredible that you want to get on your snowboard and go try it. So I try to do that on and off the hill as far as being a role model goes because I know there are kids out there and I'd rather be a role model in something like this than in something negative, like a gang or something like that. If I can help kids in some way, get stoked, or just get into something, get involved in something and be really stoked on something, that's my job and that's kind of the way I look at it. I want to be the best I can be so that others will take it even farther, take it to the next level.

Lafonte: Alright, let me break it down for you. I am an athlete and I think that being a professional for me means I'm representing a sport and I think that my sport is mostly about freedom. It's changed so much for me; it's represented different things for me like when I first started out the excitement, the newness of it all, and getting product. For a time you were riding, getting product, starting to get paid. It was a big party, but now for me being professional is serious. It's serious for me because I'm dealing with a higher level of everything. The people that are interested in snowboarding now and the people that you want to appeal to are big corporations, people that have PhDs and they don't even snowboard, they don't ski, they go to the gym for their workout. Try to go from working with people that snowboard to people that have absolutely no idea, who have never even seen snow. They are the people that are making all of the decisions now and you have to market yourself to them. Being a pro snowboarder means being versatile, kind of like an entrepreneur of your own talent.

Cummins: It means riding every day, riding super hard, not going in for lunch, not being a pussy, doing stuff, pushing what you're doing, scaring yourself each time.

WHEN IT COMES TO YOUR PERSONAL DIRECTION IN THE SPORT VERSUS THE DIRECTION THAT YOUR SPONSORS WANT YOU TO GO, WHERE DO THEY AGREE AND WHERE DO THEY COLLIDE?

Rosenthal: Pretty much my sponsors have no problems with what I'm doing. I don't think there's anything they want me to do that I'm not doing and there's nothing that I don't want to do that they want me to do. It's pretty good. I have a good set of sponsors that aren't just a bunch of idiot businessmen; they're in the sport because they know about it and because they're snowboarders themselves. They're people that know what they're doing and I have a lot of influence on most of my sponsors, like what kind of product they put out, and marketing, and whatever. So, when it comes to what I want to do, it's pretty much up to me.

Cummins: All of my sponsors back me up pretty hard because they know what I like to do and that's why I chose them. I don't choose them because I'm making the most money; I choose them because they're behind me in what I do. I don't do these TV shows or TV contests or this type of thing, I do the Mt. Baker Banked Slalom and that's it. I'm lucky enough to have good people backing me that understand the part of the sport that I'm into. Just the snowboarding part, I'm not too mixed up into the contests or the TV stuff, it just beats people down constantly.

Zellers: At first we disagreed. In the late eighties, my sponsors wanted me to maybe do something with my hair, maybe get some new clothes, get a "rad" personality, and I wanted to be in the backcountry a little bit more where you couldn't spend as much time on your hair or your clothes. So that was a big clash and they were pretty much dropping us because of that. There were a few sponsors that were thinking that way. Speaking to mostly me and Tom [Burt]. Me and Tom were not strong on image at the time. Now since I've decided to do what I want to do, it works and people just latch on to that thing and they never ask me to do what I don't want to do.

DO YOU FEEL THAT YOU ARE PAID ENOUGH FOR WHAT YOU DO?

Crawford: Definitely. It's taken me awhile to get to where I am but I couldn't be happier. I think maybe one thing, as far as the general of snowboarders go, they risk their life a lot more than a lot of other athletes, and I think that overall they should increase the pay in snowboarding if the companies can afford it. And if they can't, maybe do certain things like life insurance, health insurance, help the riders out in that regard. A lot of riders are just doing so much and working so hard and not getting adequate pay for it. But the way I look at it is if you keep working hard, somebody is going to notice somewhere, someday, and you're going to eventually get what you deserve.

Rosenthal: I'd do it for four hundred dollars a month. Just enough to pay my rent, and if I couldn't get that, I'd do it for free. It's all relative, the only reason I ever expect any more money for snowboarding is, you know, it's hard if you hear someone else is getting something, and you think you're in the same position as they are. Aside from that, **honestly I'd do it for nothing. I'd pay too.**

Lafonte: (Laughs) God, no! Hell, no. The only time I've ever really been paid, and it really wasn't even worth it was a Mountain Dew commercial I did a few years ago. The residuals I got from that were well worth it. But apparently my niche could be, or K2 thinks it is, backcountry. Anybody that goes into the backcountry, you're putting yourself at risk right away. For, say, someone like K2 to ask me for a film segment in Hatchett's movie, I gotta be out there bustin' my ass. I've gotta be one up on the guys. You know, whoever gets up there first gets it. I'm not saying it was a motivation, I'm just saying for what you do to your body and yourself and time. No, you're definitely not getting paid what you need to.

But you shouldn't have to have a middleman. It should be one on one, it's a contract, it's a handshake, you look 'em in the eye and say, "This is what I do. Do you understand this? Do you understand what's going on; the scope of things?" Which I think is probably part of the reason people aren't getting paid. Because **the people that are paying them, they sit in an office. They don't see what goes on.**

WHAT ARE SOME OF THE STRESSES THAT COME WITH BEING PRO THAT PEOPLE DON'T KNOW ABOUT?

Crawford: Number one, the travel. A lot of people when they hear you're going to all these exotic places and having a lot of fun assume that it's bluebird, sunny, and powder, and everything is carefree where in reality there is a lot of nights spent in airports, a lot of missed flights, a lot of stresses that go along with traveling that a lot of people don't really think about. Number two, injuries. When you're injured or you're hurt and there's pressure for you to do good or something like that, it's really difficult because snowboarding is a cutthroat industry and there's always that kid that's nipping at your heels that is so good, but I like that because it keeps you on your toes.

Burt: I don't complain too much. Let's see, trying to explain your daily job to people. A lot of people think that being a professional athlete doesn't take any work, but actually it is a lot of work and a lot of commitment. It's not necessarily that it isn't fun, but it definitely is a job; it's a job that I love. The only other bad thing about being a professional is that you're the first person to hit the floor when companies fall through because you're just a marketing tool. That part of it is kind of rough because you never really know.

Pitman: Actually, it's riding nonstop all the time; everyday it works your body. And just feeling obligated to ride well all the time; it's pretty stressful sometimes.

Temple Cummins, Donner Summit, 1995.

Zellers: Convincing people you work. I think that is really tough. You're out there a step away from your eyeballs freezing and it's blowing like crazy and nobody can help each other deal with frostbite because you're all just barely hanging in as it is. But you've got to get the photo because you're in the spot and the light is good and you're coming down. You've got to work in adverse conditions and you're hoping that you can get back in the snow case, get in your bag and get warmed up and that everything works out. Trying to convince people that it's a job is impossible.

WHAT ARE SOME OF THE BEST THINGS ABOUT BEING PRO?

Basich: Having the freedom to do stuff when you want to. Making your own hours. Having friends all over the world. Being outdoors. Traveling. It's a job that has its ups and downs; it makes it exciting that way, not a steady line. I like to live in the changes of the seasons.

Burt: The best thing for me is being able to see different places and ride different mountains around the world. I am totally lucky to have been able to snowboard all over the place from Europe to New Zealand to South America to Alaska. Another thing is getting to ride with the highest caliber of riders out there. I get to ride with some of the best in the world all over the place along with when I travel, I meet the local population wherever I go and get to ride with great local people who don't necessarily make it in a magazine, but they just rip. Those two experiences, meeting the people and going to the places are the best thing about being pro for me.

Cummins: Being able to stay at one place, or go to where it's really good, and knowing that you'll get some good snow if you just wait. Just to have the luxury to kick it and wait. In turn, you get to ride with the people that you've met snowboarding, who are like some of the raddest people, and you're snowboarding with them, just grinning from ear to ear, taking a run one after the other, just scared, both of you. That's super fun.

Zellers: The lifestyle is 100 percent the best. Since I've been a pro rider there have been no regrets, every year just keeps getting better. So it's this lifestyle of playing as hard as you can, then you work and when you work it's intense and you're focused and you're into it. You're not working every day at all, you've got this great lifestyle and you get to be out in the mountains. **You get to spend time doing what you love to do.**

Mike Basich, Tahoe backcountry, 1999.

MICHELE TAGGART

BY KATHLEEN GASPERINI

Let's clear one thing up: Michele Taggart is way more Marcia than Jan Brady. She wears cool clothes, dyes her hair various colors, and occasionally dabbles with chic nail polishes and henna hand-paint patterns.

She can be as beautiful as Meryl Streep or as average-looking as, well, Meryl Streep. She's inventive and chameleon-like, always coming up with the most creative concepts for snowboarding, dressing, gardening, and thoughts about the future, yet claims not to be very creative-minded. Here is look at who she is and what she hopes to be, and you know the show ain't over. She's just shedding her skin.

In the early '90s, Michele, uncharacteristically for a snowboarder, competed in both the GS [Giant Slalom] and Halfpipe: "I'd haul all these boards with pairs of softboots and hardboots up the mountains for training," recalls Michele. "OK, so it was a hassle in Europe 'cause you had to ride, like a gazillion lifts to get to the spot where we were training." But still, she did it, swapping hardboots and an alpine board every couple of hours for softboots and her twin-tip freestyle board for halfpipe training. It was worth it. No one has ever won four overall World Championship titles in a row like Michele has.

A couple of years ago, in a time of serious transition, she dropped Burton as a sponsor and decided to ride sponsor-free for a year, which got her way stoked on freeriding. But a sponsor-less Michele Taggart is like a free agent Michael Jordan. It just doesn't happen. When Bonfire/Salomon snagged Michele, she snagged a tree midair and broke her leg. Undeterred, she healed, opted for the softboot setup, and started riding in the pipe just in time to make the first Olympic snowboarding squad of 1998.

Does Michele plan on attending the 2002 Olympics? "I'm going year by year," she says. "But I'd like to be there." As for the political bullshit, Michele takes on a "rather-kiss-a-wookie" Princess Leia attitude: "It won't change, the politics of the Olympics, I mean. It'll always be the same people or same type of people running the show. I'll do my own thing and have fun. For me, I do what I do because I like it. I don't have a problem with what other people are doing, but hopefully, [snowboarding] will remain as cool as it has always been. And if I get in, I'll still do my own thing."

Mt. Bailey, Oregon, 1998.

The first time I ever met Tony Hawk—the absolute biggest name in skateboarding ever—I was introduced and without even blinking an eye he says, **"Oh hey, nice to meet you. My name is Tony."**

It's the little things like this that keep this veteran of skateboarding grounded in reality along with the rest of us. He is an exceptionally great skateboarder with an extremely positive attitude. It is impossible to turn on any televised skateboard event without seeing Tony being hyped as the world's best vert skateboarder ever. Not only has he worked like hell to be where he is today, but he also continues to promote the sport any way he can to ensure its longevity. He seems to have accepted the role of being the "spokesperson" for the entire skateboarding industry without ever getting interviewed for the position. I guess it is just the sort of thing that comes with being on the top of skateboarding for almost twenty years.

Not only am I indebted to Tony for all he has contributed to skateboarding, but I'm personally just stoked to see a man with such influence and good attitude rub off on the next generation of skateboarders. I am not here to make Tony sound like a god, but to just acknowledge the huge role he has played in skateboarding. It can't be easy to balance a business and a wife and a child and stay at the top of the skateboard world all at the same time. But he pulls it off with a smile.

WHAT'S YOUR ATTITUDE TOWARD LIFE?
I'm an optimist. I've been put in so many adverse situations that I had to learn to have a positive attitude and maintain composure no matter what. Worry will kill you quickly.

ON STUNTMEN, INJURIES, AVOIDING THEM AND STAYING HEALTHY:
I always knew of the dangers inherent in this profession. I've had other injuries that took longer to heal than my broken elbow. Some still linger. I usually feel OK in the morning, though, except after trying 900s for three days straight. Calculate your risks. Don't just try something without the experience to justify it. Even though you see guys pulling the crazy stuff in magazines and videos, they have the confidence and experience of years of skating. If you do get hurt, work at healing your injury instead of just lying around and waiting for it to get better. It will speed things up and ultimately make your body less prone to doing it again.

TONY HAWK
BY ISAC WALTER

ON BIG BUSINESS—THE GAP, COKE, LEVI'S, AND THE MILK ADVISORY BOARD VS. SKATEBOARDING'S UNDERGROUND IMAGE:

The object of doing something like the milk campaign is not entirely for personal gain. In doing so, skating reaches a larger audience that may not have ever recognized it as being legitimate. These people (or their kids) may suddenly embrace skating, which helps the industry grow and gives the skating community more opportunities.

REGARDING MIKE VALLELY'S COMMENTS ABOUT THE MUNSTER CONTEST BOYCOTT AND TONY NOT REPRESENTING THE MAJORITY OF SKATERS:

At the Munster contest there were a few key events that set everyone on the boycott campaign. First, the vert ramp and street course were mediocre. Titus [the organizer] receives huge sponsorships so there was no excuse to create anything but the best skating terrain. That mixed with overzealous security came to a head the night before the contest. Suddenly, everyone was screaming "boycott" and we walked out. I realized that Titus could tell the three-thousand-plus skater spectators that arrived the next day whatever he wanted regarding our absence. All of these people were paying a lot of money expecting to see American professionals perform. In their eyes, we were just a bunch of spoiled Americans who refused to skate on anything less than perfect. They would never know the politics and reasoning behind what happened until it was too late. The next morning I had people from Titus calling and begging me to convince skaters to enter. To appease the spectators, I asked my team to put on a demo for the crowd but not enter the event. Although they offered, we refused payment. Other teams, World, for instance, did the same. **Certain skaters** saw this as a slap in the face for what was being stood for and **chose me as the scapegoat. I accept the role.** At least the thousands of European skaters that made their way to Munster that year got to see some exceptional skating. Later they would learn why we didn't participate in the actual contest. All in all, it was a pretty shitty weekend.

ON A LONG SKATING CAREER:

I have no clue how long I can do it, but as long as I feel like I'm still improving I will persevere. Progression has always kept me going.

THE PROBLEMS OF AGING:

The only problems are the responsibilities of being a husband and father, although I don't really consider them problems. I'm sure I'll pay for all of this physical abuse later in life.

THE BIRDHOUSE VIDEO, *THE END*, TONY'S LAST VIDEO PART:

I don't make ultimatums, but I doubt I'll ever work this hard on a skating part again. I wrecked myself a number of times making this video.

MAINSTREAM MEDIA COVERAGE:

It helps get more people interested, but it also gets pigeonholed by being labeled as "extreme." People shouldn't see skateboarding and rock climbing in the same light, but they do, thanks to this newfound term.

INNOVATION:

Generally, the kids who are starting now are seeing what twenty-five years of skating evolution has brought to them. These kids learn kickflips in their first year. Imagine what they'll come up with after ten years.

HIS MESSAGE:

No, I don't try to make too many political stands or anything but I just like to see guys skating that are diggin' it, not because they think they're looking cool doing it or because they'll be accepted. The guys who just do it purely because they enjoy it, that's what I like to see. That's the only reason why I've done it—because I dig it.

WHAT MAKES HIM ANGRY:

The only thing that gets me angry, I guess, would be in skateboarding all this kind of political fighting, just bullshit that we've gone through for so long is still happening. It almost seemed like we were past it, but it's back around.

WHAT MAKES HIM HAPPY:

Watching Reilly [his son]. Just being with him. My family.

Opposite: Tweaked mute grab at the Encinitas YMCA, 1998.
Above: Taking time to sign autographs for kids.

In the late '80s and early '90s Christian Hosoi was one of the biggest skaters ever. Girls swooned over him and guys wanted to be just like him. He was a regular fixture of the Southern California nightlife scene. Tricks were named after him, like the "Christ Air." Thrasher magazine ran a cover early in the '90s with photos of Christian and Tony Hawk, with the tag line "Skater of the decade: Hawk vs. Hosoi." Christian graced the cover of Thrasher six times compared to Tony's five. But as the decade progressed and streetskating supplanted vertical-ramp skating, Tony seemed to grow in stature while Christian seemed to fade from view a bit. Not that Christian couldn't skate the street, but his focus on skateboarding was beginning to wane. Nevertheless, Hosoi was one of the all-time greats, and is now, sadly, mostly forgotten by contemporary skaters. As of this writing he's in jail for drug possession, and has fallen on hard times. Don't write him off though; while in jail he's cleaned up and reads the Bible daily. And, in the 20th anniversary issue of Thrasher both Tony Hawk and Alva cite him as one of the all-time greats who could still come back and blow everyone away.

One day in 1995, Matt Kennedy called me up out of the blue and told me that Christian had found a copy of the early newsprint Heckler and wanted to submit an article to us. The next day this showed up in the fax machine. This rambling, free-form piece of writing shows not only why Christian was all about style and creativity but also gives a glimpse into why he maybe lacked the focus to become as successful as Tony.—JB

Above: Speedway, 1988. Left: Venice Boardwalk, 1987.
Opposite, left to right: Backyard pool, 1987.
Christian at his own backyard vert ramp
in Canoga Park, California, 1989.
Winning the NSA highest air contest in Sacramento, California, 1991,
as Steve Caballero looks on.
Page 104: Hummer's Ramp, West Los Angeles, California, 1988.

My name is Christian Hosoi.

My views and experience and devotion are to keep a focus on my beliefs, I'm gonna try to make it happen no matter what it takes to get the job done.

Competition takes psyching yourself into a consistent strategic physical/mental and spiritual place for maximum concentration and confidence to perform ,at your highest potential. *I think in rhythm's timing, not words.*

I thank you (the people) who put my dream in perspective. My reality Fantasy Island gone bluegrass backyard style. Ya know what I'm sayin', huh? *Tattoo, where is that plane?* I got MIT I want to test out, I'll fly high or low and avoid the radar, I love you mom, pops for being more than just my parents.

A teacher/learner who listens, respects, and encourages your inner expression. That's understanding. I'm the explanation, open your eyes and focus to all my family, friends, lovers, girlfriends. Bob Marley, Bruce Lee, Nishi, you are true to love and life. I'm honored to have you as a friend. As much as we do business, we sure have a lot of time for pleasure.

Intellectual being is loony and animated to some extremes but to study and practice is only gonna help you succeed or fail. Understanding is something to listen and experience or think about but once understood, an explanation is not gonna matter.

It's mind over matter. If you don't mind, it don't matter.

Keys to life: living in a positive atmosphere and environment. Imagine and picture what's on your mind. Now conquer it by setting goals, values, and morals with high standards instead of high maintenance, brainwashing, and out-of-tune keys. Life is music. Now what would it be like out of tune? It wouldn't even fit in the hole. Let alone be happy.

"Let us be everything." Everything is transparent ground 'til painted. Now that's our choice to pick and choose the color we use to indicate a sign or painting not to lose. Everything's here to use and amuse, time to cruise.

Europe was incredible. Skateparks on the beach, cement bowl to bowl to spine to hip. It's the shit. I feel the positive vibrations coming out of the people and not just the guiding light.

I'm American born in downtown L.A. Japan is my heritage and my complete focus. I take pride of what I'm made of or what I'm recognized by. Attitude is characteristic behavior taken to a positive or negative personality. I'm what I've always been and will be till the day I'm not focusing.

The places traveling has taken me gave me meaning to be or make anything that I set my mind to and believe in. My cultural travel taught me to appreciate what you and I have and not take it for granted. Like life is to love. My work is original not reproduced; my personal work that is. *So from rough draft or final draft will always be my genuine draft. "I'll drink to that."*

Trade shows are ways to create illusion or facade; sometimes not always an oasis, but in classy, righteous, honest images. Identity will come out in consistency, that is time, and time is experience. Focus essential vitamin.

Focus, teach, learn, and share. Influential rock and roll model is an opportunity for you to be focused. You better recognize.

Women are beautiful, soft and supportive, fierce, wicked, loving, deadly, caring, and my mother is a woman so, let's just say I not only admire them, I love them and that if they were my mother, sister, aunt, daughter, girlfriend, or wife, I'd still love 'em. End it.

Behold the future, got-a-grip.

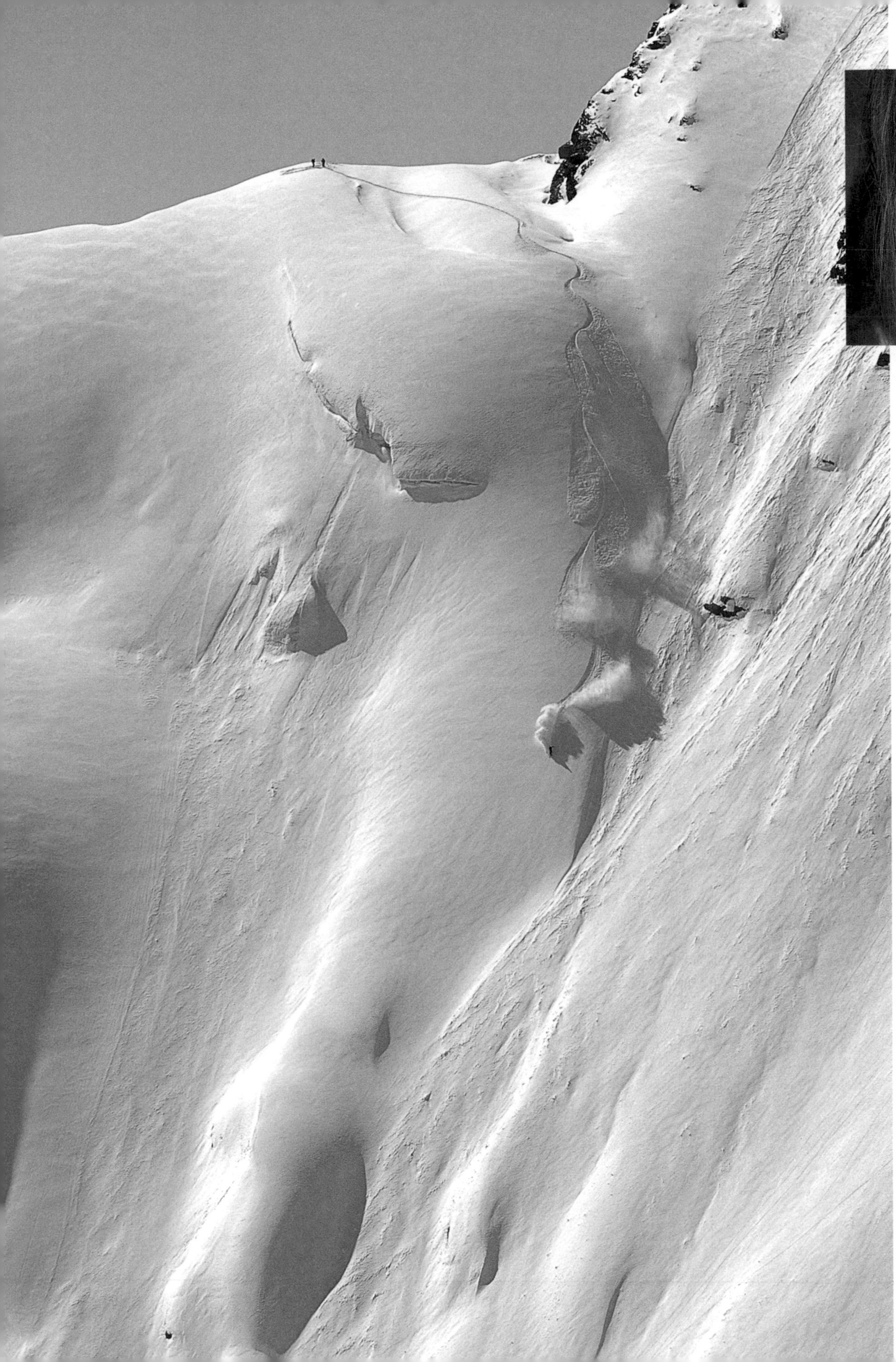

The mountain was ten minutes away, a lot closer than my school, which was fifty minutes by bus. It was '89 when I tried snowboarding and about '90 when I really started riding. When I started, I could apply what I knew in skiing to snowboarding. Plus the people I met were so low-key, open-minded, fun, and easygoing, which was the way I wanted skiing to be. The moment I started snowboarding I had a feeling I was gonna be doing it for a while. I never predicted I was gonna be a snowboarder 'til I started snowboarding. It kinda fell in my lap, in a sense. I just tried it one day with some friends. Prior to that I wasn't really interested in it. But after that day, I instantly knew that was what I was gonna do. It was such a good feeling and I thought maybe it might take twenty-five years for the masses to catch on to the sport, but they will for sure. But for me, personally, I thought that it was so much fun I didn't care if the mainstream was gonna do it or not, I wanted to do it regardless. Plus I got to be free. I got to decide what I wanted to do instead of having a bunch of coaches decide for me and tell me what I had to do all the time.

—*Victoria Jealouse,*
professional snowboarder
and big-mountain rider

THE GUIDE TO FINER RESORT EMPLOYMENT

BY GENE SUNG

Certainly most snowboarders have dreamt of spending a winter in Tahoe sculpting the vast snowfields, fine-tuning the sweet science of trickery, and inhaling unspoiled oxygen. Unless you have a few thousand dollars or are supernaturally talented and living off the expense account of a sponsor, you will likely end up working at a resort for your pass. I was one of the unlucky majority who couldn't soar like Brushie, spin like Terje, or have the style of Jamie, but I loved snowboarding as much as any pro so I dropped out of college six seasons ago to become a resort slave working on the hill. After my first season in Colorado, I returned to college with boarding virus in my blood. Each following winter thereafter, I left school for Lake Tahoe, doing the most trivial resort jobs for my "free" pass. Contrary to what any resort says, the pass is not free, but actually an employee pass with strings attached. If you show up to work ten minutes late, you could lose your pass for a week. So my advice to would-be resort employees is to buy a pass and save yourself some hassle. Sadly, like most slackers moving up to the mountains, I usually only had enough money for rent and a week's worth of ramen, so I resorted to the resorts.

Over the course of my six seasons working at the resorts I learned the ins and outs of the various entry-level jobs and, more importantly, which of these jobs allowed for maximal snowboard time. So here it is: The Guide to Finer Resort Employment.

FOOD AND BEVERAGE

Undoubtedly, working in the cafeteria is the lowest and most torturous of all resort jobs. Unfortunately, many new hires get sucked into this job because the turnover rate is high. Just imagine this: An endless sea of hungry, irate skiers and boarders screaming for that burger while you slave over a hot grill making french fries. There is definitely no glamour in flipping burgers, stocking ketchup, and mopping the tables. Girls laugh at you, parents think you're a loser, and you're the butt of all your friends' jokes who come groveling for free food on their ride breaks. My friend Bill nearly had a nervous breakdown. One day he freaked out and cried over and over again: "I dropped out of art school to stock ketchup for five dollars an hour! Where the hell is stocking ketchup going to get me? On top of it all, I hate this job because I never get any riding time!" If your main concern is riding, then definitely don't sign your name on the dotted food service line. Since the turnover rate is so high, those who are left usually work forty hours a week with few ride breaks.

RENTAL SHOP

When you walk into the rental shop during the middle of the day, you'd see one guy sprawled out on the boot-fitting bench, sleeping with a driblet of drool rolling down his cheek, and another guy with a blank expression staring at Cindy Crawford on *House of Style*. And where are the rest of the workers in this empty shop? They are all out on the slopes riding on their extended snowboard break. If there is any job on the mountain for which you clock in massive riding time and little work, it's the rental shop.

The way rental shops operate is everyone works hard in the morning when the skiers and boarders get their equipment. This is the worst part of the day since most people have no idea about what they need. It seems like they leave their brains at home because once they walk in the shop they forget their shoe sizes, names, addresses, and wallets. Usually, after several hours of chaos, all the people are successfully escorted out of the shop and onto the slopes. Then everyone in the shop lets out a sigh of relief, gives each other high fives, gets their boards, and takes the rest of the day off. Even better than getting a five-hour break every day is that the shop overhires around Christmastime.

Once the holidays are done, the resort's business is often cut in half so there are far too many people working. What the manager then does is only schedule most workers two or three days a week, and you're left with a pass that is good for your five days off. Think of that! Five days with a pass!!!

This can be heaven or hell, depending on how much you appreciate money. I've had friends in the rental shop who have earned sixty dollar biweekly checks and rode every day. The sad part is the first of the month when you have to apply your hundred-and-twenty-dollar income to rent. That's when you think: "Maybe I should get a second job." Then you think: "Nah! I get to ride every day!!!"

My good friend Rob once complained in a serious tone as he sat with a Coke in the empty snowboard shop watching *TB4* after a three hour break that "Man, this job sucks. It's such hard work dealing with skiers. It's a lot more stressful than it looks." I just looked at him and laughed at his pathetic laziness.

LIFTS

Along with food service, working the lifts qualifies as one of the worst jobs on the mountain. If you actually like working the lifts that means you never like to ride, you like freezing on the storm days, you like watching your friends ride, you like shoveling snow all day, you like getting to work super early, and you like being bored in a shack with nobody to talk to. Yes, there is little pleasure in being a "lifty," especially since there are nearly always forty-hour weeks, and you only get an hour to eat lunch and try to squeeze in two or three runs.

Aside from the major disadvantages, there are a few good perks. As a lifty you don't have to actually deal with people except when they slam getting off the lift. Usually, all you do is herd them through the line and load them onto the lift. Besides a "Hello, let me see your ticket," or a "Go that way," you don't have to talk much. On warm, sunny spring days you get a good tan and it's nice being outside. What it ultimately comes down to though is you never get to ride, so this job is not for the true snowboarder.

TICKETS

Much like the rental shop, this is a job you kill for because you get so much riding time. In the mornings you deal with a huge line of people and lots of cash, but once the lines are gone, you're on the mountain. Most of my friends who worked tickets were out by noon every day and loved it. What could be better than that?

PARKING

Who wants to get there at six o'clock in the freezing, snowing morning and put cones in the parking lot?

NIGHT JANITORIAL

Depending on the shift you're assigned, this position can mean a lot of riding or little sleep. Some resorts have the night schedule begin in the late afternoons, which is great since you ride all day then work until eleven or twelve. The mountain night life is dull: parties with the same fifty wasted guys, the same five drunk girls, and the same flat keg. So a night job is ideal. Just think, you can get first tracks every powder day, no tourists to deal with (except what they leave in the bathrooms), and you get forty hours a week. Unfortunately, the "graveyard shift" is the janitorial schedule at some resorts. Working from ten to seven in the morning can be very taxing on the constitution and will make snowboarding a very tiring experience. Graveyard janitors can ride every day, except they usually want to sleep and end up missing much of the day. Be forewarned that the graveyard shift is only for the strong of heart.

RETAIL

This is one of the better jobs because you're inside, all the reps want to give you deals, and good schedules are easy to connive. Here are some of the common questions you have to answer:

"Can I get change?"

"I thought it was on sale."

"I broke these glasses, so can I get a refund?"

"Can I get change?"

"What are toe heaters?"

"Why are the prices so high?"

"I work at _____ Ski Shop. Can I get a deal?"

"I scratched these goggles and I can't see out of them, so can I get my money back?"

The same question a hundred times an hour.

So there you have it! The Guide to Finer Resort Employment. After all, if you only wanted an honest-to-god five-peanuts-an-hour job and didn't snowboard, you could live in the city where life is much more interesting. My friend Brad once said to me these immortal words, which should be the philosophy of all resort workers: "Ski resorts are THE ONLY PLACE where you go to work to get out of going to work."

FOR THE RECORD:
DON'T TRY TO BE COOL...YOU AREN'T
BY MIKE DAY

Nineteen-ninety-four saw a huge influx of participants to the sport of snowboarding. Some people still refer to the early '90s as "the wave of snowboading that crested." Local heroes became national heroes. Small companies became big companies. As a result, the battle of "who was down back in the day" was waged. The need to fit in and be cool became greater, which created a frenzy of sorts. At the time, names like Chris Roach, Noah Salasnek, and Shaun Palmer were associated with ultra-coolness, as they were the top pro personalities of the time. To say you were friends with "The Palm" gave you instant respect and in most cases, instant friends. "Sprayin'" is what we call it, as in "sprayin' at the mouth." It's gone on since the beginning of time and it will never end. In reaction to all the fools that spray, Heckler writer Mike Day wrote the following editorial. —SM

Ride for yourself. Develop style and confidence.

You become secure and can handle any terrain or situation without hesitation. Then, bros who deserve it can have their buddies pull strings for their free ride. Remember: It's who you are, not what you are...period. Free boards don't make you a good rider. More often than not, people judge you by who you ride for. Why you ride is your personal claim. You for you...that's it. It is respectable to be low key and be the "nobody" who's schooling all of the "new school" flat-ground, name-dropping sheep, the ones who try so hard to learn the new move my friends did last season on some video that gets overplayed at your local shop. They did this with Noah and that with Roach. Everybody gets to hear junior's first time in the same state as Palmer: "We go every place and do it together, every day. Yeah, me and Chris Roach drank off the same keg, he is now my blood brother and calls me daily. He even lets me fuck his little sister. I'm cool! Joe Pro farted in a lift line and I smelled it so I'm fully down."

I've heard bros talked about like my family members by kids who are too scared to ask for a sticker, let alone just be true to their own lives. You talk about other people more than you relate to yourself. You lead a boring life if you need rumors about strangers to carry a conversation. Weak! Ride for your soul.

Sponsors are something to be proud of. Hard work gets rewarded. Don't think [Chris] Roach or Salas [Noah Salasnek] don't pay big dues. A paycheck is nice, but those guys paid years ago. Dues paid in full with those dogs, riding from the heart is why they are on top. Not a copycat image bought at Surf & Skate with mom's Visa card. Seen in the "New Fashion" article. Someone you don't know deciding how the "crowd" should dress to impress when loitering at the bottom of the hill. If it's cool, I made it so. Clothes suck, and you do too, sporting that new look everyone needs. You look cool in that eight-hundred dollar snowsuit but have you any Jones to ride?

Leave your image in the parking lot. I won't help you follow my line. You need to bleed riding. You will succeed without problems. You may never be pro, but you are not full of image. This is as good, in fact, a better goal to reach. Ability and confidence makes tough competition for a false image that you don't need holding you back. The top dogs have earned their clout years ago with soul. I know, I was there to witness the bullshit. I saw pro status become respectable. I was at Donner way back then and before, broke and disrespected on the only hill that opened its arms back when we weren't cool. Where were you?

STEVE CABALLERO

When something you love doing—like music, art, or skateboarding—becomes your profession and your sole source of income, it is easy for that profession you worked so hard to achieve to become a job with no passion, and your love for your art disappears. The first step is usually a certain jadedness wherein a lot of things about your profession really suck and there are a lot of people in your profession who are nowhere nearly as good as you are and don't deserve the success they have. Pretty soon you don't want to play music, paint, or go skating because it's work, and you'd rather do something else. Eventually you quit your career as an artist, musician, or skater, and the whole thought of your past profession leaves a bad taste in your mouth. The sad part is that you forgot the reason you started in the first place because it was more fun than anything else you'd ever done.

Steve Caballero is thirty-five years old, has been a professional skater for twenty-three years and not only does he still love to skate, but he doesn't show any signs of slowing down either. In a sea of too-cool-for-you pros with big attitudes, Steve is a refreshing oasis of positive attitude without anything bad to say about anybody. He just wants to skate.

I first met Steve in 1993 at the NSA Donner Ski Ranch contest. Later that year, when his band at the time, Shovelhead, came through town, we had a chance to get together, skate, and talk. Skating with Cab was cool because even though he was ten times better than me, I didn't feel any vibing or attitude. Steve even gave me pointers on trying to slide a rail I was having trouble sticking.

Here's some of what we talked about. —JB

Above: Backyard pool session, 1987.
Right: Crooked grind over a gap, 2000.

ON SKATEBOARDING

What's rad about skating now is the progression of the sport, how rad the tricks are, how difficult they are. Skating is still aggressive in some ways, but it's really technical in others and a lot of people can do both, can be technical and aggressive, and a lot of people just stick to technical. I like the aggressive part. Vertical skating is really aggressive because you just can't hop on a board and learn to skate ramp. It takes years to learn.

As far as streetskating these days, kids are learning the hardest trick first. They wanna catch up to everyone real quick. That's cool for them. If they're having a good time doing it, then more power to 'em. Streetskating's cool because you don't have to build a ramp or find a pool, you don't have to rely on other people or spend money to do it. I dig it, I miss riding ramps, but I enjoy what I'm doing now and that's just hanging out with a bunch of friends and driving all over the place going skating. Going to Santa Barbara or up to San Francisco.

There's lots of stuff not to enjoy about skating, but I enjoy it because I've been brought up through it. I think to be a real, real professional skateboarder I think it is a job because you have to deal with a lot of kids, and you have to deal with having a professional attitude at contests and demos. You have to listen to the boss of the company you ride for. I've been riding for Powell since 1979. My roots are there and they're still helping me out and give me a lot of support. I almost quit Powell to try to start my own company, but then I thought about it and if you start your own company, you have to quit skating and be a real businessman and I don't wanna be that. I wanna be a skater, travel, and play music.

To each his own, whatever you're into doing, that's what you're into. I've learned to adjust to anything. Usually people who don't like something, dislike it because they can't do it or they don't enjoy doing it. I guess that's it. Just keep skating and don't be narrow-minded, have an open mind and give everything a chance. Don't try to skate to be a professional, skate for fun, and if it happens that you become good enough to be a pro then fine. Don't be a follower, try and be a leader.

ON SNOWBOARDING

I've been snowboarding ever since it started, back in the Lonnie Toft days. I have my original yellow Sims snowboard, the one that you had to put a skateboard on top. I have a Sims Bert Lamar too. I used to go to Tahoe and ride the Tahoe halfpipe. Tom Sims would come out there and every year he'd have a new snowboard. The first snowboards were wood. Then they started to come out with P-tex, and then metal edges, and so on. I like just catching a lot of air and going through powder. Powder is like the best feeling. I would like to be more technical, but I don't spend that much time snowboarding. It's just a fun thing for me. I think to be a pro snowboarder, you have to really work at it. I'd have to move to Lake Tahoe, it's a four-hour drive for me. Snowboarding's just another hobby, a fun thing to do.

ON MUSIC

I've been playing music since I got out of high school. I started out with The Faction, and we did that until 1986. Then I started another band called Odd Man Out, and that was with one of the guys from The Faction and we did that until 1989. And then we got together with The Faction again. Jeff Kendall [pro skater, now Santa Cruz Skateboards' team manager], he replaced one of the guitar players. We did two shows and broke up again and then we started Shovelhead. This band is the most serious band I've been in because this is the one I've done the most to promote and make something out of. It goes both ways, sometimes I spend a lot of time on the band and sometimes I'll spend a lot of time skating. I hope something will come out of this 'cause I've taken a lot of time out of skating to make this work.

Shovelhead only released one CD and didn't last too long after that. Steve later joined Soda, but left that band after about a year to focus more on his skating. "I'm concentrating more on skating because it demands all of my attention and work," he told me in 2000. "The times that music was important in my life were when skating was slow and not very popular. Being part of the Vans Warped Tour keeps me in tune with music and gives me a chance to perform in front of thousands. Skating keeps me busy enough with all the touring, contests, and demos. I love this sport too much to give it up at this moment in my career. It's way too much fun still. Today's scene is great. Skating is becoming more respected all over the world because of Tony Hawk. He has done wonders for skating's image and popularity with the mainstream. I'm very proud of him, and I hope to someday become a great spokesman for the sport like he has.

Top: Steve signing autographs for fans at the 1999 X-Games.
Above: The Warped Tour, Boreal Ski Resort, 1997.

SHAWN FARMER

"In Huntington Beach the cops pulled me over and I had a little Glock behind the seat. They searched the car, took it and charged me a thousand in bills. It sucked! It wasn't like I was brandishing it or anything. That's why I'm late on my payments." —Shawn Farmer

Hardcore snowboarders have always kind of been slackers to some extent depending on which generation you're talking about. But Shawn Farmer was different, on another mental wavelength almost entirely. There were no walls to separate him from fear. If his hand was on fire he would fan the flames higher; go with the flow down any type of terrain and add Mach 7. He was the first to drop a seventy-five footer on a snowboard off a cornice in Alaska. Farmer's no team player. He wasn't wearing anyone's uniforms or playing by anyone's rules but his own. He was a rapper in a heavy metal band called Soak in 1993 before it was the hip thing for white boys to be. A complete believer in doing your own thing. Farm's accomplices were occasionally Nick Perata and the tunes in his own head that must have been crankin' through the roof. Here's a funny scenario from one day that we hung out. —CC

Stray stacks of finished wood now entered our path as we stumbled through a subzero temp garage that only a portion of Shawn's rent covered. "My landlords are doin' some remodeling here today," he said. This was his homestead.

I was introduced to a couple in their mid-forties—a lady named Shane and a guy named Gene. Both were the landlords and they seemed pretty levelheaded. Within minutes I was caught in the middle of a heated conversation.

Left: Tahoe, 1994. Below: Farmer reasoning with his landlords.

The debate concerned the efficiency of the ceiling in the small, downstairs living quarters, which was today's carpentry project. The question: Why such an icebox? Farmer vented his theory, "Yeah, I think a lot of the cold air drafts come from that stairwell," as he pointed towards our entrance point. In a curious carefree manner, Shane suddenly replied, "Oh yeah, where is the door that was on there?" [Farmer in a whispery low voice], "Uuhh, I broke it off." Everyone erupted in laughter.

Gene then asked curiously, "So how did you break it off, Shawn?" "Uuhh...I rode my snowboard down the stairs and grabbed onto the door so I wouldn't fall over."

Everyone laughed again as Shane made a humorous remark, "What were you on, besides the snowboard?" Farmer reacted, "I just got kind of out of control, I guess, hahahaha." Then things got heavy fast. Farmer had been out of town a lot and had been missing the landlords. Kinda missed the boat to give them some rent money. Here's a transcript:

GENE: DID YOU FINALLY GET YOUR CHECK? YOU KNOW YOU'VE BEEN LATE ON THE RENT TWO OUT OF THE THREE MONTHS THAT YOU HAVE BEEN HERE, MAYBE YOU NEED A ROOMMATE!

Farmer [stressed]: I can afford to pay the rent, I've just had a lean period. I got in trouble in San Diego. I had to give some money to the cops. It's like that takes priority over everything, 'cause it keeps me out of jail!

GENE: I HEAR YOU, BUT PAYIN' THE RENT IS A PRIORITY BECAUSE IT KEEPS YOU HERE!

Farmer [totally stressed]: You were supposed to have this ceiling insulated months ago, the TV upstairs sounds like a loud stereo down here, and I can't even hang out down here 'cause it's so damn cold! I've been seriously inconvenienced, I insulated all of this ceiling by myself and my time's worth money, if I go out on a photo shoot, I get a $150 a day!

SHANE: I'M SORRY, BUT I TOLD YOU THAT I WAS GONNA BE GONE FOR A MONTH, SO DOING THIS JOB GOT DELAYED. I NEVER GOT A RESPONSE FROM YOU SHAWN, YOU'VE BEEN VERY HARD TO GET A HOLD OF. YOU DON'T HAVE A PHONE, YOU DON'T HAVE A PHONE MACHINE!

Farmer: Well, I'm gonna get all that hooked up...soon.

SHANE: I'LL WAIVE THE LATE CHARGES AND GIVE YOU CREDIT FOR THE WORK YOU DID DO. SO IF YOU PAY GENE THE REST OF THE RENT BY FRIDAY, I'LL BE GONE, THAT WILL WORK.

It was resolved, at least for the time being.

Grraaaacjckc!...Almost tripping over boards, we made our way through the garage, through the pieces of wood. Farmer started talking: "What a hassle, I should just move out! Naw, I don't wanna go through first and last month's rent, movin' all my shit."

I added insult to injury, "Why don't you get a roommate like they said?"

Farmer said, "I don't wanna move in with some fuckhead! But I got this one guy I want to move in, he's from back East. I want to start a business with him. He's got a computer, he knows all that shit, he's good at business, I think."

"What are you gonna sell?"

"I don't know, we'll start off by selling shirts and shit. And my CDs, I've got six hundred of 'em sitting in my room, need to off them first."

"What business are you gonna do with him?" I asked.

"I don't know, I'll start with T-shirts, maybe sell these things."

Farmer handed me the new Soak CD. "This is the shit! Let's head up."

It was only a matter of time before we would get to Donner.

Time? Only 1:15 P.M. I was driving, checkin' out the new Snowave shop at the entrance to Squaw Valley. I almost rear-ended Farmer's truck! He suddenly hit the brakes to pick up a young, nubile female hitchhiker. He was now behind me. As I hit the turn signal to enter the freeway on-ramp, I glanced in the rearview mirror. Farmer went straight, right into Truckee! All I could hope was that he would show at Donner and not cheese.

Almost cresting the Summit, about a half mile from the Boreal exit, I noticed a white truck travelling about 80 mph to catch up with me. Wow, he shined the hitchhikin' girl or she shined him. Rad! We were gonna make it to the Ranch. The necessities were done to get on the hill. By chance we hooked up with our mutual friends Tim Manning and Jason Pata, they were a chair in front of us.

On the lift, Manson, I mean Farmer, started whispering, "There's a lot of ccrrraaaazzzyy people around hheeerree."

"You told the hitchhiker girl that?" I asked.

"Yeah, she was gettin' all nervous and shit, hehehe."

Suddenly he threw his arms in the air, with a smirk on his face. "Dude, I want a businesswoman for a roommate, one who will just fuck me sometimes. Yeah, that's what I need!"

As I laughed my head off, the conversation suddenly turned to music. "Our band rocks! Check that CD, put it on. You got to turn it all the fuckin' way up to hear how good the quality is!"

Bewildered, I ask, "How many tracks did you record it on?"

Farmer said, "Twenty-four tracks, old school two-inch. It's the best for live bands, guitars and shit. Analog is the best!"

Suddenly the lift stops. Thirty seconds pass. Farmer humorously yells, "Come on, Jesus Christ, were gonna go get our money back! Jump off Pata—there's a little tranny right under you!" Pata pauses ready to jump, the chair starts up again. We eventually get off the windy chair and buckle in. Manning and Pata are riding with us this run. Standing up on his board, Farmer babbles, "Yeah, my landlords are putting up tongue-and-groove board on my ceiling today."

Manning asks, "Why aren't you helping them?"

Farmer shoots back, **"I don't have time for that, man, I'm out here riding today! Hahahahaha..."**

Everyone laughs.

With heads shakin', we drop in for first tracks. It's 2 P.M.

Since that day I've heard the rumors. Farmer's not sponsored anymore. He bought some boots from a shop in Tahoe City the other day so he could go ride at Squaw. He's living with Shaun Palmer at his huge pad in Meeks Bay, as a caretaker. But the last time I saw Farmer was on a little hike into the Outer Limits terrain at Alpine Meadows. Must have been in 1999. He said hi, shook hands. Too busy riding to chat, he took off so fast through the powder and into this chute that no one could catch him. Literally! Some things never really change, do they?

How to Be a Rock Star

by Bob Klein (Superagent)

Bob "I'll make you a star, babe" Klein is sports agent to rock stars such as Shaun Palmer and Terry Kidwell and can guide you through everything from getting sponsored/signed to starting your own company to getting a Hollywood producer to do a film about you.

First and foremost, you must have the proper look. The short hairdo is in order these days, and if your color is common, dye it green.

Check your body for two things: tattoos and piercings. If you don't find either of these cosmetic enhancements on your person, *run*, don't walk, to the nearest artsy parlor to acquire these most necessary attributes to your look. It is very important to choose the proper placement: Piercing of the tongue is a requirement, as it also allows you to sound like the rock star you are becoming. Additionally, you should have a visible piercing on your face. Eyebrows and lips are good locations.

Next is the 'tude, dude. Start with the look on your face. Do not, and I repeat, *do not* ever show a smile. Smiles show weakness in character, and rock stars do not have a weak character.

Get a cell phone. You can buy the kind in the toy department at the grocery store. Most people can't tell those apart from the real thing. Talk on your new rock star prop as much as you can. When you walk into a room, say something like: "I'll have my agent look it over and he'll call you tomorrow, *ciao!*" Use foreign words to greet people and to say good-bye, as this shows you are one step ahead of the traditional "Whassup?" and "Late."

Bob Klein shows his roots at the first Mt. Baker Banked Slalom while Cory Ahtoong shows his crossover air guitar potential.

Practice carrying your board around. Switch from one arm to the other, carry it behind your back as if you are going to hike up a big hill. This is very important in your efforts to convince people that you can actually ride a snowboard. If you don't carry your board the right way, people may actually want to see you ride, and for rock stardom, that would be disaster!

When you receive all of the products from your sponsors, put the stuff on. Wear your boots and clothing around the house to give it the "ridden-in" look. That way, when you are traveling, on the chance someone sees your open duffel bag, they will see your "used" equipment. The same goes for your board. Take a flathead screwdriver and scrape the top of the board along the edge so it looks like your board has been well used.

Get yourself an agent. If you have an agent, you will get a bigger contract, because people will think you are so busy that you can't handle your own deals, and you won't have to talk to sponsors as much.

This all sounds like a lot of work, but if you do it early enough, you will enjoy a full winter of sitting on the couch and pulling tubes, without being disturbed by actual activity. If you have what it takes to be a real rock star, I am always looking to represent new talent, so give me a call.

"Snowboarding was just like skateboarding and rock 'n' roll, basically. Being a pro skater or snowboarder was just like being in a band and touring, having fun or whatever...
Now it is turning into a serious professional sport. I really do not consider myself as a professional athlete in that regard."
—**Axel Pauporté**, *King of the Hill contest winner, 1999*

JIM RIPPEY

As an amateur snowboarder Jim Rippey had a lot of ambition, a lot of talent, and a lot of personality to bring to the sport. He grew up riding the snow-covered hills of Lake Tahoe, where his riding progressed. Soon after, Jim became a poster boy for professional snowboarding. Active in contests, he has great footage in the largest films, is always present in the magazines, socializes with the public and his fans, and boasts one of the top-selling pro models for the world's largest manufacturer, Burton. A high-profile personality in the sport, he was the commentator for snowboarding's halfpipe inauguration into the 1998 Olympics in Nagano, Japan. —CC

HOW DID YOU START SNOWBOARDING?

After graduating from my hometown high school in Quincy, California, I was always riding at Donner Ski Ranch. During my first year I worked there as a lift operator and I remember the first night I went to get that job. They had the mountain lights on just for the employees and I saw these guys coming down the mountain making turns and I thought, "Fuck, that looks so rad!" The way it looked I just knew...I really wanted to try it. So that night I rented a board and went out with my friends and tried it; I had to learn the hard way about catching edges, slamming and stuff. Then the next day I didn't have to work so I went out and rode all day; I was really stoked on it right away. I rode most of that year and towards the end of the season I talked to Laurent [Northern California Burton rep]. I told him I was interested in getting sponsored and he told me to enter some contests. So I went and did four contests. I ended up with three firsts and one third. I actually won the first one I ever entered, at Homewood. It was a halfpipe contest and the pipe sucked. I just made sure to do one big air right in front of the judges, I also did a hand plant. I just tried to put a run together when everyone else was pretty bummed on the conditions. Anyway, I won it. Then, after that, I went to Laurent at the end of the year.

HOW LONG AFTER YOU STARTED RIDING DID YOU ENTER YOUR FIRST CONTEST?

About three months. The next year Laurent said, "I'll let you borrow a board for the year and I'll give you your clothes at pro-form." I was stoked because I didn't have to pay full price for the clothing I needed and I didn't have to buy a board. Up to that point I had been riding for exactly one year. I did the seven contests of the Cal Series and I did other contests around the Lake. I had fourteen firsts (pauses), one second, and like three thirds. I won overall in Racing and Freestyle on the Cal Series that year.

DO YOU FEEL YOU HAVE GRADUATED FROM SMALL SKI-RESORT COMPETITION RIDING TO BIG BACKCOUNTRY MOUNTAIN RIDING?

I'm into riding steep stuff now 'cause it's a lot more fun. I mean if you're on a steep snow face it takes a one-foot jump to do a thirty-foot air. You can look where you're gonna land and it just gets your adrenaline going. The speed involved is something you can't compare to riding in a park. It's awesome!

WHEN YOU'RE ON A PHOTO SHOOT OR FILMING, HOW MUCH MENTAL PREPARATION DOES IT TAKE?

I definitely have a thought of exactly what I'm gonna do, and one of the things I always do is make my runways packed down really good 'cause on the top of a cliff you could hook up on a rock and rag-doll over the cliff; so whenever I'm risking my life I don't take it lightly at all, I don't wanna die or anything (laughing). I just wanna do it, capture it on film, and be done with it. Not only do I pack my runways and get those all dialed, but I figure out how much speed it's gonna take to clear the cliff and land in the sweet pow spot where the cliff is the steepest. Then I think about the trick that I'm about to do off it and if I can visualize it in my head and see it happen usually I can do it, but I try and calculate things the best I can. You try and calculate everything to the best of your knowledge and take everything into consideration: the snow, the angles of the takeoff and landing. Sometimes there's one thing you didn't calculate or account for and that's when things go wrong.

DIDN'T YOU HAVE A CLOSE CALL LIKE THAT WHILE YOU WERE FILMING ON STANDARD'S *TB4* [*TOTALLY BOARD #4*]?

It was total spring snow—super slushy—and it was at Squaw. I was gonna do a frontside 360 and frontside 360s are pretty easy 'cause you can jump and then you can see the whole way around while you're rotating. So anyway, I was hiking up to go do it and I decided that I wanna try something a little bit harder and I wanted to do a fakie to forward 540. One of the things I didn't account for is that I can't ride as fast backwards as I can forwards and it was slow slushy snow. So I dropped in to do it, was bogging, didn't have the speed, and still went for it. I came up way short. I didn't think that riding backwards would affect my speed in the takeoff; I came really close to landing on my chest on some rocks. Luckily I just hit my elbow, that was it.

I REMEMBER SOME FOOTAGE SHOT IN ALASKA IN WHICH YOU PULLED OUT TO THE SIDE OF A VERY STEEP CHUTE AND THE WHOLE THING SLID INTO A HUGE AVALANCHE. DID YOU KNOW THAT WAS BEHIND YOU OR DID YOU INSTINCTIVELY PULL OUT TO THE SIDE OF THAT?

No. When I dropped in on that, that day our guide dug a snowpit and said that things could slide, they didn't look super stable. So we kinda decided as a group to stay away from anything that's really exposed where you're put out over cliffs or anything that could slide. And then for some reason the next thing we landed on was this huge face where the line on the left was pretty exposed and one on the right that was also kinda exposed. We're on the top of it and it's sparkling powder and it's like fifty degrees [pitch] and it looks so sweet, perfect. Tom Day is like asking, "Who wants to do this one for a heli shot?" And I was like, "Yeah, I'll do it. It looks rad."

So I was planning to go down the right side of this gully and do five or six turns so my slough would go down the right chute, and then turn to the left where at the top was the perfect wave with a really nice twenty-foot transition to slash on the way down. So before I dropped in Victoria [Jealouse] told me, "Be cautious if you surf that wave cause there's a three hundred-foot low angle cliff on the other side of it." I didn't even remember seeing this cliff from the helicopter. So I dropped in and made like five turns, went left, and got up on this wave of slushy sun-baked snow that the sun had been hitting, whereas the first part of the run the sun hadn't hit it. So I'm surfing down good pow and I cut over to the left, next thing I know I'm on this slushy wave and I'm just like, "What the fuck!"

So I snap a turn on it and instead of making a big plume like I wanted it to, it just dropped like three inches and fractured. So in front of me it started sliding. I went to the left and thought I'd be able to stop there and watch all this go over a fat cliff and then right as I thought that, I got hit in the back with another small slough that was actually this whole fracture—half was below me and half was above me. The snow hitting me in the back was going over my head and when snow does that it liquifies. When it turns into water it's so fucking heavy! So it hits me in the back and I'm holding my heelside edge as hard as I can, as far to the left as I can trying to avoid going with this waterfall of snow over this cliff. I held it for about a second, and then it took me with it and I was part of this waterfall thinking, "I'm gonna go over this fat cliff but I'm just gonna keep my board in front

of me and land on it instead of my head." After going with it for about a hundred yards my heel-side edge finally hit, I fought it left and got out of it about fifty feet before the cliff! Then there was like seventy to one hundred feet of just snow plume going over this huge cliff, the helicopter was hanging, and I gave 'em a thumbs-up telling 'em I was OK.

So it was pretty scary, but it was kinda tweaked though. After that happened instead of me sitting there going, "Oh my God, I could have just died." I was thinking, "Wow, that's gonna be a great shot." Which is completely warped! It's kinda weird, I never really thought I was gonna die. I thought I might go over some fat cliff and get fucked up but I never really thought, "I'm gonna die." Then the helicopter is just hanging there waiting for me to keep going and I'm thinking what Tom Day [cinematographer] just filmed from the helicopter is gonna be a great shot, but I still have a few more thousand feet of vertical right here and I can get some good pow shots. So I start going again and make three turns, come up to a cliff, ollie it thinking it's a fifteen foot cliff. I'm like thirty-five to forty feet off the ground thinking, "What the fuck!" I caught a ton of air and landed in like four inches of pow on top of ice! It was so fuckin' hard! My heart was going a million miles per hour. But stuff like that happens every once in a while and it's good. It's a slap in the face 'cause you've taken it that close to the edge and you've gotten away with it. Next time it's gonna make you think about it more.

WITH A THREE-BEDROOM, TWO-BATH HOME IN TRUCKEE, CALIFORNIA, A GLEAMING FULL-SIZE 4X4 TRUCK IN THE DRIVEWAY, AND FRESHLY SCREENED SIGNATURE MODEL BURTON BOARDS LYING IN THE CORNER OF YOUR LIVING ROOM, HAS YOUR LIFE BECOME WHAT YOU SET OUT FOR IT TO BE?

I'm stoked that I made it to a point in my life where I was able to finally do something like build my own house. Right there I knew snowboarding was paying off better than expected for me.

HOW ABOUT SNOWBOARDING AND THE OLYMPICS. WILL YOU COMPETE EVER?

I think it's just great. It just makes snowboarding bigger, and if it gets bigger then there's gonna be more money in the industry; and if the industry gets bigger it will be doing better, which is good for everyone who works inside of it, including you and I. But for me personally I'm not really too worried about expending too much energy on competing in the Olympics. It's all pipe riding and I don't focus too much on pipe anymore anyway (laughing).

SO WHERE CAN YOU GO FROM HERE? WHAT DOES THE FUTURE HOLD FOR JIM RIPPEY?

I love filming. My plans are to keep working with Burton snowboards, keep designing my board for them and try to come up with really strong graphics and a board that people are stoked on so that I'm doing my job. I wanna always keep on top of my riding for as long as my body will allow it 'cause if you get stale and people see you doing the same tricks every year in the videos no one is going to really watch you. Each year you've got to do things bigger and better even though that puts pressure on you. I am grateful for everything in snowboarding that allows me to have the opportunity to go places like Alaska and get a helicopter, or put your credit card down and not even have to worry about paying for it because you know that you have a travel budget that is going to pay for it. I'm doing things that people dream of doing and getting to do it every year.

Previous spread: Alaska, 1996.
Opposite: Backflip, Sugar Bowl, 1996.
Sequence: Donner Summit, 1993.

MIKE VALLELY:

I Skate for Myself

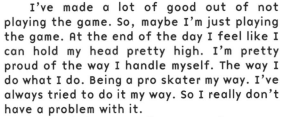

I do not want to push the idea that being sponsored and skating for a company is what it's all about. I would rather say I skate for myself because I really do. That's where I am at and that's where I think it is at. Being sponsored is a nice thing. It's a bonus on top of the fact that I skate for myself. But the more magazines you read, the more videos you watch, the more you plug yourself into the skateboard industry, the more information is fed to you about being sponsored. Just the idea of being sponsored, free products, making a video, is constantly spread to you. That becomes the goal. That becomes the goal of skateboarding. A kid would say to himself that he wants to be sponsored, he wants to be in a magazine. I was like that when I was a kid. That was a dream for me to be in a Powell video. I don't know if it's just my perspective, or where I am standing. Although that was the goal it did not get in the way.

We had these dreams but our dreams didn't get in the way of what we were doing. I might be wrong, but what I see a lot is that the idea of sponsorship, the idea of getting free product, the idea of getting in the magazine truly gets in the way of kids enjoying skateboarding for what it is. Maybe I see it that way because I'm sponsored. My views may be a little perverted compared to the views of an amateur, but maybe that's just how it appears to me. That's why I stress the fact that I skateboard for myself. Sometimes though, kids are waiting for you to rattle off who your sunglasses sponsor is, and who your hemp sack sponsor is, and who your underwear sponsor is. So, when I say that I skate for myself it can easily be misinterpreted as wisecracking.

I've made a lot of good out of not playing the game. So, maybe I'm just playing the game. At the end of the day I feel like I can hold my head pretty high. I'm pretty proud of the way I handle myself. The way I do what I do. Being a pro skater my way. I've always tried to do it my way. So I really don't have a problem with it.

I lived in a small town. The cops, teachers, and city council were all cracking down on us skaters. I never thought there was going to be a way out of that town. Skateboarding every day was such a real experience. Everywhere you went someone was telling you that you couldn't do it. Chasing you out of places. It was life with the volume turned up. It was really intense all the time. There was this daily struggle. When I read all the magazines and watched all the videos it really kept me inspired. On top of that I was having my own experiences skateboarding, all of my rewards from skateboarding. Just all the different things I was experiencing. Being on my board. Together that was so heavy. Then to pull a quote out of a Powell Peralta video, something like *Skate to Create*, that was awesome. I hope that saying that I skate for myself can do the same thing. **I look at skateboarding as an art form.** Bottom line. It's a lot of other things. It's definitely a sport, skateboarders are athletes. To me, skateboarding is a form of art. You are expressing yourself. As artists it's our jobs to inspire and to empower, if we can't do that then we are failing our audience. As skateboarders that's what we have to do. That is my calling. That's why I'm me.

Because of the Bones Brigade I think I have created my own folk-tale or legend. By enduring the shit I've had to deal with. Not everyone has had a front-row seat to it but everyone sort of has an idea that I came from someplace and I did something and I'm still around. I'm still plugging forward. If I step out I have to tip my hat to myself because it has been one massive ride. I meet people in different towns and they always want to thank me. I ask them what they want to thank me for and they say for being myself. That's like the greatest compliment. For some reason I still have a place in skateboarding. I still have this niche in skateboarding and I've been waiting for everyone to shut me down. And it hasn't happened.

Talking about people who are progressing or evolving, or people who get me psyched with the way they skate, with me it all starts with Mark Gonzales. That's really cliche to say, but for me it's the truth. I think a lot of people feel that's what they're supposed to say, but for me it's the truth. Without Mark Gonzales there would be no Mike Vallely. Period. He is the guy 100 percent. He was the artist. The poet. He was the guy. Freedom just poured out of him. He was just this guy who was overflowing with creativity. It showed in everything he did. If anybody I ever meet lives up to this famous quote by Oscar Wilde, "living is an art form," that quote was made just for Mark Gonzales. Everything he does is artistic, creative. Just sitting down eating, having a conversation with him is a form of art. I hate to be around the guy too much because that's a heavy trip to be around. He is overflowing with this stuff. I've hung out with him, I've lived with him for a period of time. I can't really pinpoint anything in particular. Everything he did is inspiring to me. Just the way he lives his life. I don't necessarily agree with the things he has said or done, there have been times when I thought poorly of him. But from a distance, man, he is so inspiring. And so awesome.

Beyond him, the other guys when I started out skating, Natas, he was so inspiring. I sort of tried to erase that memory because he's not around anymore. I don't know what he's doing, I hear all these different things. I guess that he lost his passion for skateboarding. I don't know if that's totally true but I hear it is. That's the impression that I get so I pull away from that. It's great if he doesn't have a passion for skateboarding and he's moved on. That's fine. But when someone like him, somebody that impacted skateboarding so hard pulls away for some reason, it rubs me the wrong way. It leaves me with a bad taste. He's a hero, you know what I mean? To find out that your heroes aren't going to go down with the ship, for me that's rough. I would just love to see the guy be into skateboarding. Making a contribution. Whether it's futile or not. That's just my own personal tweeknish. That's just what I want to see. The guy was one of my heroes and he's not around anymore. It's like I lost the connection with him, the way I still have it for Mark. Mark has come and gone through the years, but he's still impacting skateboarding, whether people see it or not. Natas just seems to have succumbed to business and the world of money. I am sorry. It's too heavy, man.

I guess to an extent I am a purist in that sense, the money that keeps the skateboarding industry afloat leaves the hands of the skateboard industry. I do not want to see the money that keeps the industry afloat leave the skateboarding industry. **I don't want to see companies like Nike, ESPN, and Mountain Dew come in and profit off skateboarding.** Making skateboards. They already profit off the image. Here is the difference. Some people say, "What is the harm of promoting the sport and watching it grow?" What happens with growth is people forget about protecting it. I'm not against growing, as long as we can control it. But if we don't have a say then I'm not for it.

There are people in the industry right now who are thinking in the opposite direction. They don't care about protecting the sport. I can't deal with that. I am anti that. I will fight that and see it defeated. I've already experienced that on several levels with Powell. I've spoken my piece and will continue to do so until they kick me out. I'm not against growth. I'm not against the Olympics. I'm against what that might represent for the sport. If we're in the Olympics we can only lose because our industry isn't united and we don't have a common goal. Until the big business guys in this industry get together and lay down some goals, what is skateboarding? Who are we? What are our goals? That has to happen. Do industries do this? Probably not. Do people who make up industries get together and do this? No.

The skateboarding industry is a small world. We can all get together and have common goals. That probably won't happen, but that's a dream. I won't stop dreaming that dream because it can happen. People have sold skateboarding out and will continue to do so. I'm worried about the history. I can't imagine some kid in his driveway thinking about winning a gold medal. That's not my vision of skateboarding. That's not where it's at. With stuff like the Extreme Games, it's all competition. What are they putting on TV? They're putting competition on TV. That's what they're showing, that's what they do. What can some kid fooling around on his skateboard in his driveway relate to a vert contest? That's just some vert contest on TV. Is that skateboarding? I don't think so. It's a part, a small little piece. That kid goes around his neighborhood skating with his friends. That's skateboarding. For me, that's the wrong message to be sending out for skateboarding. And I don't think kids can relate to it. As a kid, it was all about skating to have fun. It's just warping what skateboarding has been historically.

I always go back to how skateboarding affected me growing up. Skateboarding was such a positive thing, it gave me things that I needed. When I was fourteen, I had a sense of purpose and direction in my life. The kids I went to school with didn't have it. As a kid, skateboarding was a surrogate family for me. I didn't have a good family life so skateboarding was there for me. Anything could have come along and tweaked me but skateboarding was there for me. It was positive and kept me in check. That's all I want for kids now, to get into skateboarding because it's fun. It doesn't matter what tricks are going on, as long as it can be that. I don't think if we horde out in some competitions, if we got to extreme measures with the Olympics and stuff, that's why I am anti that. I'm not necessarily anti being in the Olympics, but only if we have control. If big companies come in and buy out the skateboarding companies, say Nike comes in and buys out Powell, will each company buy our names? I don't know, that could happen. It could easily happen. And I just think that's not skateboarding anymore. I was just about to start speculating on a bunch of different scenarios and I don't think I should go there. Just think about if we continue to grow and grow and grow. Watch those scenarios play out for a little bit and you'll see what happens.

I will continue to put these ideas out there. And I will continue to try and get people in the industry to see these things. If everyone in our sport right now—the people in control, the people with money and power—would just sit back for a few minutes and think, why did I get into skateboarding? What were my first exper-iences in skateboarding? I just think that would bring some revelations. When you're in business the picture gets fuzzy. And, I've seen it. I've seen people have to change themselves in order to survive. That's a part of the reality of the business side. And if they could just hold on to their origins and be able to look at them on a daily basis or where did that come from. Even if we don't talk about it, just having that idea out there does unify us. Does it? I hope so. Just think about who you are and where you come from. We're not all going to sit down and talk about it. I realize the difficulty of it, but we all got to look at ourselves in the mirror. We were all fourteen, we all started skateboarding at some point. We all got into it for a reason. If we can all just stay in touch to the smallest extent we will be alright. I hope.

(This text is from an interview that Geoff Kula did for Heckler *that never ran.)*

Slam City Jam Contest, 2000

JIMMY HALOPOFF

Not only does Jimmy Halopoff go way back, but the guy was light years ahead when it came to stylish "seatbelt" grab airs and shit like that. He was heavily influenced by Randy Walter who he travelled with extensively in a less-than-roadworthy station wagon. —CC

I was in Vegas at the trade show one year and it was just a big letdown. My sponsor at the time told me they wanted me to do the same contest series the next year. I felt I was ready to "move up" and I just wanted to do something new instead of travel around in my old beat-up station wagon. That's how we would travel to these contests, me and all my buddies.

The car had some electrical problems. **It needed a wire jump to start it and a wire jump to work the headlights and the windshield.**

It was me and Randy Walter, Trevor Snowdin, Shon Baughmann, and Phil Ferguson. It was a crack-up. We'd just sleep overnight in that thing goin' from contest to contest and we'd be like the only ones camping out in Boreal's parking lot before the contest with it snowing outside. I was freezing in the station wagon with my spacecraft mattress. There were three of us lying on the mattress so close together. It was just sickening how close together we were, with one person lying in the front seat. It was just crazy!

A lot of the people who lived in Grass Valley would drive up in the morning, others would stay in motels. We'd just be there the night before barbecuing in the parking lot. Such losers. Just trying to make it in snowboarding, it was so funny. But that was probably the funnest time in my life involving snowboarding. **Then, anytime we had troubles with the car, Rob Juistina would help us out and give me some weed so I could sell it, fix the car, and keep going to the Series.** I remember one night he had a party at his house and I took him into this room and said, "Rob you gotta help us." We couldn't even make it to the Mt. Lassen contest and I wanted to go so badly. It was one week away. I said, "You gotta front me some weed, man, you gotta front me some weed!" Anyway, we ended up making it up there for the event.

Rapid exit from the Horizon Hotel parking lot in Tahoe, 1998.

MIKE BASICH

Mike and Tina Basich are brother and sister and could almost be the Donny and Marie of snowboarding. They're a household name among snowboarders and they project a positive and healthy image. They even live in Salt Lake City. They are about ten times cooler than the Osmonds though, and they're in Salt Lake for the deep, dry powder days, not the Mormon Church. —CC

Right: Ready to compete in 1991.
Below: Utah backcountry, 1997.

MIKE BASICH: I rode for Kemper for four years and Andy [Hetzel] just got his board with them. I got second at the World Championships in Breckenridge, Colorado, and I guess my career was starting to grow, you know. Then they were gonna make a board for me. I had all my designs in to make the board when this guy approached me at the Las Vegas trade show and asked me if I wanted to ride for Hooger-Booger Snowboards. I was like, "I don't know, maybe." Then they made me a good offer and I went back to Kemper; they were always horrible about paying on time. I thought maybe this will help me out with money and I can get out of Tina's shadow 'cause I was Tina's little brother for a while as both of us were riding for Kemper, you know. I thought it would be fun to do my own thing, be completely separate. So I signed with Hooger-Booger and lost a little money on the way out with Kemper. It was probably the best thing I ever did.

WHAT HAPPENED AFTER THAT?

I was doing my own thing with my clothing company 241. I decided to completely ride for myself and silkscreened the topsheet and base for a few snowboards on my pool table. I then sent them off to to a friend at A.M.S. (American Snowboard Manufacturing) in Seattle. That's pretty much what I was riding up until I signed a contract with Elan Snowboards in May of 1999.

TELL ME THE STORY ABOUT YOU AND TINA BECOMING GOOD FRIENDS WITH ADAM YAUCH OF THE BEASTIE BOYS.

My sister met him while he was snowboarding in New Zealand a few summers ago, then he had the whole next winter off and came to Utah, that's where I met him. We were out riding and stuff; he's into the same type of riding I'm into: freeriding as much pow as possible. Then Adam moved into those Santa Fe apartments with me and my friend Chris. We lived there for the winter, hung out and rode. Then the year after that he lived at Tina's house, spent probably half the winter here. Adam's pretty into his music now and the Free Tibet thing he's doing. He's also back on his tour schedule again so he doesn't live out here anymore. I knew him for about a year and a half before I ever went and saw the Beasties play. I'd never seen 'em play before. He's super quiet, a really nice guy; but quite a different person on stage. It's a trip to go watch someone you know perform when sixty thousand people at a stadium are chanting their name (laughing).

TELL ME ABOUT THE INCIDENT WHEN YOU AND ADAM PAINTED THAT 241 PIECE ON THE WALL AROUND HERE FOR THAT POSTER PHOTO A FEW YEARS BACK.

It was when we were living at the apartments. We were bored one night. We were with this guy filming for a movie and he filmed us buying the spray paint. Then it was right down the street from here and we went out there at two or three in the morning, I did some of it and Adam did some of it, we filmed that also (laughing). We ended up going riding the next day and drove by it on the way home. We stopped for about five minutes and filmed us talkin' shit in front of it (shaking his head).

So we did that, then we went up to Taco Bell. Three cops walk in, the place is packed with kids and they come straight to us. They're all, "We got ya!" And we're all, "Huh?" We act like we don't know what they're talking about and I guess two old guys saw us filming in front of it and noticed the painting was new. They followed us to Taco Bell and called the cops.

So the cop asks to see my hands and I didn't have any paint on mine. Then he asks to see Adam's hands and he had some paint on his pinkie. So they busted him, took us outside, and searched the car looking for the spray paint. In the meantime the video camera is sitting right there with all the footage and evidence of us doing it all on tape plus there's 241 stickers laying all over the floor (laughing).

They never turned on the camera but they knew. They're telling us, "This is a major crime in Utah." They wrote Adam a four-hundred-dollar ticket!

HOLY SHIT!

We ended up talking to the owner of the property where the wall was, payed him eight hundred bucks and he dropped the charges.

DID HE MAKE YOU GUYS PAINT OVER IT TOO?

Well we offered to repaint it but he decided to take care of it himself. It was expensive, but it sure made a great 241 poster (laughing).

TINA BASICH
BY MELANIE MORENO

Tina Basich is not only one of the biggest personalities in women's snowboarding, she's one of the biggest personalities in snowboarding period. A familar face to anyone who has watched MTV and ESPN's coverage of snowboarding, Tina is one of the most recognizable names and faces in the business. She's a talented snowboarder who pushed the envelope in big mountain and freestyle riding and is also very involved in the industry, yet she has remained down to earth. When we covered Tina in our fall '95 issue, her childhood friend Melanie Moreno went to visit her at Tina's then new Salt Lake City home and wrote this piece for us. — JB

Tina Basich was born and raised in Sacramento, CA. I first met her when I was about ten years old while playing soccer together on the same team. It was a good team, we won most of our games. We didn't have any idea that we would later become good friends and fellow skateboard Bettys. And even with the success of our team, we definitely didn't imagine that Tina would someday be a professional athlete and one of the top snowboarders in the world. We didn't even know what snowboarding was.

Del Campo High School in suburban Carmichael, CA, was filled with a bunch of jocks, cheerleaders, burnouts, and drama class kids. Teenage life in suburban Sacramento could be pretty boring, especially when you didn't exactly fit into one of those categories. Burnouts were off smoking at the creek, jocks and cheerleaders were busy planning the design for next year's homecoming ball, and drama class kids—I have no idea what they were doing—but probably something we didn't want to be doing.

Tina and I were total skateboard Bettys. I'm not at all ashamed to admit it. And neither is Tina: "We never really clicked into the whole high school scene of rallies and dances. I never really hung out with too many people from school. All my friends hung out at the skateboard shop or we knew people from contests and stuff. We were always gone on the weekends anyway."

Being a skateboard Betty is not as easy as it may seem. You gotta follow all the skaters around to contests and demos, give them rides to halfpipes and pools, and hang around skateboard shops. It takes devotion and loyalty—qualities our more shallow peers did not possess. While most other teenagers were busy playing tennis at the local swim and tennis club, we were spending our free time hanging out in skateboard shop parking lots, carpet banks, coffin banks, neighborhood ramps, and ditches.

On the night of her senior ball, Tina took Sacramento skater Randy Smith to dinner and then to Go Skate skate shop where they spent all night giving friends rides in the limo.

The Basichs have a great house. They built it themselves and allocated the entire upstairs to Tina and her brother Michael, who, if you didn't already know, also makes his living from snowboarding. (He rides for Elan and owns a snowboard clothing company called 241.) There was a time when their new house wasn't done, but they had already sold the old house. For six months, the Basich family lived in a teepee on their front lawn. I spent a lot of summer days at that house. Most of our friends liked to go there because there were always toys and things: a trampoline, a swimming pool, a pool table, a pachinko game, and best of all, a big, friendly, yellow dog. To top it off, there were always snacks, or someone was always barbecuing.

Now Tina mostly lives in Utah. She was sponsored by Kemper when she first traveled there for a photo shoot at Snowbird. Most of the team members had never experienced Utah snow and vowed to return. Prior to this, she always rode in Tahoe. She likes the snow in Utah because it's very light and there's a ton of powder: "The storms come over the lake and absorb the moisture and then dump it on the mountains."

Her first two years in Utah, Tina lived in a small two-bedroom condo. Then, she decided to move into a house, where she lives with two roommates: Burton pro rider Dave Downing and Beastie Boy Adam Yauch. Her brother Michael lived in the basement for a short time but after being injured he had to move back to Sacto. Tina had to move to a bigger space because "There wasn't enough room at the condo for all our house guests."

There are about six visitors staying at her house at all times during the winter months: "I like to be able to invite friends to come visit me in Utah. It's so nice having enough room for all of us."

During the summer, Tina's house is completely empty and stays vacant until November. Pro rider Shannon Dunn, one of Tina's closest friends and roommates, Dave, and Tina practically have the same schedule: "We all go to the same contests and stuff. It's cool 'cuz I have someone to travel with. We pretty much do everything together during the winter."

When I went to visit Tina in her new house just outside of Salt Lake City this summer, all the roommates were missing and we had the run of the place. Her family had recently been there to build a deck in the backyard and to do some minor repairs. The Basich family is very close and her parents have always taken an active interest in both her and Michael's love of snowboarding. The house in Utah has a panoramic view of the mountains where Tina spends most every winter day. Sparsely decorated, you can tell it's Tina's house. On the walls hang photos of her friends and all the furniture in the house has either been built or fixed up by a Basich family member. They're very crafty like that. She didn't use the kitchen in her new house until four months after she moved in: "There are a lot of good restaurants around here—Brackman's Bagels in the morning and Thai for dinner." The kitchen works fine, though. We had a gourmet-style barbeque dinner the night before flying back to CA.

SPONSORSHIP

Coming from a nonskiing family, Tina first got into snowboarding when her mom came home and told her about a snowboard she had seen on display at some store. The next weekend, Tina and Michael rented boards in Sacto and drove up to Soda Springs. Snowboarders weren't allowed to ride on the lift, so they spent the day hiking up the ice-covered hill. Not discouraged one bit, she went out the next day and bought a Burton Elite, the standard of the time. (Tina later sold that board to Casey Doggin for a hundred bucks, but ended up buying it back broken a couple of years later for memory's sake.) From then on, every weekend was spent snowboarding.

She originally only rode at Donner Ski Ranch, but later started checking out different places. At that time, Boreal required snowboarders to get certified before they could ride the lift. You had to demonstrate you could turn and stop before being issued some laminated card with your picture on it. She recalls, "I was so stoked when I got my intermediate pass. That meant I could ride the big lift!" Boreal actually ended up sponsoring her one year, and she got to ride for free.

In 1987, Tina was flown her first board: a Sims Pocketknife 1450. And, at the end of the 1988 season, after avidly snowboarding for four years, Kemper sponsored her. It wasn't until her last year with Kemper that she got her own model. Tina has always had a hand in the design of her boards including supplying the artwork for her graphics. Before Tina began designing her first model, she went to Europe, where almost all snowboards are manufactured, to check out how they actually produced snowboards: "Visiting the factories really helped me understand all that goes into the design of a board. I remember getting a voice mail message from someone who was getting a pro model and wanted me to call and explain how to design it. I laughed because I feel like that's not something you can just explain over the phone. **Anyone who is getting a pro model should be able to design it and understand how it all works.**"

She's currently riding for Sims Snowboards. When Shannon Dunn left Sims to ride for Burton, there was a vacancy that Sims wanted Tina to fill. Since Kemper had changed ownership during her last year, she felt the timing was right.

Tina attributes a lot of the growth of her snowboarding skills to riding with Andy Hetzel. They both rode for Kemper and always rode together. She saw an improvement in her snowboarding from riding with him: "I really try to ride with people who push me. Instead of leading the pack, I like to try and keep up with someone that is better than me. Freeriding in good conditions is the best. I love Utah because the mountains are big with different terrain."

Tina has entered the World Cup for the past five years, and last year won at Mt. Saint Ann in Canada. Next year, she wants to concentrate more on freeriding. She only entered ten contests last year and this year she plans to do only four: "Contests are getting a little silly. I don't like the competitiveness of it. People are getting too serious—it used to be fun, now it's a bunch of waiting around for your turn. The last contest I did, it didn't even feel like I snowboarded at all. Five years ago, to make money, you had to win contests. Now you can do photo shoots and film all year and make a living."

Summers for Tina used to be time for resting and spending time with her family. She would return to Sacto for the majority of the summer, take a couple of classes at American River College (tennis or photography—"mainly so I could use the darkroom."), and visit friends. Since getting her pro model, she hasn't felt like she has had that summer break. Board designs, graphics, clothing designs, and ad designs have used up her summer. She often feels like she has got too much going on, and she has had to turn down projects that she would have liked to do. Camping at Mt. Hood used to be the extent of Tina's summer riding. But this year, she rode out of the country a lot: "I was fortunate enough to go to Chile and New Zealand and ride winter conditions. I rode Mt. Hood for a couple of days. I don't know about that whole summer snowboard scene. It's a little too hectic and crowded for me."

Early in the summer, I went with Tina to the Beastie Boys concert at Cal Expo. It was like I remembered in high school. The whole Basich family went, along with a couple carloads of friends. We met at a pizza parlor, ate dinner, and caravanned over to Cal Expo. Tina picked up a handful of tickets and brought Adam's jacket to him along with some other essentials he had left at home in Utah but needed for the remainder of the tour. When Tina went backstage to deliver the stuff, she didn't stay back there long because she preferred to hang out with her friends where all the action was.

The thing about Tina is that she's still the same girl I remember from my soccer team. A lot of people can really get affected once they get a taste of fame. With the popularity of snowboarding, there are a lot of people out there that have an inflated view of self-importance. But Tina keeps it all in check: "Snowboarding is becoming so popular—everyone wants a piece of the action. I even saw a girl holding a snowboard in a Victoria's Secret catalog. With all the money being made and hype around the sport, sometimes you have to remind yourself, it's just snowboarding."

Opposite: Wallride, Snowbird, Utah, 2000.

CIRCE WALLACE

In the early '90s, snowboarding slowly progressed out of its Day-Glo phase of the late '80s and images of wide-stanced snowboarders sliding over handrails dominated print media advertising. Two-page spreads were thrown up in the mags like punk-rock flyers. Insignia blazed belt buckles, lighters, and tent-sized, chain-wallet-fitted pants religiously reigned throughout a snowboarding community that was defining the word "hip." One of the riders and trendsetters of this era was an aggressive and fearless female named Circe Wallace. After moving on from the pro-snowboarding circuit, Circe has been heavily involved with an agency called The Familie. She's now an agent for professional snowboarders. —CC

WHAT LED YOU INTO SNOWBOARDING?

I had these two friends named Sandy and Thatcher. They were like what you could call total party animals (laughing). Thatcher was a trust funder who had like the nice [Volkswagen] Jetta and all the new equipment. He loaned me a board and we went to Hoodoo Mountain, a tiny little ski area [between Eugene and Bend] in Oregon. I wore my Nike Air Jordans and rode a Burton Woody board (laughing). I was kind of a skate rat at the time and it was like a natural progression; I immediately liked it. That's where I snowboarded for the first time. That was pretty much the beginning of my love for snowboarding.

WHAT WAS GOING ON AT THAT TIME IN YOUR LIFE, WERE YOU INTO THE "HIPPIE SCENE" IN THAT PART OF THE NORTHWEST?

No, not at all, I was more into the "punker scene." I guess you could say I was totally in love with skating. I had a friend named Anita Testison; she was actually my best friend and she was really good. She was like a gymnast who could do double kickflips and stuff. We would just do drugs and skateboard all night—that was kinda what you did in the small town of Eugene, Oregon.

WHAT TIME FRAME WAS ALL THIS?

That was around '85 or '86. I was in ninth grade and I went to Roosevelt High School. We would always say, "We got to get out of here, we're caught in a time warp!" Everybody's parents smoked weed, it was like this total subculture within but being in the valley and far enough away from Portland it totally had and still has its own identity. I went to my freshman year of high school with Anabell Garcia, Jerry Garcia's daughter, and Page Scully, whose dad was the manager of the band [Grateful Dead]. But Eugene is a total hippie town for sure. But I don't think that's really a bad thing. I mean, the drugs were kinda gnarly cause they were so free-flowing and that's kinda harsh, but in general the people there are really mellow; it's a good vibe. I graduated from that high school in 1989.

TELL ME ABOUT YOUR EARLIER DAYS. WHERE DID YOU GROW UP?

I grew up in various locations. I was born in Eugene, Oregon, my mom and dad divorced when I was two. Then my dad became somewhat of a nomad and I lived back and forth between my parents, but my mom was still living in Eugene. I lived in Portland for fourth grade, and Nashville, Tennessee, for sixth grade. Then I moved to Seattle after my freshmen year in high school and that's where I was up until about seven years ago when I moved here to Encinitas, California.

YOU'VE SEEN A LOT OF GROWTH IN THE SPORT.

It's been an interesting time in our sport and I've been snowboarding for almost fifteen years. **In an eight- to ten-year period I saw it go from where you know every single snowboarder and person on the hill to where 95 percent of the people on your local mountain are anonymous snowboarders.** That's a really crazy thing to see happen in such a short time.

WHERE DID YOU DO MOST OF YOUR RIDING WHEN YOU LIVED IN WASHINGTON?

When I was in school we would do a lot of night skiing on Snoqualmie Pass at Ski Acres and Pac-West; that's where all the snowboarders would go shred. Then on the weekends we would usually go to Mt. Baker where the terrain was much more aggressive and challenging. It got to the point where I wanted to learn more and that's where we kinda had to go.

SO WAS RIDE SNOWBOARDS YOUR FIRST SPONSOR?

I was actually on Burton Pro Form [a sponsorship for discounted boards through a rep] for like a year when I was really young. Then Lib Tech picked me up and I rode for them for two years. Things were going really good, I had my first really good video segment in *Roadkill* [Fall Line Films 1992]. Ride Snowboards came about and wanted a woman for their team and they were based in Seattle. I had really good relations with Tim and Stephanie Pogue who were at the core of the company at that time. So they made it happen for me. They stepped up and pushed me, and gave me the

opportunity to ultimately pursue my dream. I think the progression that I've gone through has been a natural one, from the Ride-sponsored freestyle-park-pipe-handrail kid which I was into at nineteen until the present. Ultimately, Ride's biggest time was when we were perceived as the cool hardcore company that had this great team. The dynamics were incredible. **Snowboarding is an image-driven sport. No one can deny that. For Ride, that's all it was.** We didn't have any World Cup contenders, we didn't have any Olympic hopefuls, but we had great charisma and good marketing.

WHEN AND WHY DID YOUR DIRECTION IN THE SPORT CHANGE?

In January of 1995 I tore my ACL [ligament in the knee] in the park at Big Bear [a resort in southern California]. That was a big change for me and I had a lot of time to think about what it was I wanted to accomplish and what my goals were in snowboarding. I wondered if the contest scene was something that I wanted to be a part of or not. I questioned what I wanted out of snowboarding. I kinda came to the conclusion that for me it was always about riding good snow. I wanted to ride powder, I wanted to hit the jumps, I loved that and it was fun but things changed. I became different as I got older. I wanted to apply the things that I learned in the pipe or in the park to real mountain terrain. **Now I feel that the most rewarding snowboarding I've done has been in the backcountry hiking or heli-skiing in Alaska.** And that's as gnarly as it gets, you're putting it all out there. I think that's a common progression. Out there it requires a lot of skill and knowledge and maybe that's why I chose that course for my future.

DID YOU EVER GET INTO CONTESTS?

Just the Northwest Series contests, and that was years ago. But then I started working with Dawger [Mike McIntyre, cinematographer] and Fall Line Films. Filming was performing to me. That was the best way I thought to prove myself; if I had a good film segment no one could deny that. It wasn't a judge deciding how I did. The general public had the opportunity to look at that and decide whether I was a good rider or not; that to me was the ultimate reward. Plus I got to promote my companies as well.

DID A LIFESTYLE BASED AROUND SURFING MAKE YOU WANNA MOVE DOWN SOUTH?

I started surfing up in Washington and really fell in love with it. My downtime seemed dismal up there and in my off seasons at this point in my life I wanted to spend time down here in Southern California. I get to see Washington and Tahoe in the winter anyway.

ANY MEMORABLE CONTESTS THAT YOU'VE ENTERED OVER THE COURSE OF YOUR CAREER?

I did the Baker Banked Slalom, which I got fourth in years ago. But that's the most prestigious event. To actually win that would be a big accomplishment for me. That's the type of event I like because it shows true accomplishment, there's no one judging you. It's all about your freeriding capability. If you can bank those turns and win that event [pauses], I think it's one of the most prestigious events in snowboarding, for sure.

(LAUGHING) YEAH, SITTING THERE WAITING IN THE LINEUP WHILE IT'S DUMPING OUT AND THE SNOW IS AWESOME.

Plus it just doesn't register with me, it's against the whole antiestablishment thing that snowboarding has always been about. Screw all this bullshit, let's go ride, you know?! That's what it will always be about for me, call me "old school," whatever. I've always considered snowboarding different and that's what I've loved about it. It was not something that you could schedule or put down on paper in a points system. It was about freedom of expression; ultimately just goin' out there and just lettin' it ride, you know. Without that it just wouldn't be the same for me. If I was on the Olympic Tour or Olympic Trail, whatever they call it, I wouldn't love snowboarding because that's not what it's about for me. I have no desire to hold up that gold medal. I don't care, it's all hype! You could have the best run of your life and still not win that gold medal because it's all about judging and being judged.

WHAT REPRESENTS A CHALLENGE FOR YOU AFTER ALL THESE YEARS OF BEING INVOLVED IN THE SPORT?

I found personally that the hardest thing to do in life is to balance success and integrity. And to just stay successful in itself is a challenge.

Opposite: Tahoe, 1998.
Above left: Alaska, 1998.
Left: At home in Encinitas, California, 1998.

JEFF TOLAND

By Chris Carnel
& Arlie John Carstens

As streetskating began to explode in the early '90s, Jeff Toland was an up-and-coming and respected member of the new ranks of pros. He skated aggressively and technically at the same time. He then started snowboarding and was quickly sponsored by Burton. Toland had the skills to become a big-name pro in either, or both, sports. But he also had the skills to party harder than anyone else and have more fun doing it. As the job description that comes along with being "pro" got more demanding as the industry grew and consolidated, Jeff moved on. It just wasn't fun anymore.

This interview took place in the winter of 1995 when Jeff was making a bid at pro snowboard status and living in the pro-seeking mecca of Truckee, CA. Chris Carnel and straight-edge vegan musician and pro snowboarder Arlie John Carstens dropped by Jeff's house one afternoon.

"Come in, my name is Jeff."

Jeff Toland introduces himself to Arlie John Carstens, "My house is kinda crazy, we get drunk and break glass."

"Is this Patsy Cline?" Arlie asks as the music spills from the stereo.

"Yeah, this is good drinkin' music," replied Toland.

"Especially when you got cabin fever," blurted a gentlemen affixed to the couch sitting next to me, who vaguely introduced himself to us as Keith.

He continued, "It's been raining and snowing for three weeks up here. We have yet to see the sun."

Looking towards a large number bottles in the windows, Arlie was amazed. "You drank all of those yourself?!"

Toland responded with a nod and a smile, "In less than a month."

Arlie's face turned sour, he shook his head and commented, "I hope you drink a lot of water when you're drinkin' that stuff... That shit will give you an ulcer!"

"Naw, it's already in the alcohol. I'm a pro, I got it goin' on. I mix it with Coke," Jeff casually responded.

"Wow, that's fuckin' harsh!" The straightedge Arlie was blown away.

The stereo's volume was muted. The Weather Channel became the primary focus. Five more days of stormy weather flashed on the screen and Toland planned his dismal future accordingly. "We're gonna try and go ride in this shit today at Boreal in a few hours."

"Have you guys built any quarterpipes out in the yard?" I asked.

"No, but we got that snowmobile out there. Let's go check it out." Toland was motivated. The weather changed from rain to snow, warm one minute, cold the next, and as we scoped out the snowmobile, it was buried.

Back indoors, Jeff went into a semi-karaoke to live music by Johnny Cash, "I've been flushed from the bathroom of your heart..."

The stereo prevailed. A T.V., ironically in synch, depicted houses being washed away by flash-flood rivers. "I got all my roommates into this music, it's bad!"

Suddenly Jeff was intrigued with the images, "Is this Sac.?" The T.V., still on the Weather Channel, showed segments of Northern California's Rio Linda, a victim of severe rainfall. Toland added his two cents, "That's 'Spinda Linda' meth capital, now their meth labs are all shot...(laughing)."

I suddenly changed into journalist-boy mode and sprouted some questions:

CHRIS: WHEN DID YOU GET INTO SNOWBOARDING?

Jeff: I tried it years ago when Don Bostick worked at Go Skate. They had a deal for thirty dollars: a bus ride, a lunch, and lift tickets to Donner Ski Ranch. I tried it, but I didn't really like it. I kinda got mad at all the Day-Glo and stuff. I was a little punk rock kid so I was "anti" for years. Then I started hangin' out with Card [John Cardiel] and them, which I did before, but I remember seeing footage of him doing backflips and stuff. I started boarding with him and he wasn't wearing Day-Glo. Then when we had the big storms like two years ago, I started comin' up a lot with Noah [Salasnek] and Matt Kennedy. Noah hooked me up with a board and Gerry and Artie at FLF [Fall Line Films] gave me boots and bindings. They helped me out. That's when I started riding.

CHRIS: WHEN DID YOU START SKATING PRO, LIKE WHEN DID YOU START SKATING FOR CHAPTER 7?

Jeff: I turned pro for Think. That was about 1990. Fausto decided to put me on and turn me pro for the "Disco in Frisco" contest.

CHRIS: WAS THAT THE FIRST ONE?

Jeff: No, I think it was the third one. Butterflies from hell, I was so scared. Then **I just got burned out, it became a job doing skateboarding stuff after that.** Except for traveling.

CHRIS: WERE YOU MAKING ALL OF YOUR MONEY FROM SKATING?

Jeff: I was makin' money at that. I really didn't make that good of money from Think. They were a small company starting out and I was getting like two hundred and fifty dollars a month or something. But I lived at home, at my grandma's house in Sac. It didn't matter.

My friends down around the corner have a bunch of music equipment, they're over there playing right now. I like to go over there sometimes, get drunk and scream... "As I step down from the train..." [Toland sings to classic Johnny Cash lyrics.]

I like to avoid the total snowboarding attitudes sometimes. It seems cooler with all the people that I know, like Jamie [Lynn] and stuff, Ranky [Mike Ranquet] and all those guys. Those guys are super cool! They're down to earth and riding with 'em is fun, you know. Like Rocket, that's my drinkin' partner, he likes to get me scared when I go riding with him.

CHRIS: WHAT KIND OF STUFF HAVE YOU BEEN BOARDING, TOLAND, HAVE YOU JUST BEEN FREERIDING?

Jeff: Yeah freeriding. I don't like parks that much, especially Jibassic, I don't like landing on flat. I'd rather go out and find stuff, it's so much more fun. Just go cruise around. Also, you're just by yourself, basically. You don't have a bunch of kids hangin' around. I hate when there's a pack of guys and they all stand above the kicker, I call 'em "Packistands."

CHRIS: TELL ME HOW YOU CAME UP WITH THE NAME "JIBASSIC PARK."

Jeff: I was at Noah's one night and we were all just sitting around this table all hammered and I saw this newspaper with this ad that said "Name this snowboard park and win a season pass." So I thought "jib" and at the time *Jurassic Park* was like the big thing. So I told Brett Sigur who worked at Boreal at the time and he was stoked. Boreal liked it, and I won.

ARLIE: THAT NAME GETS GURNED SO HARD, ALL OVER THE COUNTRY.

Jeff: It's just a joke too. "Jibassic," "jib," bro! Stances twenty-eight wide and shit... [Everyone starts laughing.]

ARLIE: SO DID YOU WIN A FREE SEASON PASS?

Jeff: Yeah, I got a free pass.

ARLIE: SO YOU ARE PSYCHED!

Jeff: Yeah, but now I gotta work there 'cause I'm not pro anymore.

ARLIE: WHAT'S IT LIKE WORKIN' THERE?

Jeff: Overworked, underpaid. But it's cool though. My roommate Antho is my supervisor. I work with him doin' whatever. My manager is my friend Pete, and this guy Mike Box, the main guy, is totally cool.

ARLIE: THE BEST THING THOUGH IS THAT YOU GUYS LIKE PATSY CLINE AND JOHNNY CASH, THAT'S FUCKIN' PUNK!

Jeff: And Hank Williams Junior and Senior. I don't even watch MTV anymore, I watch TNN. They have drag racing and drag boat racing. And the Discovery Channel. They have a show called "Weekday Wings," with World War II planes. All kinds of planes.

After walking around the neighborhood in search of terrain to ride, we came up empty. The next thing I knew we were back at the house again while Toland's roommate, Christin, did the basic chores of cleaning, laundry, and vacuuming. Jeff felt inclined to show us his bedroom and his bed, the "Tollbooth"—a basic mattress with a door on the side of it to avoid noise and roommates while he sleeps his days away. He also has a rad pair of boots with chains attached for icy conditions he called his chain-shoes. All in all, it was a fun lazy day. Arlie and I bailed to the nearest restaurant to eat. Jeff concluded, all sprawled out on the couch, with, "Well, guys, I guess I'm not goin' to Boreal now. What the hell am I gonna do?" The vacuum sucked glass as Christin labored and made circles around the Toland couch.

"I guess I'll just sit here, I don't even have beer!"

Opposite: Boreal, 1996.
Left: Roseville, California, 1994.

THE DISABLED SKATER

NAME: ERIC FRANKS

aka: The Disabled Skater
Age: 14
Skating: 3.5 years
Other activities: Rock climbing with just his arms
Home: Valley Springs, CA
Message to other skaters: "No matter what your problem is, keep trying."

While at the Yuba City, California, skatepark one sweltering day in 1998, I noticed a kid with defective legs in a four-wheeled-chair-type contraption. "Wow," I thought. "This guy's out here doing it, working with what he's got." He was going up the various transitions, doing these little kickturn-type moves, fakies, and basically just rolling around. **It inspired me in a totally different way** than say Chad Shetler snapping an ollie to fifty-fifty on the tennis court fence bar and dropping back into the tight tranny; or Kip Sumpter blasting over the monstrous concrete wave at high speed. It reminded me that all the bullshit that I deal with—people, deadlines, attitudes, vibes, stress, just basic crap—is petty and shouldn't get me down. —SM

IT'S SIMPLE

At its core, riding a board, especially a skateboard down the street, is a very simple thing to do. Just you and your skateboard making the best of society's leftovers. However, board riding culture is far from simple—it's a huge multi-million (billions if you count fashion) dollar industry that employs hundreds of thousands of people and uses millions of dollars of resources, like cotton, leather, plastic, wood, etc., which indirectly employs thousands of more people.

Does such a pure and simple activity need so much infrastructure?

As we enter the next century, hedonistic self-gratification is very much in vogue. Especially in the case of the young American male as evidenced by the best-selling lifestyle magazines like *Maxim, Gear, Bikini,* and even TransWorld's *Stance,* which is specifically aimed at boarders and whose motto is "gear, gadgets, girls." (It's interesting that the only human item, the one that you might actually be able to interact with, is last.) As I travel around the world, I'm often dissapointed to see that this is also the only thing we export to other countries, culturally speaking. The dotcom boom and a stock market that some say is too healthy, has combined to create an America that is more affluent than any past, with the gulf between the rich and poor greater than ever.

As multimedia artist Barbara Kruger has noted, Corporate America tells us "I shop, therefore I am" and "You are what you buy."

But, while much of the world is looking over the fence to see if their neighbor's grass is greener, there are some dissenting voices. The anti-*Maxim* could be *Adbusters,* the magazine that takes corporate America to task for their sins. Thomas Frank, the editor of *The Baffler,* published a book titled *Commodify Your Dissent* that examines how grass root scenes and cultural movements are appropriated by the marketing departments of Pepsi and Coke. While they may be preaching to the converted and a bit heavy handed, these minority views seem to be slowly catching on. In the October 2000 issue of *Skateboarder* magazine, editor Aaron Meza comments on the current trend of skaters copping the pimp daddy trend: **"Eventually, bragging and boasting will be looked down upon in the mainstream, everybody will stop pretending they're millionaires, and people will adopt a humble approach to life."**

Taking things to an even further extreme, there are those few people who've forsaken their high-paying jobs and fast-track careers and downscaled their material needs in order to live a simpler life and spend more time with their families and friends. They refer to their new lifestyle as the "Voluntary Simplicity Movement." These people claim that America is suffering from "Affluenza," and that they are much happier having left the rat race and the keeping-up-with-the-Joneses mentality behind them. Ironically, there's now a magazine, *Real Simple,* that takes this premise as its focus, but then bends it back towards consumerism, advising its readers on what they need to buy in order to "simplify" their lives.

A related and parallel, and equally unpopular, train of thought is the resources themselves, and the impact on our environment. Snowboarding is dependent on snow, and few would argue that the natural beauty of the mountain environment is a great deal of the attraction to the sport. But unthinking consumption runs counter to enjoying the Earth's natural resources, as it uses them up at a pace faster than they can be replenished. Global warming is changing the Earth's weather patterns.

Where does this leave those of us who find that moving sideways on some sort of board makes our lives seem more fullfilled? Skaters and snowboarders have always been kind of outsiders, but have we let our own "culture" trap us a little bit? Ignore the environment if you'd like since it's a complicated and big issue, but consider this: Would you rather have a brand-new board, clothes, car, etc., and always be on top of the latest fashion trends, or would you rather work fewer hours and take three months off to actually ride your board? —JB

IT'S FREE!!!

One of the perks of working at a magazine, (and actually one of the reasons we started *Heckler*) is that you get lots of free stuff. "Free lift tickets, bro. Let's start a mag!" Yep, if you work for a magazine, big or small, you will get, in varying amounts, free clothes, free CDs, free snowboards, free skateboards, free subscriptions to other magazines... I think you get the point. It's actually not free, however, because there are usually strings attached ("did you review that new hardcore-punk-polka-hip-hop-ska CD we sent you?") or it's in exchange for some kind of service.

At first you're like, "Whoa, check out this sun-visor I got from Sega and this CD from this speed-core band." But pretty soon, you have enough clothes, shoes, boards, etc., and you've stoked your friends out and sold the extra CDs at the used record store.

At this point, you're probably going, "What an ungrateful jerk, why doesn't he give me his job and I'll get all the free stuff!?!?"

Now, maybe it's just me, but I reached a point where when people would offer to give me free stuff, I would say no unless it was something I really needed. But new products keep relentlessly coming out and companies really want to give them to you as a way to promote their "new and improved product line." But it seems wasteful for me to get a new snowboard (and all the petrochemical resources within) if my old snowboard is still working pretty well. Even if it is free.

Rule number one: Get a new one of everything

every year if you possibly can. It doesn't matter if your old one still works, because it's not as good as the new ones and besides, it's last year's style.

I'm sure I'm jaded, but I remember the specific time when these thoughts that had been in the back of mind moved to the front. Tommy, our office manager, had a catalog from a shoe company that he was showing around the office and to our interns and anyone else who happened to come into the office. "Hey, do you want some free shoes? These guys said they'd send us as many free shoes as we need."

This catalog was from a new company trying to break into the lucrative skate shoe market. Now I must confess, I love skate shoes. I hoard at least two pairs at a time when I find a shoe that feels really good to skate in. But, I looked through their catalog and not a single one of their shoes looked like anything I would want to be seen wearing nor did they look like a functional skate shoe. I decided that I didn't want to just get a pair of shoes because they were free. What would I do with them? How could I justify the waste of resources?

I guess I was the only one in our office who didn't order any shoes, because a few weeks later our UPS guy shows up with this huge box of shoes. Everybody busts them out and pretty soon I'm hearing, "These shoes seem kind of funky, I don't know if I'd really wear 'em."

My thought was that they would make good shoes for homeless people because they had the thickest soles of any skate shoe I'd ever seen, almost a platform skate shoe, and they should last a homeless person a really long time. Luckily I found a few pairs lying around the office later that week and we gave them to David, a homeless guy pushing his shopping cart through our neighborhood.

I suppose my point here is that everything I said above is even more important if you don't get shit for free. Because then you're spending your own hard-earned money. If you're at all like me, you have only a limited supply of money and the more stuff you need, the more time you have to spend working, which means you have less time for actually riding that board you bought. Now with that in mind, ask yourself do you really need a new snowboard every year if your old one is still serviceable? Do you really need a new pair of sunglasses/ shoes because your old ones aren't the latest model but they still work fine? It's your call, but most people including myself, would rather play than work. And the less you need, or think you need, the less you have to work. Simple huh? —*JB*

> *"It was a morning like other mornings and yet perfect among mornings."*
> —Kino in The Pearl, by John Steinbeck

HOW TO SAVE ENOUGH MONEY IN ONE YEAR TO GO ON A TWO-WEEK TRIP TO ANYWHERE IN THE WORLD YOU WANT TO:

Buy used CDs, clothes, boards, books, cars, etc., whenever possible. By buying something used you are not only saving yourself money, but you are reducing the demand for more new products to be manufactured. Reduce, reuse, and recycle. Cook your own food instead of eating fast food. Ride a bike, skate, walk, or take a bus instead of driving. If you think you need a new board/wheels/shoes/etc., wait a few days and then ask yourself if you really do need that new whatever.

CHAPTER 4. THE SUITS MOVE IN

Corporate America buys advertising space on human snowboarders,
the Gravity Games, 2000.

The Suits Move In

by John Baccigaluppi

In our Fall 1995 issue we ran an editorial entitled "Alternative or Independent: Do You Know The Difference?" It was at the peak of "Alternative" music's popularity and if one thing was clear, the alternative was now the mainstream. Large record labels now embraced music they ignored only a few years previously. Even more strange was how large corporations like Anheuser-Busch and Pepsi aligned themselves with large concert tours, and proclaimed themselves the "alternative" beer and soft drink. An oxymoron? While some bands were prescient enough to smell a rat, most weren't and quickly signed on with the major labels and MTV. After years of struggle and living near the edge of poverty, who could really blame them? It was only a few years later that most of these bands were dropped from their contracts as the big labels consolidated and popular music moved on. Only a few people in the scene, like recording engineer Steve Albini with his essay "The Problem with Music" raised a dissenting voice.

With its meteoric rise to popularity on the cultural radar screen, snowboarding was only a few years behind the music scene. It started with people who had more in common with the indie music scene than the corporations who controlled the ski industry. But as the sport grew at an amazing pace, the ski industry wanted in. People like Jake Burton and Mike Olsen who started the sport now found themselves competing with the same people who once scorned them. The ski resorts that once banned them from the slopes now catered and marketed to them. In 1995, almost all snowboard maufacturers were independent companies run by snowboarders. By 1999, K2, Salomon, and Rossignol—all ski companies—were market leaders. It was almost too easy for these larger, more experienced companies to come in and put most of the independents out of business. But despite all this consolidation and big business, the market leader is still run by a snowboarder. Yep, Jake Burton is still independent and still number one. This is a very good thing.

Now skateboarding is bigger than it has ever been, and the mainstream is chasing it just like they chased punk rock and snowboarding. I still hold out hope that, because skateboarding is so difficult, it will stay in the hands of its founders. You can buy the skater look, but you can't buy the ability to do even a simple trick like an ollie, a kickflip, or going back and forth on a mini-ramp. You can take a guitar lesson or a snowboarding lesson, but aside from a few summer camps (that are more like group-training sessions) you can't really take skateboarding lessons. As of this writing, it's still too early to tell where the skateboarding business will end up. Although K2 bought Planet Earth skateboards and Adidas and Nike have pursued the marketplace, skateboarding's most visible spokesperson is Tony Hawk, and Tony has more than paid his dues. His roots, purity, and dedication to the sport are undeniable. I take comfort in this.

For the record, I don't feel like things should always remain small and underground. What's the point in making a great album that only a few-hundred people hear? I think that if everyone skated, the world would be a better, happier place. But, as I've watched music and then snowboarding gain mass-market acceptance, **it's inescapable that the people who laid down the roots were often trampled over and discarded while something, some sort of soul, was lost in the process.** I'd like to think that great ideas that come from small groups of people can reach more people with their essence still intact. But I'm repeatedly proven wrong. Nirvana has been supplanted by the Backstreet Boys, and only those who never flirted with the mainstream, like Fugazi, survived.

It's like this I guess—any party of a small group of intimate friends that is crashed by a bunch of frat boys and sorority girls just isn't the same after they've arrived. There are inevitable clashes of culture, and even when the jocks and cheerleaders have left for another party, you can't erase their presence from the house.

Always an optimist, however, I still hold out hope. Small microlabels like Jade Tree are putting out great music (Promise Ring, Jets To Brazil) that sells well, while their bands ignore offers from bigger labels. Have we, the collective "good" music scene, learned something? I think so. I hope so.

And no matter how "Extreeeeme" snowboarding and skateboarding gets—even if Tony Hawk becomes a spokesperson for the Burger King Whopper 900 X-Treme Meal Deal—one thing will always remain true: ollieing to a grind on a curb will still not only be fun, but it will also be yours and yours alone. The feeling you get when carving a big turn in two feet of fresh powder will always be yours despite how many corporations and sponsors brought it to you. And, when you connect with an artist whose music moves you, that connection is real, and it's between the two of you, despite the fact that several thousand other connections almost exactly the same exist. That's the beauty and lasting strength of art.

"I DON'T MEAN TO GURN ON YOUR THING, MAN, BUT I REALLY HATE YOU FUCKING PEOPLE."

BY RHINO T. GHERRING

I'll probably never ski or snowboard ever again. I wasn't injured, no ACL reconstruction or hip displacement. I just don't seem to get it anymore. I've seen what it does to people. I work at a place that is overrun during the winter months by the masses: nylon-clad, delusional adventurers. Because I want to remain employed, I can't give the name or location of the place because this little ditty would surely get me fired (which also explains the pseudonym). I am the ski-crowd bartender. The place is on the way home from a resort, so when the lifts close, they flock to my bar. THEM. It's not really an age thing, or a generational or gender thing. All walks of life are pretty much equally represented, and all are just as equally annoying. I'm thinking maybe the top three most annoying percent should be hunted for leisure—to replace that recreational urge of mine to ski and board.

"DUDE!" a high-pitched, hell-bat skater shouts. "Fuckin' in-TENSE day du-day, man!" they yell at each other, meeting up inside at the bar.

"YAUGH!" high-five, high-five, high-five, high-five...high-fives all around the group. "Fuckin' whirly, brah!" more high-fives.

"Let's get a fuckin' beer, dudes!"

"Gimme' a fuckin' Extreme, dude!" a goatee yells at me.

"Yeah, brah, fuckin' Bavarian Alps Extreme!"

"Sorry guys," I say in my best mock-apologetic (which I was never very good at to start with due to my general lack of that thing called "giving a shit"). "We don't carry it."

"No fuckin' Extreme?!"

"DUDE," a synchronized chorus of voices bands out across the bar.

"What else ya got?"

I run through the entire menu of beers and the same disgusted, condescending look runs over the faces as I go through the domestics and popular imports. When I get to the microbrewery selection, looks of genuine interest grow under ratty goatees, and other under-twenty-five, experimental facial hair.

"No fuckin' Heckler Brau?"

"No Sierra Nevada?"

"Sorry."

"DUDE," the synchronized chorus sounds out again.

"Gimme' a fuckin' Pondo!"

"Yeah, brah, an' a fuckin' Sierra Nevada Pale Ale!"

"They don't have Sierra Nevada."

"Dude!" goes the chorus.

"Jus' gimme the Pondo then, I guess."

"Pond-erosa?" I ask.

"Yeah, the Pale Ale...an' a fuckin' Wild Boar."

"You want a fuckin' glass with that?"

"Na."

"How about some fuckin' appetizers to go with that?"

"Give us a few on that, wouldja' brah?"

"A few fuckin' minutes, or a few fuckin' appetizers?" I got a few smiles from the others crowded around the bar, but the spokesman and his majority didn't seem to notice he was being dicked with.

"Minutes," their spokesman finally answered, puzzled, after giving the matter far too much thought.

This piece showed up pseudonymously in our mailbox one day. —JB

I collected—all on daddy's credit card...But I have seen the sign. The all-seeing, all-knowing groundhog has finally reared its ugly head. He has seen his little shadow in the dirty field, and he won't be sleeping much longer. This terrible white shit that modern man assaults with polysynthetic equipment is going to melt and go away. Then all the shred-punks will go home, and I won't have to deal with them again...At least not until next year.

In 1995, the Washington, DC-based band Jawbox released For Your Own Special Sweetheart on Atlantic Records, which is part of the WEA conglomerate. Their two previous records, Grippe and Novelty, were on the DC-based independent label, Dischord (Fugazi, Minor Threat, Shudder to Think). At the time, fans of the band were extremely divided in their opinions of the band's move to a major. One disenchanted fan actually sent them a letter berating them for signing to a major label and said that he hoped they would be killed in a fiery van accident while they were on tour. Others felt that Sweetheart was the band's best effort yet and were stoked that the band would be able to focus on their music full-time and quit their day jobs. Heckler's music editor at the time, Sean Schroeder, interviewed J. Robbins and Bill Barbot at a show they played in Sacramento on July 27, 1994 at the El Dorado Saloon. We ran the interview on the left half of a spread, with Steve Albini's classic essay, "The Problem With Music" on the right half. —JB

THE PROBLEM WITH MUSIC
BY STEVE ALBINI

Whenever I talk to a band that is about to sign with a major label, I always end up thinking of them in a particular context. I imagine a trench about four feet wide and five feet deep, maybe sixty yards long, filled with runny, decaying shit. I imagine these people, some of them good friends, some of them barely acquaintances, at one end of this trench. I also imagine a faceless industry lackey at the other end, holding a fountain pen and a contract waiting to be signed. Nobody can see what's printed on the contract. It's too far away, and besides, the shit stench is making everybody's eyes water. The lackey shouts to everybody that the first one to swim the trench gets to sign the contract. Everybody dives in the trench and they struggle furiously to get to the other end. Two people arrive simultaneously and begin wrestling furiously, clawing each other and dunking each other under the shit. Eventually, one of them capitulates, and there's only one contestant left. He reaches for the pen, but the lackey says, "Actually, I think you need a little more development. Swim it again, please. Backstroke." And he does, of course.

Every major label involved in the hunt for new bands now has on staff a high-profile point man, an "A&R" rep who can present a comfortable face to any prospective band. The initials A&R stand for "artist and repertoire" because historically, the A&R staff would select artists to record music that they had also selected out of an available pool of each. This is still the case, though not openly. These guys are universally young (about the same age as the bands being wooed), and nowadays they always have some obvious underground rock credibility flag they can wave. Lyle Preslar, former guitarist for Minor Threat, is one of them. Terry Tolkin, former NY independent booking agent and assistant manager at Touch and Go is one of them. Al Smith, former soundman at CBGB is one of them. Mike Gitter, former editor of the *XXX* fanzine and contributor to *Rip*, *Kerrang,* and other lowbrow rags is one of them. Many of the annoying turds who used to staff college radio stations are in their ranks as well.

There are several reasons A&R scouts are always young. The explanation usually copped to is that the scout will be "hip" to the current musical "scene." **A more important reason is that the bands will intuitively trust someone they think is a peer,** and who speaks fondly of the same formative rock and roll experiences. The A&R person is the first person to make contact with the band, and as such is the first person to promise them the moon. Who better to promise them the moon than an

idealistic young turk who expects to be calling the shots in a few years, and who has had no previous experience with a big record company. Hell, he's as naive as the band he's duping. When he tells them no one will interfere in their creative process, he probably even believes it. When he sits down with the band for the first time over a plate of angel hair pasta, he can tell them with all sincerity that when they sign with company X, they're really signing with him, and he's on their side. "Remember that great gig I saw you at in '85? Didn't we have a blast?"

By now, all rock bands are wise enough to be suspicious of music industry scum. There is a pervasive caricature in popular culture of a portly, middle-aged ex-hipster talking a mile a minute, using outdated jargon and calling everybody "baby." After meeting "their" A&R guy, the band will say to themselves and everyone else, **"He's not like a record company guy at all! He's like one of us."** And they will be right. That's one of the reasons he was hired. These A&R guys are not allowed to write contracts. What they do is present the band with a letter of intent, or "deal memo," that loosely states some terms and affirms that the bands will sign with the label once a contract has been agreed on. The spookiest thing about this harmless-sounding little "memo" is that it is, for all legal purposes, a binding document. That is, once the band signs it, they are under obligation to conclude a deal with the label. If the label presents them with a contract that the band doesn't want to sign, all the label has to do is wait. There are a hundred other bands willing to sign the exact same contract, so the label is in a position of strength. Those letters never have any term of expiration, so the band remains bound by the deal memo until a contract is signed, no matter how long that takes. The band cannot sign to another label or even put out its own material unless they are released from their agreement, which never happens. Make no mistake about it: once a band has signed a letter of intent, they will either eventually sign a contract that suits the label or they will be destroyed.

One of my favorite bands was held hostage for the better part of two years by a slick, young "He's not like a label guy at all" A&R rep on the basis of such a deal memo. He had failed to come through on any of his promises (something he did with similar effect to another well-known band), and so the band wanted out. Another label expressed interest, but when the A&R man was asked to release the band, he said he would need money or [percentage] points [of the profits], or possibly both, before he would consider it.

The new label was afraid the price would be too dear, and they said no thanks. On the cusp of making their signature album, an excellent band, humiliated, broke up from the stress and the many months of inactivity.

There's This Band

There's this band. They're pretty ordinary, but they're also pretty good, so they've attracted some attention. They're signed to a moderate size "independent" label owned by a distribution company, and they have another two albums owed to the label. They're a little ambitious. They'd like to get signed by a major label so they can have some security—you know, get some good equipment, tour in a proper tour bus—nothing fancy, just a little reward for all the hard work.

To that end, they got a manager. He knows some of the label guys, and he can shop their next project to all the right people. He takes his cut, sure, but it's only 15 percent, and if he can get them signed then it's money well spent. Anyway, it doesn't cost them anything if it doesn't work. Fifteen percent of nothing isn't much!

One day an A&R scout calls them, says he's "been following them for a while now," and when their manager mentioned them to him, it just "clicked." Would they like to meet with him about the possibility of working out a deal with his label. Wow. Big Break time. They meet the guy, and y'know what—he's not what they expected from a label guy. He's young and dresses pretty much like the band does. He knows all their favorite bands. He's like one of them. He tells them he wants to go to bat for them, to try to get them everything they want. He says anything is possible with the right attitude. They conclude the evening by taking home a copy of a deal memo they wrote out and signed on the spot.

The A&R guy was full of great ideas, even talked about using a name producer. Butch Vig is out of the question—he wants one hundred g's and three points, but they can get Don Fleming for thirty thousand plus three points. Even that's a little steep, so maybe they'll go with that guy who used to be in David Letterman's band. He only wants three points. Or they can have just anybody record it (like Wharton Tiers, maybe—cost you five or ten grand) and have Andy Wallace remix it for four grand a track plus two points. It was a lot to think about.

Well, they like this guy and they trust him. Besides, they already signed the deal memo. He must have been serious about wanting them to sign. They break the news to their current label, and the label manager says he wants them to succeed, so they have his blessing. He will need to be compensated, of course, for the remaining albums left on their contract, but he'll work it out with the label himself.

Sub Pop made millions from selling off Nirvana, and Twin Tone hasn't done bad either: fifty grand for the Babes and sixty grand for the Poster Children—without having to sell a single additional record. It'll be something modest. The new label doesn't mind, so long as it's recoupable out of royalties.

Well, they get the final contract, and it's not quite what they expected. They figure it's better to be safe than sorry and they turn it over to a lawyer—one who says he's experienced in entertainment law—and he hammers out a few bugs. They're still not sure about it, but the lawyer says he's seen a lot of contracts, and theirs is pretty good. They'll be getting a great royalty: 13 percent (less a 10 percent packaging deduction). Wasn't it Buffalo Tom that were only getting 12 percent less 10? Whatever.

The old label only wants fifty grand and no points. Hell, Sub Pop got three points when they let Nirvana go. They're signed for four years, with options on each year, for a total of over a million dollars! That's a lot of money in any man's English. The first year's advance alone is two hundred and fifty thousand dollars. Just think about it, a quarter of a million dollars, just for being in a rock band!

Their manager thinks it's a great deal, especially the large advance. Besides, he knows a publishing company that will take the band on if they get signed and even give them an advance of twenty grand, so they'll be making that money too. The manager says publishing is pretty mysterious and nobody really knows where all the money comes from, but the lawyer can look that contract over too. Hell, it's free money.

Their booking agent is excited about the band signing to a major. He says they can maybe average one or two thousand dollars a night from now on. That's enough to justify a five-week tour, and with tour support, they can use a proper crew, buy some good equipment, and even get a tour bus! Buses are pretty expensive, but if you figure in the price of a hotel room for everybody in the band and crew, they're actually about the same cost. Some bands (like Therapy? and Sloan and Stereolab) use buses on their tours even when they're getting paid only a couple hundred bucks a night, and this tour should earn at least a grand or two every night. It'll be worth it. The band will be more comfortable and will play better.

The agent says a band on a major label can get a merchandising company to pay them an advance on T-shirt sales! Ridiculous! There's a gold mine here! The lawyer should look over the merchandising contract, just to be safe.

They get drunk at the signing party. Polaroids are taken and everybody looks thrilled. The label picked them up in a limo. They decided to go with the producer who used to be in Letterman's band. He had these technicians come in and tune the drums for them and tweak their amps and guitars. He even had a guy come in and check the phase of all the equipment in the control room! Boy, was he professional. He used a bunch of equipment on them and by the end of it, they all agreed that it sounded very "punchy," yet "warm."

All that hard work paid off. With the help of a video, the album went like hotcakes! They sold a quarter-million copies! Here is the math that will explain just how fucked they are: These figures are representative of amounts that appear in record contracts daily. There's no need to skew the figures to make the scenario look bad, since real-life examples more than abound.

Income is underlined, expenses are not.

THE BALANCE SHEET
This is how much each player got paid at the end of the game.
Record company: $710,000
Producer: $90,000
Manager: $51,000
Studio: $52,000
Previous label: $50,000
Agent: $7,500
Lawyer: $12,000
Band member net income each: $4,031.25

The band is not a quarter of the way through its contract, has made the music industry more than 3 million dollars richer, but is in the hole $14,000 on royalties. **The band members have each earned about one-third as much as they would working at a 7-Eleven, but they got to ride in a tour bus for a month.**

The next album will be about the same, except that the record company will insist they spend more time and money on it. Since the previous one never "recouped," the band will have no leverage, and will oblige.

The next tour will be about the same, except the merchandising advance will have already been paid, and the band, strangely enough, won't have earned any royalties from their T-shirts yet. Maybe the T-shirt guys have figured out how to count money like record company guys.

Some of your friends are probably already this fucked.

This piece was originally printed in the Baffler. Much thanks to them for letting us reprint it. For a complete copy of this article including a very cool section on recording along with lots of other great thought-provoking articles send $5.00 to:

The Baffler
Post Office Box 378293
Chicago, IL 60637

End Figures
Advance: $250,000
Manager's cut: $37,500
Legal fees: $10,000
Recording budget: $150,000
Producer's advance: $50,000
Studio fee: $52,000
Drum, amp, mic and phase "doctors": $3,000
Recording tape: $8,000
Equipment rental: $5,000
Cartage and Transportation: $5,000
Lodgings while in studio: $10,000
Catering: $3,000
Mastering: $10,000
Tape copies, reference CDs, shipping tapes, misc. expenses: $2,000
Video budget: $30,000
Cameras: $8,000
Crew: $5,000
Processing and transfers: $3,000
Offline: $2,000
Online editing: $3,000
Catering: $1,000
Stage and construction: $3,000
Copies, couriers, transportation: $2,000
Director's fee: $3,000

Album artwork: $5,000
Promotional photo shoot and duplication: $2,000

Band fund: $15,000
New fancy professional drum kit: $5,000
New fancy professional guitars (2): $3,000
New fancy professional guitar amp rigs (2): $4,000
New fancy potato-shaped bass guitar: $1,000
New fancy track-of-lights bass amp: $1,000
Rehearsal space rental: $500
Big blowout party for their friends: $500

Tour expense (5 weeks): $50,875
Bus: $25,000
Crew (3): $7,500
Food and per diems: $7,875
Fuel: $3,000
Consumable supplies: $3,500
Wardrobe: $1,000
Promotion: $3,000

Tour gross income: $50,000
Agent's cut: $7,500
Manager's cut: $7,500
Lawyer's fee: $1,000

Publishing advance: $20,000
Manager's cut: $3,000
Lawyer's fee: $1,000

Record sales: 250,000 @ $12 = $3,000,000 gross retail revenue
Royalty (13% of 90% of retail): $351,000
Less advance: $250,000
Producer's points (3% less $50,000 advance): $40,000
Promotional budget: $25,000
Recoupable buyout from previous label: $50,000
NET ROYALTY: -$14,000

RECORD COMPANY INCOME:
Record wholesale price $6.50 x 250,000 = $1,625,000 gross income
Artist royalties: $351,000
Deficit from royalties: $14,000
Manufacturing, packaging, and distribution @ $2.20 per record: $550,000
GROSS PROFIT: $710,000

JAWBOX
BY SEAN SCHROEDER

You're starting a tour with Stone Temple Pilots in three days, how did this come about? Was there any question as to whether you should do the tour, or was it like "We're going to do this major label thing and we're going to give it 100 percent"?

No. Part of our approach to having signed to a major label, and now being on a major label, is to try and do it in as much of our way as possible. We don't want to give everything up that we've worked so hard on. The idea was, if we're going to sign to a major label, we don't want to have to turn the reins over to somebody else. We wanted to get on a bigger tour at some point and it just so happens that this seems like a really good time to be doing that, plus STP asked us. Nobody else that is on tour right now asked us to do it. So we thought about it and figured we might as well do it. It's a lot different than any other tour we've done before because it's so much bigger. Up until now we've always toured with bands we were friends with, and it has been a really egalitarian type of thing. This is going to be our first brush with the "Big Rock" biz as it applies to playing shows because Atlantic really hasn't exercised any influence over what shows we play at all.

So they give you freedom to do whatever you want or because...

It's because it's not their thing to be involved in, necessarily. **We have a really good relationship with them, it's very cool.** They've been really supportive of things that we want to do, and they've helped us do a lot of stuff that we want to do, and they haven't told us that we have to do anything. They've just been really cool.

They give you full reign over what you want to do with artwork and all that stuff?

I did the artwork myself with my friend Steve.

Have you received any more hate mail like you did with that fiery fan letter?

Maybe like one every three weeks to the effect that we betrayed some kind of faith that someone placed in us, and "how dare we?" It's fair enough in a way, you know, but in the end it's really just us who are going to have to live with the decision. We chewed it over a million times to try to make sure we could do it in a way that we could still be true to ourselves. So it's a shame if someone is upset about it. On the other hand, tough break.

Do you answer all of the letters you receive?

Yes, we answer every letter we get. I would rather have a dialogue with people too. You know, if someone says "You stood for something, in my eyes, your band meant something to me, and now that you're on Atlantic Records it doesn't mean something to me." I would rather have a dialogue about that because I can kind of understand it. But I'm of the opinion that every case is different. I don't want my band to be accidentally waving a flag for major labels allowing people to say, "Oh look, Jawbox, they were on Dischord Records, and then they thought it was ok to go to a major label, so it must be just fine, major labels must be just plain cool" because, the truth is, no matter what you do you have to take it with a grain of salt and be skeptical about it. Multinational corporations are basically not cool, but our decision was a practical one and I think we are just really lucky. It was a decision based upon the desire for our band to thrive. It was a decision that we made with the intent of keeping control over what we do, but we also wanted to be able to sustain ourselves. If nothing else, we'd like to show other bands that this is a choice you can make, you can do it and still put out good records and still have control over what you're doing and still do things the way you want to do them. Thus far, it's been that way for us.

It's something that Atlantic deserves a lot of credit for because the people that we've been working with there have been really cool. They're really great people just to deal with on a personal level. I feel like we are getting respect from them and we have respect for them too. I mean, they're helping us do what we want to do.

They're adapting the way that they are used to doing business to our situation.

We have to kind of talk out of both sides of our mouth because we're having a really great experience, but at the same time every situation is different.

Do you think that there is any validity to the argument that there actually are only one or two paths to take once you do sign to a major label?

I don't know if that's true, but I think those are all bridges that you have to cross when you come to them. There is a lot of precedent for a band to get signed then suddenly get dropped because it's not making any money, or for a band to get signed and suddenly suck because someone is telling them what to play. But I think we all think that every situation is different. You have to think that way, if you don't think that way you run the risk of being an idiot, of being so doctrinaire that you don't have your eyes open. I mean, literally, all you can say is so far, so good. Compared to the kind of horror stories people like Steve Albini want to tell, we're having a fucking bitchin' time!

In 1999, Eric Stenman interviewed J. Robbins after Jawbox broke up and he had formed a new band, Burning Airlines.

Were there specific causes behind the end of Jawbox and the beginning of Burning Airlines?

The big reason was that Jawbox's drummer, Zach, quit the band to go back to school. His presence was very critical to the way we put music together. Also, our process of songwriting had become very argumentative. We were trying so hard not to repeat ourselves. We felt like Jawbox was what it was. We felt like the band had gone through a lot of changes and that its identity had finally solidified. Dealing with Atlantic Records had really worn us out too. Dealing with the labyrinth of corporate red tape was a bummer after a while. A lot of people thought we broke up because the band got dropped from the label. What would be closer to the truth would be that we broke up because we were sick of being on a major label. That's a big generalization and I hate making generalizations. A lot of people have great experiences being on major labels. We had a good one to begin with. Things changed after they figured out that we weren't going to be a cash cow. Jawbox was hoping to have our cake and eat it too. We thought that we were in a very unique situation. **In the end, we discovered that major labels don't allow for unique situations.** I'm glad that I've moved on. During the final days of Jawbox, we had all become so concerned with the business side of the band and our lives that we were forgetting about the music.

KEVIN SECONDS

As the founder and lead vocalist of 7 Seconds, Kevin Seconds is one of the forefathers of the DIY punk movement. In the early days of punk rock, he worked with Henry Rollins and Ian MacKaye helping each other book shows. I got to know Kevin when I produced the Ourselves CD for 7 Seconds on Restless Records. Since then we've worked on quite a few albums together and have become good friends. Kevin has also been a regular contributor to Heckler, and has written music reviews and features and added his artwork to the magazine. This is an excerpt from an interview I did with him for Punk Planet in 1998. —JB

LET'S TALK A LITTLE BIT ABOUT WHEN 7 SECONDS SIGNED TO IMMORTAL/EPIC/SONY.

Yeah, yeah well, you know, it was just an experience. At the point just before signing with Immortal, we were going to record an album regardless and we were just hoping that we wouldn't have to do it on a label that was going to sit on it, which is what's happened in the past with other labels we've dealt with. So we sent out a couple tapes to some of the bigger hardcore punk labels and indie labels and there just wasn't anyone biting. I think we're sorta regarded in that hardcore scene as being these guys who have been around forever and have maybe had our day and that day's past or whatever. I kinda understand that way of thinking—I don't agree, but I can kind of see how we're looked at because we

have never been consistent and we don't come out with an album every year. So then our friend Brent Spain was acting as our manager and he started sending out tapes to some other labels, including some majors, and the interest started coming mostly from major labels for some reason.

I think a lot of it was because at that point it was the crest of the big punk thing: Green Day and then Offspring and Rancid. So, I guess in that respect we were in a good position because we are established as a band, people know who we are so we'll be able to sell a really decent amount of records. And that's just how it was. They started coming around asking—different labels—and we were just basically blowing it off. We weren't really taking it that seriously.

Then Immortal, they kept calling and they came up to some shows and they were the ones that seemed the most interested. They came up to Sacramento and we talked and it started to make a little more sense. Here was a smaller record label that had some success with bands like Korn, a family-oriented kind of a thing, but they had the whole Sony/Epic thing. So we talked about it and said look, maybe it's time to think about this more seriously. I mean, we didn't really have a lot of options at that point. They wanted us to come down to L.A. and record at some well-known, big rock studio or whatever and we had known that we wanted to record at Enharmonik and they had to deal with that because that was just part of the agreement. We recorded with who we wanted to record with. So we did the record with you and I love the record. I think it's one of the best we've done in a long, long time. I mean, it's consistent, it's solid, it's a good hardcore record. I'm proud of that record and I think that, now looking back on it, had it been on a label like say, Epitaph, or one of the bigger, independent labels or whatever, I think it would have done a lot better just because it was more geared to that kind of thing.

But they [Immortal] just didn't seem to know what to do with it. We did all the things we were supposed to do; we toured our butts off and we talked to radio people and did all the radio interviews and in-store record store appearances and all that stuff. We wanted to make an effort to try and really get this record out there and they just kinda fumbled the ball—Immortal did. They just kinda sat on it. I don't know what they were thinking, they just sorta lost focus on how to market the record. We got off the tour after working on it for a few months and there was talk of doing a music video, which we never did. They said, "We're not rushed for time. Let's just take it slow."

We were like, "Well, wait a minute, the record's been out for a few months, we've been touring, and it's been gettin some radio play. If we're going to do this, let's do it now."

And they just kept kinda pushing it back and so we just got sick of the situation. We looked for ways to—basically, we wanted out of the deal. We didn't want to get dropped, really, but we wanted to be able to figure out a way to get out of it. Anyway, we basically got out of the deal. We left on our own terms which is cool and even got them to pay us money for a record that we never got around to recording with them which was kinda cool. And **it was just a big relief when it was all over with.** I'm not going to say I regret it cause I don't—it was an experience that I think I needed to go through. It's easy to sit around and talk about how evil major labels are when you've never even dealt with them just because that's the punk thing to do or whatever. But, now I realize that yeah, it is pretty evil, but there are some cool people and I don't know, it was a good—I'm glad we experienced it. Now we have something we can point to as to why it's a bad idea.

Opposite: 7 Seconds in Reno, Nevada, 1997.
Right: Green Day at Gilman Street in Berkeley, California, 1991.

When people say we aren't "punk rock" anymore, I agree. It's kind of an oxymoron to say "punk rock" and "hockey arena" at the same time. We definitely come from a certain element, and we have a certain idea of what we like. We carry our morals, our ideals, our ethics, everything with us from where we come from. But I can't say I am the same person I was five years ago. I'd be kidding myself. I think that's the most important thing you can do to be a real person—be honest with yourself.

—*Mike Dirnt, Green Day*

SLEATER-KINNEY

BY SILJA J.A. TALVI

By embracing and living by the DIY ethos of punk rock, Sleater-Kinney has become one of the most vital and interesting bands of the late '90s. While punk as a genre has become stale and formula for the most part, SK demonstrates how the ideas behind punk's roots are still very valid.

In the Capitol Theater bathroom at Ladyfest, August 5, 2000. Below: Los Angeles, 1998

IN TERMS OF YOUR MUSICAL BACKGROUND, YOU'RE ALL HIGHLY SKILLED MUSICIANS...IT SEEMS TO ME THAT YOU WERE TRAINED AS SUCH. AM I CORRECT, OR ARE YOU ENTIRELY SELF-TAUGHT AS MUSICIANS AND SINGERS?

All: Self-taught.

AT WHAT AGE DID YOU START TO TAKE UP INSTRUMENTS THEN?

Carrie Brownstein: I started guitar when I was sixteen.

Janet Weiss: I started guitar when I was seventeen, but I started drumming when I was twenty-two.

Corin Tucker: My dad's kind of a folk musician, so I always sang, but not very well. I started playing guitar when I was about seventeen.

WHAT ARE YOUR THOUGHTS ON THE COMMERCIAL SUCCESS OF LILITH FAIR AND ON THE NOTION THAT IT SOMEHOW REPRESENTS WHAT WOMEN IN MUSIC HAVE TO OFFER? WHAT'S YOUR TAKE ON IT? WOULD YOU PLAY IF YOU WERE INVITED TO?

Carrie: We have actually been invited...

SO WHAT EXACTLY HAPPENED?

Carrie: We said "No thanks."

WHAT ABOUT THAT WHOLE LILITH FAIR PHENOMENON? DO YOU FIND IT IRRITATING?

Carrie: There's a couple of people—Missy Elliott I find really talented and Bonnie Raitt is really awesome, but I think it would be very alienating for our fans to see us and have to pay thirty-five dollars.

I THINK IT'S CLOSER TO FIFTY DOLLARS NOW.

Carrie: That's ridiculous.

Janet: I don't think that they have anything to offer us that we can't achieve on our own terms, at our ticket price, under ten dollars.

Carrie: And not have to do Levi's and Biore ads at the same time.

Janet: Plus, musically, we aren't of that genre. They aren't really our peers. It's out of our reality.

DO YOU HAVE A PREFERENCE IN TERMS OF PLAYING IN FRONT OF THE ENERGY OF YOUTHFUL AUDIENCES OR THE SOPHISTICATION OF OLDER AUDIENCES?

Carrie: Definitely all-ages shows. In terms of the physicality of a space, I like to have the young fans up front who do really like dancing and reflect their enjoyment of the music in a really physical way. That's great, because I do really enjoy the immediate energy flowing between the people in the front and the band. But then it's also nice to feel like we're playing to people our own age. I like to look out and see people of all ages enjoying the music. Definitely, our best shows are in all-ages places. We have played, rarely, twenty-one-and-over shows, and they're never as exciting.

PUBLIC ENEMY

Public Enemy has had more effect on rap than anyone else to date. Coming from Long Island, New York, Public Enemy was part of a revolution of hardcore hip-hop spawned on the East Coast and by 1987 were known as the "Black Panthers of Rap." But when their second release came out in 1988, It Takes a Nation of Millions to Hold Us Back, every white boy in America's suburbs was singing, "Bass! How low can you go? Death row. What a brotha knows." With lyrics that were blatantly sharp and to the point, frontman Chuck D has experienced his share of controversy. However, being banned and denounced by the media did not stop the PE force from selling millions of records on Def Jam records and becoming the most-toured group in hip-hop. Having gone on the road with rap superstars such as the Beastie Boys and thrash metal icons Anthrax, Public Enemy was one of the few rap groups that crossed the musical genre and race barrier, winning fans of all walks of life.

But by the mid-'90s, not all was well with their longtime label, Def Jam. Chuck D states, "Well, it was just philosophical differences. We signed in '86 and the people that we were with in '86 were different from who were there in '94. Nineteen-ninety-four, you know, the so-called family atmosphere after the sale from Sony to PolyGram, to me had been hypocritical and that was fine with me. It's just that I had to leave, so I began a five-year process of murdering my contract and obligations."

In 1997, Chuck D released a remarkable solo record entitled Autobiography of Mista Chuck. Then he wrote an amazing autobiography called Fight The Power: Rap, Race and Reality. In 1998, PE was back to write the soundtrack to Spike Lee's awesome film He Got Game. At the end of the decade, Public Enemy signed to a label that sent the music industry and record retail into a stir, Atomic Pop. Trying to bridge the gap between artists and consumers, Atomic Pop offers downloadable music from their Web site, atomicpop.com. Now living in Atlanta, Chuck D plans on releasing his next book which will be a journal covering five-hundred days starting in 1997. You never know what will come out of such a visionary and motivated artist such as Chuck D, the "Hard Rhymer"; you only know it will be hardcore.

The following are some excerpts from an interview with Chuck D in late 1999. —SM

WHAT IS THE PROBLEM WITH RADIO?

The problems with radio are that it's limited and it's bought out by bigger situations that want to dominate it. So therefore, they don't give any other situations the time to breathe, especially 89 percent of the rap game, which is not mainstream.

ARE THERE ANY LYRICS IN THE PAST THAT YOU REGRET?

None. No lyrics I regret. Because every lyric, I don't go off the top of my head. I think them out clearly and I have very focused topical situations. So no, I don't regret any lyrics.

WHAT ARE THE PRIMARY MOTIVES AND MOTIVATIONS OF THE RECORD INDUSTRY?

To come up with numbers and to move units. If they could sell saucepans and hubcaps for seventeen dollars, they would! The bottom line at the end of the year is profit over loss, not art over art.

WHAT DO YOU FEEL IS THE ULTIMATE MESSAGE YOU WOULD LIKE TO CONVEY TO PEOPLE WHO LISTEN TO PUBLIC ENEMY?

To think for themselves and not to be a robot. I think that's human quality, to use your brain. When you're programmed, that means you're waiting for shit. To me, that's a robot. So use your own opinion to actually shape your movements.

YOUR LYRICS HAVE ALWAYS ADDRESSED RACISM, BOTH INTERNAL AND EXTERNAL TO THE BLACK COMMUNITY. IF YOU WERE TO EXPLAIN IT TO SOMEONE WHO IS NOT AWARE, HOW WOULD YOU DO THAT?

I would do it in song (laughs). I've explained a lot of different things. I've covered a lot of different topics. Number one, I'm gonna cover things from my point of view as being a black person in America. I've got this overt thing like, "Well, Public Enemy covers race!" Every song I do does not cover race; it's just the perception to me. We should not believe all the hype and perception. We should also go into the thickness of the matter, and I'm very topical. I cover topics and I try to cover any topic and try to put it in a rap joint. That's what I try to specialize in.

WHAT ARE THE COMMON CRITICISMS YOU HEAR FROM THE HIP-HOP COMMUNITY ABOUT YOU AND PUBLIC ENEMY?

Umm, umm, too deep (laughs). Maybe the criticism that the music might be just too noisy, but I like that. Maybe just the thing with the perception of everything that we're gonna say is gonna be, black, black, black, black, and I'm sayin' yeah, that's obvious, but that doesn't mean that we can't make a good song and have a good time. It's just a song that you're gonna actually pick up a little bit more from as opposed to just being a song that's just gonna be sitting out there. I really don't pay attention to criticism too much. We just do our thing and just get down, you know?

WHAT ADVICE DO YOU SEND TO ALL RAPPERS AND MUSICIANS?

Try and never repeat yourself and do the same thing twice. Especially on the same record!

WHAT IS THE WORST THING YOU'VE EVER SEEN?

The worst thing I've ever witnessed is ignorance.

FLAKEZINE

In 1995, the snowboard industry was booming. Both hardcore riders and big business types were pretty much embracing the boom. And why not? All the hard work was finally beginning to pay off. Heckler itself had gone from twenty-eight pages to sixty-eight pages over the course of a year. In our fall issue the previous year, we traded away the back cover for a snowboard from Sims, one of the largest companies of the day. Not counting the back page, we had twenty-one advertisers in that first issue. Starting in 1995, we had sixty-nine, many of them full pages. Burton, who graciously advertised in our first issue (Jake actually rode, and still does), went from a third of a page to a full page. Everybody was happy. Love and joy were in the air. There were no dissenting voices...except one.

Someone anonymous, yet very much connected, very much on the inside, was posting long, stinging, and gripping diatribes on the fledgling Internet newsgroup, rec.skiing.snowboard. Nobody in the industry wanted to acknowledge this poster, who went by the name of "Flakezine." We contacted him via email and agreed to print some of his writings. Our advertising went down a bit the next month. Looking back on it today from the post-Olympics, post-consolidation, post-boom, and post-bust days of the snowboard industry, I realize that Flakezine was not just amusing and cool, but prophetic. Several years ahead of the Adbusters crowd, Flakezine told it like it was—but nobody listened. —JB

The Destructive Power of Mainstream Press and Advertising
by Flakezine

"Society is something like a cybernetic system that is ruled by various governors. One of the most important regulating mechanisms is the advertising industry. Advertisements function like templates that control psycho-social processes by channeling energy and guiding activity."

—From Imagologies: Media Philosophy *by Mark C. Taylor and Esa Saarinen*

Snowboarding is being embraced by pop culture at an alarming rate. No sport, it seems, has ever been more closely aligned with the icons of pop style than snowboarding has in the past few months. Recently several items surfaced in the media that deserve closer inspection:

The September 1994 issue of Britain's *The Face* magazine featured a story titled "The 100 Most Powerful People in Fashion." At number 96 on this list was Greg Arnet (misspelling his name, it's actually "Arnette"). In what is becoming the popular blend of snowboarding fashion and rock 'n' roll they said he "created the hottest shades this summer. With the silver 'Beastie Boy Arnets' now deleted, he becomes cult property."

Everyone knows the part snowboarding played in taking Arnette glasses into the world spotlight. In ads featuring Steve Graham, Todd Messick, and Greg, photographer James Cassimus captured the essence of cool through snowboarding. In fact, Mike D was probably introduced to the chrome Arnettes by fellow Beastie and snowboarder Adam "MCA" Yauch. Mike D even wore the shades at Board Aid, *Warp* magazine's snowboard/rock 'n' roll fund-raiser for LifeBeat held at Snow Summit in spring of 1994, an event that MTV used as a location for their Top 20 Video Countdown with right-wing, virgin VJ Kennedy and guest VJ Emilio Estevez.

In the same issue of the *Face* in an article about street style being at a standstill and the emergence of micro-fashions, style journalist Ekow Eshun wrote: "Come winter they [street-style trend-setters] will probably have switched to high-performance outdoors wear by labels like Northface and snowboard companies such as B13 [Burton's clothing line in England]."

This style appropriation of all things snowboard has not been overlooked by U.S. publications either. In the style section of a recent issue of *Rolling Stone*, a Burton product manager named Heidi was featured in a section on style trendsetters that blurred the line between advertising and editorial. Snowboarding was touted as "hot hot hot," in the piece.

"The Ad-dict buys images not things."
—Imagologies

On the advertising side, outerwear giant Columbia Sportswear Company of Portland, Oregon, ran an ad for their new line of "snowboard"/wear in the October issue of *Spin* with copy that reads, "Mother Boyle says snowboarding rips....Next time you catch some air, grab your Convert first." They also ran the ad in the December issue of *TeaWorld* [sic, TransWorld]. Not to be outdone, Nike advertised their Air Krakatoa in the October issue of *Snowboarder* magazine. Interestingly, *TeaWorld* ad sales-people claim they would not allow Nike to advertise in their pages. Why? Who knows. Apparently, the advertising staff felt that the Nike ad was somehow inappropriate for the pages of a snowboard magazine, while a full-page ad for Ice-T's new Album *Born Dead* or a half-page Public Enemy ad is. Incongruities in advertising policy, however, are nothing new for that magazine.

Far and away the largest hit to snowboarding in a while is the Molson Ice beer ad featuring Steve Graham, Damian Sanders, and Tex Devenport. For its first national run, it dropped in during Monday Night Football on September 26, 1994, when the Broncos were trailing the Bills 20 to 27. Molson's advertising agency purchased the footage from Gerry and Artie at FLF (Fall Line Films, creators of this year's *Gettin' Some*).

This isn't the first time snowboarding has been used to sell beer. Coors Light used Bert Lamar and others in ads back in 1987, and more current bits in an ad running this winter, however, Coors has always used snowboarding as part of a "winter sports montage." The Molson ad is entirely snowboarding from beginning to end, and will probably put snowboarding into the forebrains of more people than anything else this winter.

That Columbia, Nike, Coors, and Molson are using snowboarding as a sales vehicle shows how important (monetarily speaking) snowboarding's image has gotten. Because they are so crafty when it comes to influencing consumers, advertisers and pop-media outlets create a hype spiral. They tap into snowboarding's image by telling people that snowboarding is cool. People then make the logical jump to thinking that both snowboarding, Columbia, Nike, and beer are cool.

As with all growth spirals, the downside is that as the spiral climbs higher and higher it gets smaller and smaller. As snowboarding gets bigger and bigger, the number of companies involved in an industry will fall off, making snowboarding much less diverse. In a large market, only the very large companies have the cash to compete. Look at shoes, soft drinks, computers, and beer for example. There used to be many companies in each industry, but they were all bought up by the big guys. This is the main reason Ride Snowboards went public and Avalanche sold 80 percent to a rich businessman. Both companies understood that in order to survive in the "popularized" world of snowboarding they needed large amounts of cash.

Currently there are more than one hundred "brands" of snowboards being manufactured at between ten to twenty factories worldwide. It's only a matter of time before the companies that actually manufacture their own products squeeze out the smaller companies that are having their boards built by someone else. Manus—like Morrow—are already putting on the squeeze with their Slickfty line of boards that retail for $399, bindings included. This will force smaller companies to be much more efficient. Many on the microlabel level just won't be able to do it and will go down hard during the next five years.

The reason we're discussing this is because so many people seem to get excited when they see snowboarding being recognized by the "mainstream" pop culture. "It's helping to promote the sport," they say. "We'll all make more money." But it doesn't work that way. **In the hands of the "mainstream," snowboarding will become exactly like skiing, golf, inline skating, NASCAR, and tennis. Boring, dull, and staid.** Sure, snowboarders, snowboard companies, and the snowboard media will make a lot more money (yippee), but it will be in exchange for their souls, creativity, and individuality. You can count on it.
—October 5, 1994

Above: Mike Ranquet and Shaun Palmer just having fun long before any of the aforementioned diatribe even mattered, Bend, Oregon, 1987.
Opposite: The first ad Burton put in Heckler *and another infamous ad from that era.*

THE 2 FRESH PRINCE
BY GENE SUNG

"DAMN, YOU LOOKING SHARPER THAN A TACK," screamed scrawny little Myko, as he checked himself out in the bathroom mirror. *Gotta look good out on the hill today,* he thought to himself. With three feet of fresh powder outside the Squaw Valley slope-side condo that his parents rented for the week, Myko was checking his new buzz to make sure it was even. With only his L.A. Kings boxers on, which sagged loosely over his chicken legs, he kept running both hands across his stubbled, light-blond hair. *Damn, mirrors don't lie, and you be looking so fresh they should have your name all over the produce aisle at Safeway. Hhhaaa, he laughed, that's a good one! I've gotta remember that one for scamming at the arcade tonight. I'll be like: yo, baby, you so fresh I've seen your name all over the produce aisle. Damn, you so hard-looking, you don't even need no lines to get the bitches. Shit, in reality I just another member of LBC, ready to pull a 187 on an undercover cop.*

Yep, Myko (or Michael as his parents call him) was the downest of the down at West Beverly Hills High School. *Shit, I'm so down I don't know what's up. Wait?* said Myko. *Take that one back 'cause that just makes you sound dumb,* who took no grief from no one 'cause they best check themselves before they wreck themselves. He no longer went by Michael 'cause that name's straight embarrassing. Now he's known as "Mack Money Myko" 'cause that just sounds plain street-tough. *I should just start calling myself: "The 'G' Formerly Known As Michael Smith."*

Ha! You as funny as you're good looking, laughed Myko, trying to pop the zit on his pale, white nose. *Man, you such a comedian you could give Pee Wee Herman a pointer!!! HA HA!!! PEE WEE HAD TOO MANY POINTERS!!! HA!!! YOU IN RARE FORM TODAY, BABY!!! DAMN, GIVE ME SOME SKIN, MY MAN,* yelled Myko as he high-fived his reflection in the mirror.

Looking around him, he faced the tough choice of choosing what to wear today. A few days before their vacation, his dad took him to "The California Image," a hardcore skate/surf/Rollerblade/bikini/snowboard/alternative clothing store located in the heart of Bel Aire Mall. One-stop mallternative convenience where you can buy Manic Panic, a chain wallet, a "Kurt Cobain 1967–1994" T-shirt, and the new Jim "The Ripper" Rippey model. "Bored of your uncool self?" screamed store owner Big Wave Dave on his major broadcast commercial. "Come on in as a geek and leave as a rude boy, a shredding skater, a thrashing boarder, a tagger, a gnarly punker, or whatever new identity you choose."

Good ol' pops bought him a Jib X9 Storm Jacket, a Bonk T2 Spring shell, some Frontside-Indy Avalanche pants, a Burton fleece, a Sims long-sleeve, a Burning Snow union suit, ten T-shirts, and a beanie with a pot leaf embroidered on the front— all size XXL, of course. Equipment-wise, Myko didn't fair too badly either. He got a pair of Airwalk Freerides, Burton Custom Bindings, and last but not least, the Jim "The Ripper" Rippey model. And to top off the five-hour-long shopping spree, the hardcore little G walked out with two new pairs of Rollerblades.

Well, it's really cold today so I guess I better wear my Jib X9 Storm Jacket. No, forget that 'cause it'll look like Mack Money Myko can't hack the cold, so I'm just gonna wear my black long-sleeve, with a T-shirt over it. Shit, what goes good with black? I could wear my blue "Girl Skateboards" T-shirt, or my brown "Rollerblade Soul Grind" T-shirt. They both match pretty well with my gray pants. Well, blue goes good with the black long-sleeve, so I'll wear the "Girl" shirt. Plus, my partner back in my B Hill 'hood told me that in order for snowboarders to look legit, they have to be wearing something skate related 'cause snowboarders who don't skate aren't in the HHHEEEOOOUUUSSSSEEEE! as Snoop Dog would say. Man, "Girl" is the freshest skate company there is. Damn, I heard that Mark Carroll and Ray Howard own the operations, and they's the best there is. **If anyone asks about my skate history, I'll just say I was hanging with the Gonz back in '86.**

Man, I wish Rollerblading was seen as legit because the shit we do is as down as any skater's. You can't tell me that a "quarter cab-soul-grind-cross-fingered wheel grab," or a "front-flip crotch grab to e-brake" ain't tough. I guess it's just 'cause most rollerbladers are just these little pussy white boys. Shit, I might be white but I ain't no pussy like all the other kids at West Beverly Hills High. Just two weeks ago, me an' some of my partners formed a bladers gang: "ESSE WEST SIDE!!! REPRESENT!!! HA HA!!!" Representing not only West B Hill, but also the West Coast 'cause CALIFORNIA KNOWS HOW TO PARTY!!!

Representing my would-be partners Snoop, Dre, and 2pac—Rest In Peace. Standing up to those East Coast fools like Biggie Smalls and his wacked Notorious B.I.G. posse, with their weak-ass beats. I bet you a million dollars it was Biggie who set up 2pac and got him killed in that drive-by. I heard Biggie was behind the first attempt on 2Pac's life when he took four slugs to the body. Man, Biggie Smalls' just jealous of the Long Beach/Compton Funkadelics because his beats are like my lawn at around 5 pm—plain watered-down. Man, that Clinton Muthafucka sure dropped some tight beats with his P-Funk All Stars. Yeah!!! Bill Clinton's P-Funk representing the West Coast. Keeping it real!!!

After dressing tight and finally choosing his Black Fly's Nasty Girls shades—"'cause the frame's in the shape of a ho's tits"—over his Arnettes, Dragons, DSOs, or Oakleys, Myko was ready to step out. Just as he was leaving the bathroom, he glanced back and saw his Beanie with the embroidered pot leaf sitting on the counter. *SHIT!!! I can't forget that or else peoples on the Hill will think that I don't represent the Chronic. They'll think I ain't down when I want it legalized as much as the next G. Shit, presidents that built this country smoked the Chronic. I heard that our first President had fields of that shit. What's his name? It's the dude who chopped down the cherry tree...George Clinton! Yeah, he also drafted The Declaration of Dependence. Yeah, him and his wife Martha, was down with the Chronic. Damn, and what about Bob Marley. That Jamaican G sang song after song about getting blunted, feeling irie, and "jammin to da rhydm." He also talk about some shit called human rights, but that shit's not fun. If it ain't about partying, it ain't about me. He was into some religion called Rastafari, where he smoke the Chronic for Jah. Damn, a religion of weed is a religion indeed!!! Yeah!!! HA HA!!! Myko, you a poet and you don't even know it!!!*

Adjusting his beanie so that it sat perfectly above his eyes (that hard-ass Venice/Suicidal look), he put on his boots, grabbed his board, and stepped outside into the cold, sunny morning. As he walked the whole fifty yards to the lifts, Myko began to stress for the first time this vacation. *Shit, how do I get into one of these snowboards? The last few days I been riding them Big Foots. They like rollerblading on snow. Damn, I can't even remember if I'm regular- or irregular-footed. Man, I want to Big Foot again; but peoples were laughing at me, so I got to snowboard. If for anything, just for getting better puss, 'cause there be all these fresh-ass girlies doing it. Well, I'm just going to put my left foot forward.*

He strapped into the binding, but now the graphic's backwards, so he unstrapped and put his right foot forward. *Damn, I hope that's right.*

After pushing and tripping over his feet and his snowboard, Myko barely crawled to the lift. *Damn, that was tough. Thank God there's nobody here to see me looking like a fool.*

The only people around were the lift-op and the dark, gorgeous, blond he was talking with.

Shit, that bitch is finer than fine. Um, um...wouldn't it be nice to doggy-style that! I'm gonna have to bust out a smooth line, and steal her away from that stupid hippie-looking lifty. Yeah—a smile crossed his face—*I know just the line to use. Gets 'em every time.*

Floundering through the gates, Myko finally got to the lift-boarding area. "Excuse me, baby," he said suavely, interrupting her talk with the lifty.

"Like, hi...Do I know you?" she said back.

"No, you don't, baby. I just wanted you to know that there's a toilet seat around your neck."

"A what?" she snapped back.

"Yeah, there's a toilet seat around your neck, AND IT'S THERE BECAUSE YOU'RE THE SHIT!!!"

"SCREW YOU, YOU LITTLE PRICK!!! GO BACK TO THE ARCADE!!!" she screamed at the top of her lungs, as the lifty-lifty started dying of laughter.

Damn, it usually works—I could've given her a pointer or two. Nothing but her loss, thought Myko as he pushed out to get on the lift. Seeing the lift approaching, he started to panic. *Shit, how do I sit on one them chairs with a snowboard? Am I suppose to sit down like a Big Footer or do I sit down sideways?* Completely clueless, the chair swung around and knocked him on the ground. *SHIT!!!* Freaking out, he reached up and grabbed the chair, and then it started dragging him on his back. The lifty was still talking to the girl and didn't even notice as Myko got dragged off the lift ramp and into the air. *SHIT!!! SHOULD I YELL FOR HELP? NO, DON'T YELL 'CAUSE PEOPLE'LL LAUGH AT YOU. Cube would never yell in this situation. He'd just keep his cool.* Soon Myko was five feet in the air; then fifteen; then thirty.

Then he heard "STOP THE LIFT!!! MY SON IS CAUGHT ON THE CHAIR!!!"

With tears in his eyes, he looked down and saw his mom and the lifty both making a dive for the red "Stop" button. The lift grinded to a halt and Myko was stuck hanging onto the lift for dear life. A crowd started gathering under the lift as everyone was pointing and laughing at Myko. *Oh my God, what should I do? I'm so high up, I just can't drop to the ground. I'll break a leg, or worse yet, I could die. I'm destined to die as a champ and not a chump. Destined to go out like a G, not a Wee. If you fall to the ground, just get up like it didn't hurt. Act like nothing happened. Damn, I feel like I'm about to scream or something. Just don't scream Myko, just don't scre...*
    MMMOOOMMMMMMIIIEEEEEE!!!!!
    HHHEEELLLPPPPPP!!!!!!
    HHHEEELLLPPPPPP!!!!!!

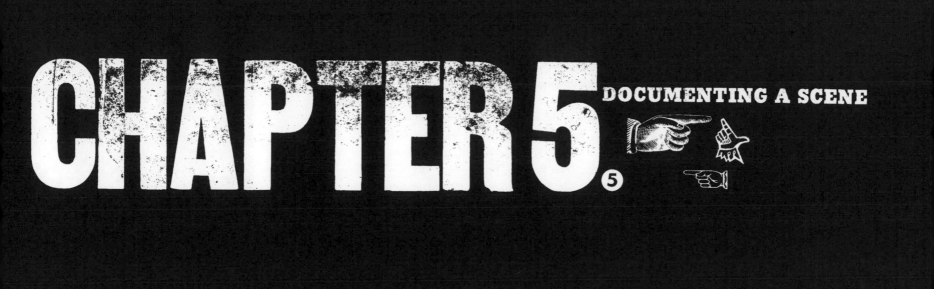

CHAPTER 5. DOCUMENTING A SCENE ⑤

Photographer Aaron Sedway, self portrait.

Documenting a Scene

by Bryce Kanights

There's something distinct to be said about the individuals behind the images that you regularly see in magazines. Over the last three decades, assorted photo jockeys have submerged themselves within the culture of these then illegitimate sports and developed relationships that have endured over time. Sleeping in cars and on floors and couches during road trips, laying in the gutters, dodging security guards, risking their lives in the face of Mother Nature, and most importantly having their cameras readily accessible in order to capture scenes and events at a moment's notice, it's all part of the process in order to get the shots.

The origins of documenting the action and culture of "alternative" (for lack of a better adjective) sports began with surfing during the '50s and '60s, but as the equipment was very antiquated, usually these images did not reflect ground-breaking action sequences. However, they did establish a benchmark for the sport and played a vital role in helping to push surfing's progression. Similarly, in the mid-'70s, as skateboarding began to experience a surge in popularity, soon photographic images of skaters were being captured and placed within the magazines at a rapid pace. These images became one of the principal drivers for the growth and progression of the sport and helped to shape skateboarding into what it has become today. At the time, there were no videos, televised shows, or websites exhibiting skateboarding; it was the powerful action images in the magazines that fueled the worldwide skating community. Veteran lensmen such as Glen E. Friedman, Craig Stecyk, Warren Bolster, Craig Fineman, Ted Terrebone, and Bill Sharp routinely documented significant skate sessions and events and kept the fire alive. During the '80s, Mofo, Grant Brittain, Bud Fawcett, Rick Kosick, Chris Ortiz, Chris Carnel, Tobin Yelland, Trevor Graves, Daniel Sturt, and others took to the scene lugging around weighty packs full of gear across the planet to document significant events. Their creative records are now of historical importance and value.

Over the past decade a new generation of skate and snow photographers has emerged to capture the energy and culture of our sports. Like their predecessors in the past, Lance Dawes, Scott Serfas, Jody Morris, Derek Ketella, Atiba Jefferson, Gabe Morford, Mike Burnett, Mike Blabac, and others reflect the same passion that accurately and creatively chronicles the various situations as they happen.

Sure, as our "board riding" (still lacking a fitting adjective) sports have gained mainstream attention there are now perks of world travel and the rewards of sleeping on actual hotel room beds, but there's no way any photographer can capture meaningful and compelling images by just being there, uninvolved. Just take a look at the majority of newspapers and mainstream magazines covering our sports globally and it's readily evident.

Very often, these mainstream photographers shoot poorly framed action images with no reference point (coping or lip) in their photographs. Specifically, they usually miss the key point of the action. It's painfully obvious that the media circus that routinely shows up for the X-Games doesn't have a clue.

As our sports and cultures continue to progress and propagate over time with subsequent generations, surfing photographers will stand to face the powerful forces of our mother ocean. Snowboarding photographers will continue to confront the bitterest of winter storms along with sketchy and unstable snow conditions. Skateboarding photographers will persist to deal with temperamental security guards, cops, and civilians of ill will. It's all relative and comes with the territory.

One skater, seven photographers. John Cardiel at a demo in Golden Gate Park, San Francisco, California, 1992.

DAVE SEOANE
BY BUD FAWCETT AND CHRIS CARNEL

Terje Haakonsen riding, Dave filming, 1996.

In a largely conglomerated world of high-budget movie production hype, shock value, and sensationalism came a do-it-yourselfer named Dave Seoane. Living above Donner Ski Ranch in a tiny shack-like studio in the winter of 1987, he quickly bypassed the normal learning curve of snowboarding and was soon doing some of the first skate-related frontside inverts and Caballerials in the halfpipe. Within a few years he held a winning streak throughout the California Series events and was riding pro for Look Snowboards. A few more years passed as the sponsorship with Look began to vanish and Seoane was shooting a 16-millimeter movie camera for fun. He shot a lot of the footage for Fall Line Films in the movies Roadkill and 8 Tracks. He was soon designing his own board for Rossignol and spending time in places like Jackson Hole riding a lot of powder. At home in Tahoe he made cool metal sculptures in his spare time and started thinking heavily about cinematography. Then, out of the blue, he was absent from a whole winter season of snowboarding while he attended the New York Film Academy.

Now Dave has Cinemaseoane, which started out with Subjekt Haakonsen (a journalistic action movie based on the life of Terje Haakonsen) and the follow-up that was later released called the Haakonsen Faktor. Dave Seoane is never in Tahoe anymore, even though he claims residence there 'cause he's too busy following the top five snowboarders around the world to produce his highly artistic and creative vision of our sport. He sees things from a true snowboarder's perspective. His work is unique and artistic. He sets up quickly and has a great eye for detail. Photographer Bud Fawcett and Chris Carnel asked Dave some "serious" questions before he boarded another flight.

CHRIS: IS IT HARD FOR YOU TO SEPARATE A DAY OF SNOWBOARDING FROM A DAY OF SHOOTING?
If you snowboarded every day you'd burn yourself out. If you shot film every day you'd burn yourself out. It's just good to balance it out. **It's frustrating when it's a powder day and bluebird when you're supposed to be on a snowboard and you end up shooting.** That's kind of a drag.

BUD: WHO IS YOUR FAVORITE RIDER YOU'VE EVER SHOT, ON THE BASIS OF THE WAY THEY RIDE?
I really like shooting with Terje Haakonsen 'cause he's really consistent and compresses (riding-wise) a lot. Jim Rippey, I like shooting with him. Guys like (Bryan) Iguchi and Jamie (Lynn). I work with those guys a lot. Sometimes it's easier when you're traveling on the road to go with people that you get along with. It helps a lot (laughing).

CHRIS: DONNER HAS CHANGED A LOT. A LOT MORE PEOPLE ARE RIDING THERE NOWADAYS. DO YOU STILL RIDE THERE?
I swear to God every time I go there I have the best time, it has the coolest spirit. Like Norm [Sayler, who owns Donner Ski Ranch], however old he is now it doesn't matter; we've got to get Norm snowboarding, he's by far the king of the mountain.

CHRIS: HOW DID YOU EVER GET INTO FILMING. WHEN DID YOU START?
The first thing I ever shot on film was [Shaun] Palmer on his motorcycle. I had a chance to go to Chile and the only way I could go was if I was to be a cameraman. So I said OK and I had to go shoot a test roll of Palmer two days before I went. I got lucky and it worked out.

CHRIS: YOU NEVER SHOOT HI-8 VIDEO AND ALL THAT STUFF?
Oh yeah, just for fun though. I had a bunch of photography classes I took, that kind of set me up for it. But filming is a lot easier, though, you just set it on infinity. Unlike with stills you don't have to pull focus or anything. You have so much light coming through the lens from a bright sunny day that it gives you a bunch of depth of field. Everything's in focus.

BUD: SO YOU'RE SAYING WHEN YOUR SIGHT STARTS GOING, YOU JUST FILM MOVIES 'CAUSE YOU CAN'T FOCUS ANYMORE (LAUGHING).
Yeah, you just follow the blob in the middle of the frame (everyone laughs).

Standard Films & the Hatchett Brothers

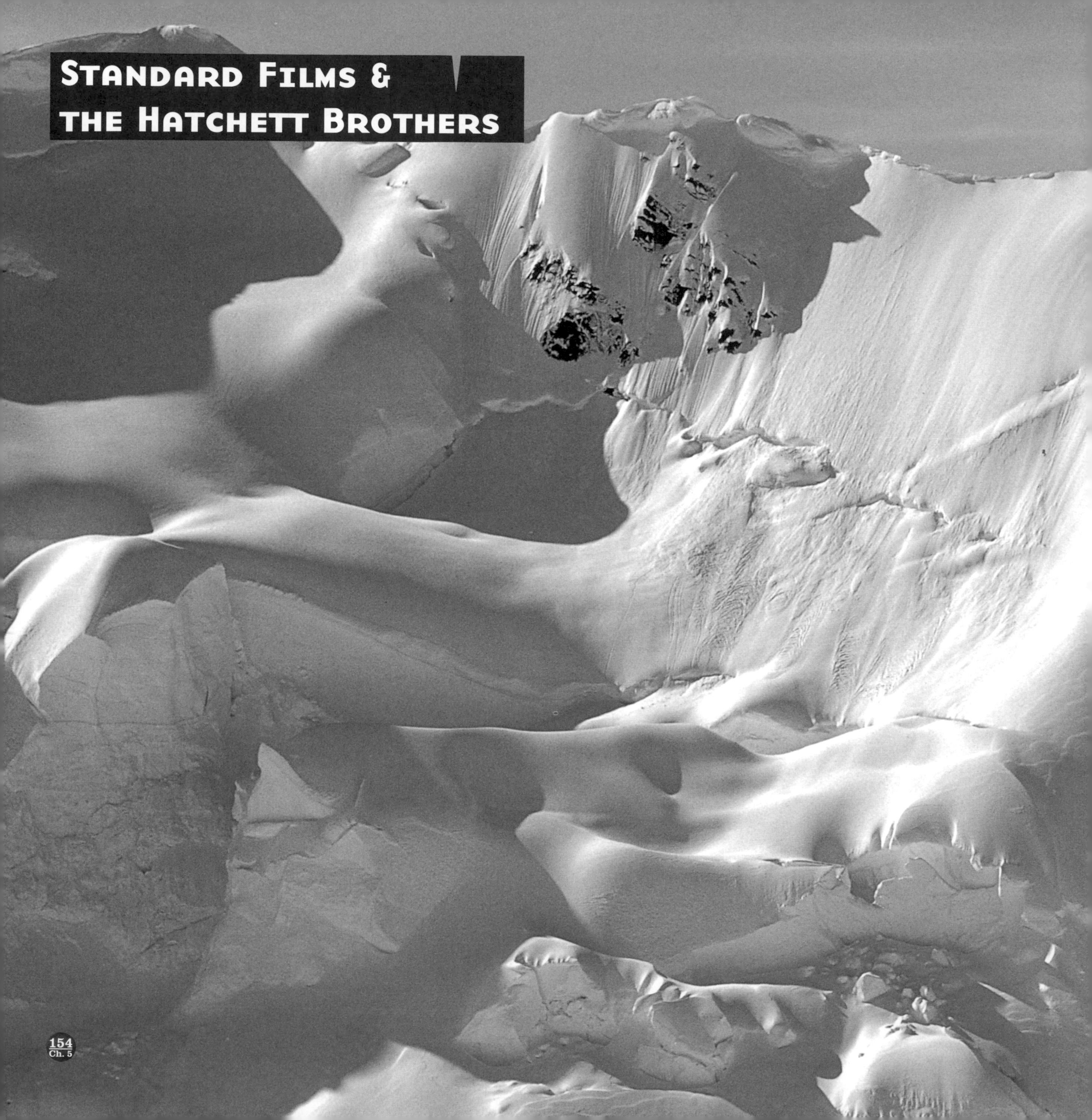

Twin brothers Mike and Dave Hatchett out of North Shore, Lake Tahoe started Standard Films, one of the world's largest and most deeply rooted snowboard film companies. With a decade of cinematography, snowboarding, and mountain experience behind them they've consistently produced the most action-packed film footage of snowboarding in the world. As sure as the sun is gonna rise in the East a film will be produced annually by them that is top notch.

The Hatchett brothers were born five minutes apart in San Diego, California, where they spent their wild youth before moving to their current home, Lake Tahoe: "We were getting in trouble a lot in San Diego, like most teenagers do, and just figured moving to the mountains would clean us up, which in the long run worked pretty well," Mike recalls. The early days in Tahoe were fun but rough. Dave once printed and matted some rock-climbing photos he shot and traded them for food to a local Tahoe restaurant, where they still hang today. As Standard Films' success grew due to their phenomenal snowboarding movie series called "TB," as in Totally Board. TB1 debuted in 1990 and starred Dave Hatchett, Nick Perata, Shawn Farmer, Damien Sanders, Jim Zellers, Bonnie Leary, Andy Hetzel, Noah Brandon, Jeff Brushie, Dan Donnelly, and Aaron Astorga. Brother Dave, a long-time Burton rider, can be seen both behind the lens and in front of it, riding some of the world's best terrain.

Gathering footage is very hard work. Getting to a peak at six A.M. on a ruthlessly cold winter morning, standing in fresh snow up to your calves, and looking towards a gray muted sky that's lit only by the sun's dim December glow takes conditioning. Organizing the world's best riders takes management skills. Operating cameras in adverse elements takes technical skills. The Hatchetts have these skills and more. The following discussion with both brothers was in Heckler's final newsprint edition, the "Family" issue, which was released in March of 1996. —CC

DID YOU EVER SKATEBOARD BACK IN SAN DIEGO AT ALL THE PARKS AROUND IN THE EARLY EIGHTIES?

Mike: Totally. I had a membership at Del Mar Skate Ranch for three years. I grew up surfing also. I just never got that good at skating. It was pretty much just fun for me.

THEN YOU MOVED UP TO TAHOE?

Mike: Dave moved up here and got into rock climbing that summer and then got into snowboarding that winter. He met Tom Burt, Jim and Bonnie Zellers, and Damian Sanders. We used to see Tom Sims up on the Pass [Donner Summit] with some snowboards on the rack of his car and that was a rarity. There were only a couple of snowboarders around back then.

THAT'S RAD. HOW DID YOU GET TO THE POINT OF FILMING 16 MILLIMETER AND DOING CINEMATOGRAPHY?

Previous spread: Dave in Valdez, Alaska, 1997.
Above: Mike during the filming of TB5, 1996.
Opposite: The Hatchetts rock out in Tahoe City with Fortress, 1991.

Mike: I went to Palomar College in San Diego for three years where I studied still photography in the late eighties. Then near the end of that in September of that year, Dave went rock climbing at Joshua Tree National Monument. So he invited me to come out. I got super stoked on climbing the first day and took black and white photos of it for my class. I got my photos back and they came out awesome; I thought I could possibly shoot photos and climb. Then sometime that December on Christmas break I went skiing with my family at Donner Ski Ranch. Dave talked me into trying boarding and I was like totally into skiing. I had done it for eight years and I'm like "I don't know, man." He kept saying, "Try it, I guarantee you'll hang your skis up!" So I tried it that afternoon and at the end of the day I just got home and basically chucked my skis. I was like, "I'm over skiing for good!" So I got into snowboarding that winter and right off the bat I quit school and moved to Breckenridge, Colorado. That's where I met Shawn Farmer, Nick Perata, and Pat Salomon. I was shooting stills, bussing tables, and I bought a [Colorado resorts] Summit Pass. Pat had gone to film school, knew I shot stills, and was like, "Let's make a snowboard movie next year." I didn't think we could do it, didn't know how or anything. FLF, actually called "Fall Line" at the time was just making *Western Front* that spring, and then the next winter they made *Exile* and that's when we made our first *Totally Board* movie. I picked up a 16-millimeter movie camera and just started shooting my brother with it. I had only done stills up to that point.

HAD YOU EVER SHOT VIDEO PRIOR TO THAT, LIKE VHS FORMAT?

Mike: No, I immediately went to 16 millimeter and pretty much the learning curve was just filming the first *Totally Board* movie. I've shot some rock climbing on video since then, but never shot anything of snowboarding in video ever. Then, after we made *Totally Board* I worked for Fall Line Films for two years and I learned a lot working for those guys; worked on *Riders on the Storm* and *Critical Condition*. They had the budget to send me wherever and pay for the film stock. That helped me out. I ruined a lot of film (laughing). Then I met Mack Dawg [Mike McIntyre].

THAT WAS HOW LONG AGO?

Mike: Nine years ago. He did a few of his own films but had never actually shot 16, only 8 millimeter and video up to that point. That was basically why we hooked up is because he originally wanted to learn 16 millimeter and also the freestyle/extreme mixture between us worked out really well. Then we kind of went our separate ways. We're still tight but Dawger does more of the freestyle-jib stuff in the sport.

TELL ME ABOUT YOUR CLIMBING MOVIES.

Mike: Climbing's a real fun thing to do. I climbed for about eight years before I even thought about making a video about it. I started doing the rock-climbing movies when I was working for Fall Line before we did *TB2* and I've done three of them since. Rock climbers are real interesting people. It's a real low-budget sport and the people who do it, do it 'cause they love it. They don't make anything close to what some professional snowboarders make, in comparison. Most climbing movies were all "la-de-da" with slow acoustic guitar in the mountains and stuff. So we made ours all aggro with fast music and guys goin' off cause there are a lot of climbers like that. Like the late great Dan Osmond. He was an inspiration for sure.

I'VE NOTICED THAT YOU GUYS HAVE HAD A LOT OF FAST MUSIC IN YOUR FILMS ESPECIALLY AROUND *TB4*, BANDS LIKE MEGADETH AND PANTERA.

Mike: We used that Pantera song "Cowboys from Hell" in the European part of *TB4*. The soundtrack as a whole in the movie ended up pretty heavy, pretty rock 'n' roll. I didn't mean it to be that hard but we did it on a computer, nonlinear, and we just kept putting parts to a fast song and it sounded cool. Then when the movie was laid out there were no slow parts (laughing). I think all different types of music go rad with snowboarding. Sometimes metal's the call.

YOU PLAYED BASS.

Mike: I grew up playing music in cover bands in San Diego. We were about thirteen or fourteen years old and we would play at high school dances. We wrote some original songs and played some covers like old Iron Maiden and Judas Priest. You know, boppy metal stuff.

DID YOU AND DAVE GROW UP ATTENDING ROCK CONCERTS?

Mike: I've seen a lot of metal bands over the years. Judas Priest I've seen eight times, Iron Maiden I've seen about eight times and the Scorpions I've seen multiple times. But Pantera one time in Reno years ago put on one of the best shows I've ever seen.

The first time I ever met Dave Hatchett was at Donner Ski Ranch about eight years ago. Dave was searching out untracked powder lines under the main chair and playing in their set of cliffs referred to as the "Palisades." I'd see him around Tahoe over the years.

TELL ME ABOUT ALASKA SINCE IT PLAYS A BIG PART IN YOUR MOVIES.

Dave: That's one of the highlights as far as big mountain-riding. We go up there every year. The best snow, the longest runs, the best terrain. It's also way hit or miss, a lot of bad weather days, and it's a lot more dangerous than your typical riding—you gotta weigh your options. There's a lot of different ways to look at Alaska. You look at it as a rad powder place with the most epic terrain you've ever ridden, but at the same time you've got to have a lot of respect for it. Every year I go up there, I think about it more and more: you're playin' the odds, you gotta really have respect and be as careful as you can 'cause there's a lot of crevasses, cornices, exposures over rock bands. There's so many ways to fuck up when you're up there. I dig it and it's a killer place to ride but at the same time it's also a nerve-racking place to ride, even on the easiest runs. Getting in the 'copter, that's dangerous as it is. A lot of people die in helicopter crashes, those things go down all the time. So that's scary.

HOW ABOUT AROUND THE TAHOE AREA?

Dave: I have a lot of fun at Squaw Valley on a powder day 'cause you can push it more and not worry about a crevasse or an avalanche. I mean you risk hitting a rock or a tree and that can take you out, but that's your fault. I couldn't ask for more on an epic powder day than KT22 at Squaw. It's a killer mountain.

DO YOU HIKE BACKCOUNTRY A LOT?

Dave: Any kind of backcountry adventure with good snow is the best. Good snow is the key. To hike and/or snowmobile in search of good powder, that's the quest.

AS FAR AS RIDING IN AND ALSO DOING YOUR OTHER WORK FILMING FOR STANDARD, IS THAT A JUGGLE?

Dave: Well, yeah. I'm kinda juggling things being a rider and helping film and working for the company—filming and being filmed. I try to do my share, editing and whatever. I think down the road I will be more involved with filming and such but I have at least a few more years of riding left in me (laughing). I want to do it for as long as my sponsors will help me out. I'm into the longevity of it. But who knows how that will change. With surfers, if the motivation is there it seems the sponsors keep them on—look at Gerry Lopez and Gary Elkerton: guys like that have been doing it forever! They've been surfing for twenty-five years and they might make more money now than they ever did. It would be cool if that happens with snowboarding. It would be cool to see Craig Kelly have a shot in the magazines ten years from now. We'll see what happens. I'd like to see snowboarders' careers as longevity last, I'd love to. As long as the riders are out there riding and riding well, it doesn't matter who is "new school" or whatever cause everyone has made their mark, everyone's good in their own way. Terry Kidwell, Craig Kelly, Jim Rippey, whoever. That's what's rad about snowboarding is that everyone has their own little things and their own unique styles. I think that's the part that will always last.

JEM COHEN
BY DARREN DOANE

Jem Cohen is an award-winning short filmmaker who has also worked with musicians like R.E.M., Elliott Smith, the Butthole Surfers, Jonathan Richman, and Vic Chesnutt. His first full-length feature film, Instrument, *documents the band Fugazi, whom he has been friends with since their inception. We asked filmmaker Darren Doane (he did the feature film* Godmoney *and has done videos for Pennywise, MxPx, AFI, Blink 182, Guttermouth, and others) to interview Jem. —JB*

HOW LONG HAVE YOU BEEN WORKING ON *INSTRUMENT*?

The footage goes back to the start of the band. There is footage from '87—some of the earlier shows, so I've been working on it personally for eleven years. I was just shooting for myself. It wasn't like I started making a documentary eleven years ago. I pretty much shoot all the time, so it was natural that I would be documenting Fugazi. I'm kind of guessing that it was around '92 or '93 that I got together with the band and we concretely decided to make it a collaborative project. I started to realize that I had quite a lot of material that I started to tinker away with. You know, little bits and pieces of sections that I might want to cut and how I might want to do it. I had always been close friends with those guys and we had done some collaborative work before, particularly with this short film I did called *Glue Man*. So we had a connection. I had also edited another piece

called *Black Hall Radio* that I did with Ian where we built the soundtrack together. So I had a history of working with those guys and it just made sense that I would eventually do a Fugazi project, but I don't think we realized that it would be such an enormous project.

WHEN DID YOU KNOW THAT YOU WERE GETTING CLOSE TO FINISHING? DID YOU JUST HAVE TO EVENTUALLY SAY, "WE'RE GOING TO STOP AT THIS GIVEN POINT."

It was really difficult because I wasn't able to just put everything aside and work on it constantly, or six months or a year at a time. I mean if I had, I would have been done a lot sooner. But I also kept shooting and the band kept getting involved, and different things kept coming up. Footage from other people would surface. The project kind of became more and more monumental and therefore more difficult to wrap up and, eventually, we just realized that it had to stop. We weren't looking to put a cap on their career, so it really wasn't a matter of we have to wait for some definitive date just so we can finish it. It was just like, ok, this is a project which covers the workings of the band up until this date and the band is still working, so we might as well make every effort to tie it up now before it gets any more unwieldy. So we really put in serious effort in the past two years. In the past year I had band members coming in and editing with me for weeks or even months at a time. So that was the final push and it was still really hard to finish it up.

IS THERE A STRUCTURE IN ANY WAY AS FAR AS THE VIEWER WATCHING IT? AM I GOING TO FEEL A STRUCTURE, AM I GOING TO FEEL A BEGINNING, A MIDDLE, AND AN END? OR AM I JUST GOING TO BE IN THIS WORLD?

Well, I think that it's primarily kind of a collage piece, but we certainly beat our heads together trying to give it some loose, but real structure. We really wanted it to work as some kind of a movie, we didn't want it to just be completely a patchwork but we're dealing with a million different formats and sources and time periods and fragments, so by nature it had to be a kind of collage. But it is a collage that has sort of a beginning, a middle, and an end. But it's not like a movie.

SO, AS A FILMMAKER, YOU LOOK BACK AT ELEVEN YEARS OF YOUR WORK. WHAT DID YOU SEE WHEN YOU WATCHED THIS FILM?

Well, I kind of came up with that band. I grew up in DC, went to high school with Ian, and I left DC in '80. I kind of missed, uh, you know I went to college, but I also moved and so I sort of missed a lot of the...the kind of grand middle period of the DC punk scene, except for seeing Ian come to where I was or occasionally visit me. And there's no doubt that there is a real parallel between what was going on with that scene and what was happening with my becoming a filmmaker. I mean basically it's a similar kind of do-it-yourself tradition and I became a little more aware of that as I made the film. Then I realized that, if I look back at the earliest footage, which was really raw, Super 8 silent stuff, and then as we got to middle period I started to do film, 16-millimeter stuff and then sometimes towards the end it would be back to the really raw Super 8 stuff. I could definitely see that my path as a filmmaker was very much interlaced with their path. Not only as musicians, but as people who kind of had to forge a different way of dealing with things because they couldn't and didn't want to follow a traditional route with the traditional industry. So there's no question in my mind that, when I look back at their work, it's not autobiographical and about me at all, but in terms of my own history **it's very much about how different mediums, music and film, have certain parallels, and how the punk scene affected their growth.**

How do you think the punk scene affected you as a film maker?

It totally affected me because that's partly where I got my inspiration in general. I mean I grew up completely obsessed with music and bands, particularly local bands and homegrown music and watching my friends pick up instruments and learn how to play them when at first they didn't have a clue. When I realized I was going to be a filmmaker, I kind of had to do the same thing. I had a model. It wasn't like, "Oh, you know you can't make a Hollywood film so you can't be a filmmaker." It was like, "Fuck, it's so expensive and so hard and I can't make a regular film. Wait a minute! I know what to do, pick up a camera and start working. Do it a different way, do it separately, and see what the benefits are." And it turned out that the benefits for me were greater than the deficit. Music has always been really important to me. I have a lot of friends who are in bands and I listen to music all the time, so I can't really separate the music thing from the film thing.

Over the course of making the film, like you said, you've known these guys for a long time. Obviously, Ian has gone through a lot just as a musician and is an icon to a lot of people. He coined the term "straight-edge" and there has been a whole subculture based on one lyric. Is that discussed in the film?

You know, the film is about Fugazi. It's not about a unit, it's not about "straight-edge." All of that stuff figures into their history, whether they like it or not. But we really kind of made a decision. We've got enough interesting subjects without having to delve into that, because frankly, Ian's belt was up to the ears and it's sort of unfortunate that people sort of still don't get it. But, in the film, we didn't see any need for it to take that turn. There were times that it popped up when I was shooting and there were times when it was clear that it was hard for him to escape it. But, we had our hands full with Fugazi and we didn't have any need to address their history.

You've spent a lot of time with them and I'm wondering how much that creeps up. How have you seen them change? These are people who've made a conscious decision in regards to their work that they're going to commit to this. Do we see the band change throughout these eleven years as people?

I think that you do, but I think that in a way, you don't as much as you do. And there are two reasons for it. One is because the movie is not a personal life exposé. The movie concentrates on musicians working. I hang out with those guys all the time and I'm quite familiar with their home lives and their private lives but that's not what the movie was about. It wasn't that we were trying to hide anything, but I did want to respect a certain degree of privacy because **we were all fed up with this kind of celebrity culture where every magazine has every person giving the details of what's in their medicine cabinet and who they're hanging out with and all that kind of stuff.** So we definitely did not want to get into that kind of, "Oh, let's see what the bedrooms of the Fugazi guys are like." It's not anybody's business and it doesn't really affect their music-making too much. And the other thing is, in terms of their changing, Brendan has a kid now and him and Jill are married and things are certainly different. We're all in our mid-thirties. The more interesting thing is that in the degree of musicianship and passion there is very little change. The earlier shows in some ways are more amped because the audience is more amped. But there is no slowdown to the band's degree of total full-on commitment, and I find that really extraordinary. I mean, it's like, it's a pretty amazing thing to be able to look at that time line and say, "Well, ok, things might have seemed a little bit more jacked and maybe there were more fast songs back then." Things are different partly because of the way that I was shooting it as well. But when I get to a later period, there's no decrease in intensity. In some ways the intensity may have increased. The musicianship certainly went through some extraordinary changes. But I have to say, I saw that band play a lot of times, and I never saw them suck and I never saw them where they didn't put out, not once. Never. There are plenty of shows that they're disappointed in. But I've never seen a show where I said, "Wow, that's not Fugazi last night."

You can't obviously dictate it, but what would you hope that someone who sits down and watches this film, what would you want them to walk away having experienced?

Well, I feel like they should have two things. One of them is that they should have a real good sense of this band's working process, of the way that they play, whether they're practicing in the studio or playing live, which is sort of their main thing. I think people should have a much broader and deeper sense that these are working musicians rather than the stereotype of, "Oh, aren't they like a hardcore band that is sort of into a political thing?" And I think

that in the course of the movie, you get to experience them as people with a great sense of humor, people who work really hard, people who get really tired, people who you know, get a sense that it's not particularly easy, yet they're very happy being musicians. But I also think, on another level, I wanted people to get a sense that a music film or music documentary doesn't have to be like a music video at all. It can be like a lot of other things. So aside from Fugazi, the way that the material is treated hopefully will give the viewers some sense of possibility, a little bit of contrast from all the other stuff that they're seeing. I'm not saying that it's better. I'm saying, personally, I get really tired of bands portrayed in a kind of hyperkinetic fragmented way where something is sort of being manufactured but you never really get to watch them simply do what they do. That's what I tried to do in a lot of this movie. It's not all that way, but there are long stretches where we did sort of say, "Hey, here's them doing what they do and let's deal with it instead of like, let's break it up into a million angles and give people some sort of angle. You know it's 1992 and the band is into this style and let's make a look for that and film it that way." It's much more straight up and that's something I hope they come away with. There are parts of the movie that are kind of weird and out in left field and that's part of it as well.

Previous pages: The film and video stock from Instrument and Jem at the Dischord offices, holding a picture of himself and Ian. Right: Fugazi at Gilman Street, Berkeley, California, 1991.

CYNTHIA CONNOLLY, BUD FAWCETT & GLEN E. FRIEDMAN

Washington, D.C., February 1999: I'm standing in the infamous Dischord house. Surrounding me are the photographers Cynthia Connolly, Bud Fawcett, and Glen E. Friedman. They all have two things in common: They were each present to document the beginning of scenes that would later become landmark movements symbolizing a generation and an era. And, they are all still shooting. —SM

CYNTHIA CONNOLLY grew up in Los Angeles and moved to D.C. where she witnessed the birth of the D.C. punk scene that included the pioneer band Minor Threat. She spent several years booking bands as a promoter. As well, she was integral in the evolution of the world's archetype of the DIY ethic, Dischord Records. She has self-published the book, *Banned in DC,* that documents the punk scene in D.C. from 1979–1985.

BUD FAWCETT moved to Lake Tahoe from North Carolina when snowboarding was an illegal activity. Bud became a staff photographer for the first ever snowboard magazine, *International Snowboard Magazine.* His images of snowboarding defined the emerging sport. He, along with other founding fathers of snowboarding, has photographed many first descents, mountains never before ridden. His photos have been published in books and magazines worldwide. Currently, he works as the art director for Palmer Snowboards.

GLEN E. FRIEDMAN has been shooting skateboarding since his preteens. Having grown up in the Dogtown area (West Los Angeles), he witnessed and photographed the birth of aggressive skateboarding and its evolution. He was also one of the first to document America's hardcore punk scene on both coasts. He also documented the beginnings of hardcore hip-hop and gangster rap. He currently lives in New York City and has self-published three critically acclaimed books entitled *Fuck You Heroes, Fuck You Too,* and *The Idealist.*

Getting these three artists together for one conversation was no easy feat. Once it happened, what took place that evening in DC was an historical event and a phenomenal experience to witness. Following is the document from the discussion that took place.

YOU'VE ALL WITNESSED MANY FIRSTS. WHAT COMES TO MIND WHEN THINKING BACK TO WITNESSING AND DOCUMENTING THINGS THAT HAPPENED FIRST?

Glen: Well, I've got a lot of them. I could talk about the first time I saw someone get hit in the head by a police officer, the first time I saw Tony Alva do a frontside air, it was the first time anyone had ever done an aerial. The first time seeing Stacy Peralta do a kickturn on vertical, how could anyone do a kickturn on vertical? That was radical to me.

Bud: First time I was watching all these snowboarders load in to Tahoe and try to live "the life," cramming into one house, like twelve people, and just destroying a house. The first halfpipe in the snow, that was cheesy compared to today's halfpipes in the snow. My background as far as California goes and the first time I ever saw a Glen Friedman photo was when I was working for Sims Skateboards back in '77.

Cynthia: Well, some of my first things are the first time going to a punk show in L.A., but it wasn't a punk show, it was at the Starwood in Los Angeles, and it was terrible. But then I figured out that's where I needed to go to go to punk shows. To me, that was like a really big first thing for me.

CAN YOU GUYS TELL ME ABOUT HOW EACH OF YOU GOT INVOLVED IN PHOTOGRAPHY?

Cynthia: I got involved because when I moved from L.A. to DC in 1981, I saw the scene, the sort of music scene here is so different than that of L.A. L.A. was so huge and sort of separated, and D.C. was so focused and really small and for some reason I thought it was something really important—that there was something going on, and I had no idea what it was. I couldn't believe that nobody was taking pictures at the time and I just took somebody's camera and flash and just tried to take photos of stuff because I thought that something should be documented even though I don't think I was doing a very good job. To me it was so full of energy and there was something there that just had to be done. That's how I started.

Bud: I have little experiences of photography from high school and college, but the first time I really strived to do something with photography was documenting, starting to document snowboarding because it was new and people weren't doing it, weren't documenting what was going on and it wasn't really planned, that's just the way it worked out. That's where I really learned a lot of my technical ability, was shooting snowboarding. And so most of my photos in my first year of shooting snowboarding are kinda bogus because they're either overexposed, under-exposed, or out of focus (laughs). And I finally figured that out after a couple of years, but it's unfortunate that some of my best images are pretty cheesy.

Glen: Just like everyone else, I always loved pictures. Everyone loves looking at pictures from the time they're little, but I got a Polaroid camera when I was ten years old, took a couple pictures with it; they came out perfect. And I just thought, "OK, maybe one day I'll try taking pictures again." About three years later I asked for a real camera for my birthday or something like that, got one, and it got stolen.

But before that, I took a class in seventh grade at Paul Revere, which was a really cool skate spot. In the class, I learned about lenses and how to develop and print film and proceeded to get a "D" in photography at Paul Revere Junior High. **The reason I got a "D" was because I only shot pictures of my friends skateboarding and stuff like that.** Everyone around me was getting really famous for skateboarding, or famous in my eyes. The whole crew, the whole Santa Monica Dogtown crew of people, and everyone I would see every weekend down at Kenter or Paul Revere was getting in magazines, and I wasn't really a good enough skater to get in the magazines. I said, "I got to get in the fuckin' magazine somehow!" So I started taking pictures of them. And I also thought I could do a better job than what I saw in the magazines 'cause I was seeing guys do stuff that I didn't see in the magazines.

I found this pool and brought Jay Adams there. I borrowed a camera and I got slide film and I got black and white film, and I shot pictures there with the right stuff one day, and the shit came out really cool. I sent it to *SkateBoarder.* Finally, I

Three photos by Glen E. Friedman, clockwise from right:
Jay Adams, 1976;
Ice T, 1986;
Henry Rollins with Black Flag, 1981.
(Also see the pieces on Tony Alva and Public Enemy
for more of Glen's photos.)

had the film, what they needed, and the first time I sent them photos, they published them, and it was a full page: Jay Adams for a subscription ad. That's kind of how I got started. Once I got that, and I got a credit in a magazine and a full page with my name on it for a subscription for *SkateBoarder* when it was only six dollars a year, and it was bimonthly, I was just stoked beyond belief. I was fourteen years old, and I got the check, and I was like, this is the greatest thing that could ever happen to me.

LET'S TALK ABOUT WHAT IT TAKES TO BE A PHOTOGRAPHER, BOTH PHYSICALLY AND MENTALLY.

Cynthia: For me, mentally, it takes a lot. I have to be into what I'm taking photos of, I can't take photos of stuff someone asks me to do and I'm not into it. I can't do topics or people or anything I'm not into at all 'cause mentally I'm not there, the focus isn't there, and it just doesn't work at all. It's terrible, it's torture, it's the worst thing. Mentally it's really hard. You have to understand what it is that you really like and what you don't like, and understanding it sometimes is hard to know, until you're already in that position and you realize that this just sucks, this is not what I want to do at all. And the focus, I don't think a lot of people understand that you really need to concentrate a lot of times and people think it's just taking a picture; it just happens. But I think there's more to it than that.

Bud: I think, physically, it's a real interesting story. When I first started taking photos, I didn't have many cameras, so it was just a matter of throwing the camera in a bag, going up on the mountain, and going around. Then I went to my first contest at Mt. Baker. I had a 200 millimeter, and Wow! I put it on a camera, put it in my bag, and I was in a mogul field; I slammed, broke the lens off the camera, and it was an unusable camera in my bag. And as the years went by more and more equipment was added, and I got this Lowe Pro pack that weighs forty pounds, and I'm hauling that around on my back, and believe me, I started streamlining a little bit and getting less and less equipment again because you have to be able to move fast. What was the other part of the question? Mentally, I'm the type of person that's slow production-wise, because I always take a lot of time to find the right spot or the right light, or the right person, usually the right spot, or just the right look. So I don't produce a lot of different work.

Glen: I think that to be a really good photographer, it takes a lot of sincerity. I think what everyone's talking about, that's one of the things that probably ties us all together, maybe more than anything else. We shoot things that we live, that we're interested in. That really is what it takes to be a good photographer. After that, you need to learn and you need to have a little bit of technical ability and understand the medium and your equipment that you're working with.

I think if you're just shooting a lot of stuff that you're not really interested in, it's obviously not going to produce anything with any character or content or really interest other people. I'm sure anyone who's shooting pictures for a skateboard magazine or a snowboard magazine, they love what they're doing, they got to, I'm sure. 'Cause I have that much faith in most skateboarders and snowboarders, and people involved in those cultures. They must love what they do, but it takes a little something extra; a little more intensity to really know how to capture the character of the people that are in the images. It's more than just catching the action. **The idea to me is to get the shot and also show some character, show something interesting about what's going on at the same time.** And that's with the action even, I really try and concentrate and see people's face, even when I'm shooting skateboarding. I would shoot people doing backside wheelers and kickturns from inside the pool, not from the coping, just so you could see the expression on the person's face and get more of an idea of the style.

And when I'm shooting music stuff, anyone can shoot a band with a fuckin' microphone stuck right in the person's face. And especially lately, or the last ten years for me, it's more about showing the band with the audience, and how they relate to the audience. And God knows, I don't want my photos to look like they were taken at a soundcheck, I want my shit to have the real action, the real intensity, what's really going on. I think that that's what's important about photos, that they express a certain amount of reality to people.

Cynthia: So many photographers can't do that. I'm not saying that I do, I don't know, but, for example, I work at Dischord Records and I get a lot of live band photographs that people just send in, and so many of them are not...there's something missing. And all of a sudden you get something, it's probably like one in fifty or sixty photos that you get, and you just know this person is into the music, there's something about it, they're really into it, they're focused on it, and they're understanding what's going on, and they're actually wanting to express what their music or the band is through their photograph, which is something that's really hard to do.

Glen: It's definitely not easy. I don't think you can get a camera and just fuckin' be a photographer. But at the same time, you don't need a good camera to be a photographer. It's something that you really have in your heart, and even if you have it in your heart doesn't mean you're gonna do it, you really gotta fuckin' practice and just deal with it. I think shooting skateboarding since I was twelve years old really helped me learn a lot about capturing intensity in that particular moment and showing it in just the right way 'cause skating was so fast, and moves were so minute compared to what they are now. I really learned to get my sense of timing from that. Also being the younger person in the whole crowd, there would be days at the pool where Tony and Jay would be just like trying to do flyaways and hit me in the head with their board! Just 'cause they're all a bunch of fuckin' wiseasses and I'm just a little squirt, you know, you learn how to hang out with the tough guys, you gotta fuckin' really prove yourself. I had a real proving ground and I know a lot of people don't have those opportunities or have those tough guys pushing them, but I think that I was really pushed in a lot of ways by the people who were around me.

And then again, like Cynthia or anyone else, when you're around people that you respect and they respect you, it also helps you get good photos because you have this appreciation for each other and it helps you express yourself that much more clearly.

If someone starts talking to me about photos, or about photography, or about art, or about music, and they haven't seen my books, or they never heard of Black Flag or Tony Alva, or whoever, it's like I can't talk to this person. It's frustrating, it's really fuckin' difficult. I can try and do it and I can try and be polite, but generally speaking, I'm not that social. I've got a real specific interest, and I'm gonna go for that, and I'm gonna try to share it with other people, and you really gotta believe it in your heart, you gotta really feel it, and then you really gotta practice it. I was fuckin' devoted to the people that I shot. I wanted to help them share their ideas. It wasn't about me. Early on, I did want to get in a magazine, but at the same time, I wanted to fuckin' share with the world. I thought I was the fuckin' man to fuckin' do this. I had to bring it to the

Cynthia: I don't even care if I get published. For me, it's just for me, and somehow for me to teach myself or to understand how to express whatever it is I'm taking a picture of—to think that I'm doing it rightfully to show who the person is, or what the thing is, or what it is I'm seeing. So I can take a photo and print it and know that it's how I remembered it. I don't actually concern myself about the publishing part of it.

Glen: Nowadays, it's definitely much more for myself, but everything I shoot I do for myself, I shoot it because I want to do it. But, early on when those movements and cultures I was so involved in were just spurting up, I took the photos for myself, but it was equally important at the time that I was doing it for other people to see. I want to share these images with other people. I created them in a way that I would appreciate, that I was always very selfish in a way thinking that I appreciate it, other people will appreciate it. If I do it this way, the way I think is right, it is right. And this is what I need people to know. It was definitely a little bit self-centered or egotistical to think, "I know what the fuckin' shit is, and I'm gonna force it down everyone's throat, 'cause this is what's right." It is because of the subjects that I did it, because the subjects were so important.

people. It's how I really felt, like a missionary, man. I wanted fuckin' people in *Sports Illustrated* to see what Tony Alva did; I wanted people in *Rolling Stone* to see what fuckin' Black Flag and Minor Threat were doing. I wanted people in the rock magazines, in the mainstream press to see what fuckin' Run-DMC and Public Enemy were doing. I started shooting those people before they had any white press. I got them their first white press. Again, from the heart, I wanted to show other people that something special is going on here, and it's something I fuckin' really love. I loved it so much, I had to do it justice. I had to do my subjects justice, and that motivated the hell out of me.

Bud: Oh yeah, totally. When I started shooting snowboarding, it was more about the athlete than it was me at any one time. It was about what they were doing. I was learning photography, I was secondary. I wanted to get these guys in front of the magazines. I had always admired other photographers' work, and I was trying to copy their abilities. Finally I started getting published; just stuff that I had in the can already. But I think it's very important that the person in the photograph be rewarded by being published.

WHEN YOU'RE SHOOTING PHOTOS AND GETTING YOUR PHOTOS PUBLISHED, WHAT PERCENTAGE OF THE MOTIVATION IS FOR YOU PERSONALLY, AND WHAT PERCENTAGE IS FOR AN AUDIENCE?

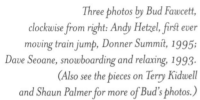

Three photos by Bud Fawcett,
clockwise from right: Andy Hetzel, first ever
moving train jump, Donner Summit, 1995;
Dave Seoane, snowboarding and relaxing, 1993.
(Also see the pieces on Terry Kidwell
and Shaun Palmer for more of Bud's photos.)

Bud: Everything from the beginning was totally for me because there wasn't a market for snowboard photos. There wasn't anybody really publishing too much snowboarding.

Glen: Let me interrupt for one second. Just so you know, when I shot punk rock photos, there was no market for them originally. And even hip-hop photos, these were things I believed in, I had to force it on people, believe it or not. Now people hear about Minor Threat and Black Flag. Years before anyone ever talked about them in the press, I was sending pictures of these bands. And even skateboarding, I sent skateboard pictures to *Sports Illustrated*, thinking I gotta expose it to other people. So really, I didn't want to interrupt you, but I just want people to know that there wasn't the opportunities that there are now for stuff to be published. It wasn't easy. When I started getting published in 1976, there weren't so many magazines as there are now.

Bud: Well, in the beginning it was totally for me because like I say, I was learning and it was interesting. It was interesting just being out with people snowboarding and learning how to take photographs, and then later it was for an audience. Mainly because those guys, or girls, should be in the magazines.

Cynthia: Did you snowboard?

Bud: Yeah, I snowboarded. All the time.

Cynthia: So you were snowboarding with these people anyway.

Bud: Yes, yes. Actually, snowboarding for me, as a photographer carrying a bunch of equipment on the mountain, it was less about snowboarding than just keeping up with most of the people I shot.

Glen: You were a snowboarder beforehand anyway. That's what you already loved.

Cynthia: That makes a big difference.

Bud: Yeah, it coincided with my photography, though. Almost the first day I went out to snowboard, I had a camera with me.

Cynthia: So you really just wanted to document what was going on?

Bud: That's why I took the camera.

TELL ME ABOUT THE DARK SIDE OF SHOOTING PHOTOS?

Cynthia: Sometimes I take photos of people and I say it's for something, and all of a sudden somebody else wants to use it for something and then I have this sort of like, well, I told this person it's for X, Y, and Z, and then it's gonna be used for something else. I have this really intense sort of guilt or something about having things used where they're not supposed to be used, and it's almost too over the top or something.

Glen: I think there are disappointments in photography. Especially when people don't use the shots you want them to, and they use shots that you don't like instead that you know aren't good. For example, I threatened to scratch the fuckin' front cover photo for Public Enemy's second album cover. The shot they used, I was really bummed. I had scissors right on the negative. They told me that if I did that, they would never use me again. So I didn't cut it and I let them use it. It's funny when people appreciate shit that you don't. Or when they miss the point of your photo. It's kind of a bummer, but it's nice if people say, "Oh, it's beautiful and this and that and that and this," but you know what, they almost never see exactly what you see, so that's the dark side right there.

Bud: I think maybe missing a shot that you really wanted to get. Or maybe having so much material in your files that you know that you'll never get caught up and go back to some of the images that you really wanted to print. I mean, those for me personally are probably the hardest two things.

Cynthia: How about when you have something, and you develop it, and for some bizarre reason the negative is fucked up because of whatever processing happened. I swear, some of my most favorite photos are just destroyed.

Bud: Like Glen said, it's really nice having the face in shots because you get the emotion, and sometimes you'll take a photo and you know it's perfect, and then you find out that the face is hidden. You've just missed an important element of the photograph. That can be a dark side.

TELL ME ABOUT YOUR FEELINGS THE FIRST TIME YOU WERE PUBLISHED?

Bud: First time I was published, my photo credit wasn't put on the photo, and I don't know if that was important or not. I guess it was as far as having a little pride in the photo. The second time I was published, the second photo ended up being published in three different places at the same time, which was a nightmare because one was an ad, and one was an editorial usage, and boy, you learn quickly how you're supposed to do business in photography when a mistake happens early in your career. I think it was a shot of Shaun Palmer. One was in a Sims ad, and one was in a magazine, a full page in *Thrasher*, and then another was somewhere else. I can't ever remember.

Cynthia: I actually really don't remember that clearly, but I know that it was in *Flipside*. I used to do a scene report, and I would just send them the photos and they would print them. I think that the only time after *Flipside* that I remember is the *Banned in DC* book that I did. That was like two years of my life pretty much devoted to making that book and when that thing came out I was terrified to see what it looked like and what thing had been created, and how the whole thing was. I had no idea. It was a really big deal for me.

DISCUSS THE SACRIFICES THAT YOU GUYS MADE TO ENABLE YOURSELF TO PHOTOGRAPH THE SCENES THAT YOU WERE EACH INVOLVED IN.

Bud: As far as snowboarding goes, I got to move to a really great place, so it wasn't really a sacrifice.

Glen: Well, I'll tell you, I sacrificed a lot. I feel like going to shows carrying a camera is a sacrifice.

Bud: Yeah, that's true. On some of those snowboarding days, it's a big sacrifice, those powder days, for sure.

Glen: That's right, there you go. There's a sacrifice. I don't like carrying a camera. I fuckin' don't like it. I don't like being a nerd with a camera (laughter). I sacrifice being cool, just being a fuckin' loser carrying a camera. And I sacrificed being able to slam dance a lot of the times 'cause I had a camera. And that's the truth. I sacrificed not skating because I had to worry about my camera equipment. I sacrificed not having a lot of fun at a lot of shows 'cause I had to carry my camera around.

Bud: Yeah, you're damned if you do and you're damned if you don't. If you make a choice not to take a camera out, you're sorry that you didn't, and if you make a choice to take the camera out, then you're sometimes at a disadvantage of having a good time or being worried all night, or whatever. But that's just part of the game that you have to play to capture the moment.

ANYTHING MORE YOU WANTED TO ADD OR DISCUSS?

Bud: I think that my interest in snowboarding created my interest in photography. For that reason, I'm very grateful to all snowboarders I've photographed in the past. Without the best snowboarders in the world appearing in front of your lens, your photos will be second rate. Those of you that are the best know who you are.

Two photos by Cynthia Connolly,
opposite and below: Rites of Spring, 1984;
Elliott Smith, 1997.
(Also see the pieces on Fugazi, Jem Cohen, Steve Albini,
and Sleater-Kinney for more of Cynthia's photos.)

Cynthia: Glen Friedman inspired me indirectly to do photography but also just seeing his photos when I visited him once, I think in 1985, and saw some of his skate photos on the wall. It just really inspired me to understand the expression of what he was doing. It got me to thinking about doing something similar to that. You know, really understanding how he really captured it and what I could do that was sort of like that in some way.

Glen: That's cool. You weren't even a skater. See, then something's accomplished. You get someone to understand what you're doing who doesn't even have any idea what the fuck is going on relatively. At the same time, people who are deep into it could also appreciate it. If you could do both those things, that's the shit. I'm stoked, if I could do that every time. If the most hardcore skater, punk rocker, hip-hop artist could look at my photo and say, "That's the shit," and then someone who has nothing to do with anything, some old fart looks at my shit and says, "That's the shit," that's dope! You just gotta like what you're doing yourself. That's the most important thing, otherwise it's not even worth doing, right?

Cynthia: It's true, that's true. That should be your last statement.

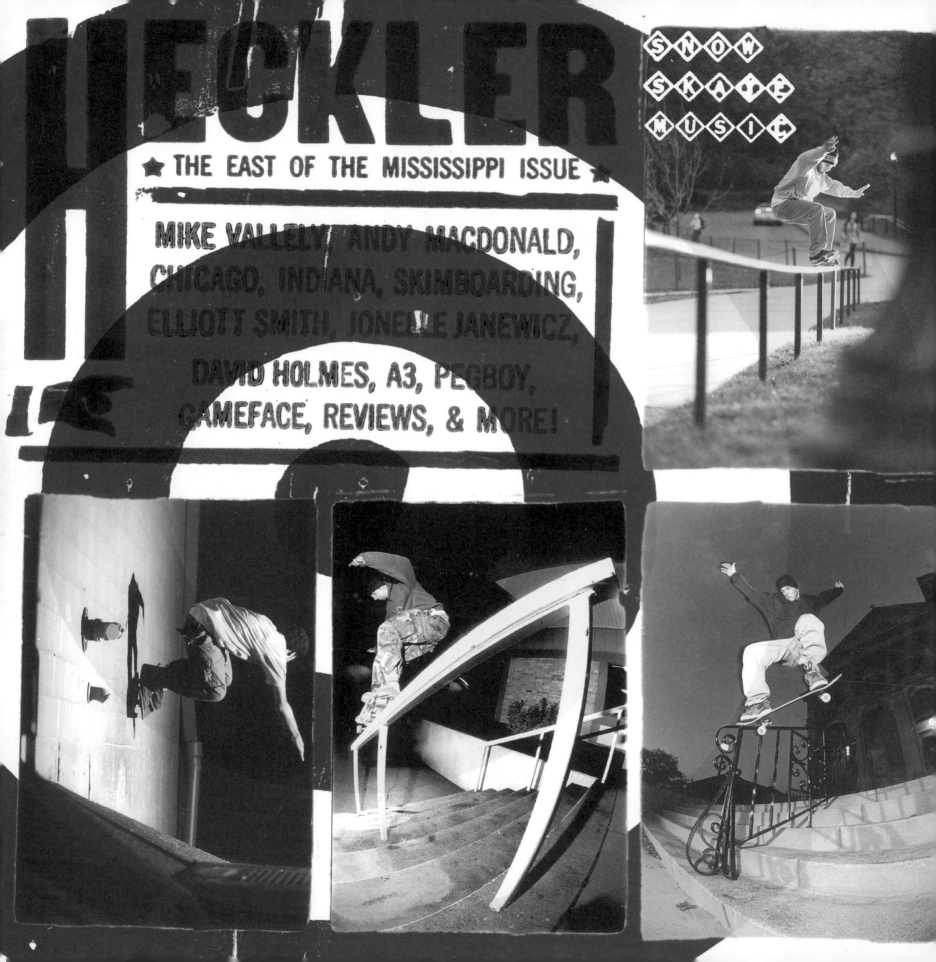

HECKLER

★ THE EAST OF THE MISSISSIPPI ISSUE ★

MIKE VALLELY, ANDY MACDONALD, CHICAGO, INDIANA, SKIMBOARDING, ELLIOTT SMITH, JONELLE JANEWICZ, DAVID HOLMES, A3, PEGBOY, GAMEFACE, REVIEWS, & MORE!

SNOW SKATE MUSIC

CHAPTER 6. ART OR SPORT? ✳✳✳

6

One of the aspects of **Heckler** that I enjoy the most is the art direction and the graphic design. Aside from the enjoyment of doing design, I really like collaborating with other artists and designers. Scattered throughout this chapter are a few of the more successful collaborations.

Hatch Show Print is one of the oldest letterpress printers in the United States. I met Jim Sherraden who runs the shop at an AIGA design conference in New Orleans. I was really impressed with the workmanship and handmade quality of their work and asked them to do a cover for us, which is shown at left. Jeremy Maynard designed this cover and the skaters are (clockwise from top) BJ Sellhorn, Jason Poole, Chad Hitzeman, and Chauncy Collins. —JB

Sport or Artistic Expression?

by Sonny Mayugba

On one hand, skateboarding is a physical sport supported by an industry. Most companies have teams, just like other more popular sports. The purpose of these teams is to promote the sport and sell product. Skateboarding team members represent their sponsors by using specific products and wearing branded clothes, which basically becomes their uniform. Some teams have matching uniforms, much like other more popular sports.

On the other hand, skateboarding is a 100% individual, creative outlet for expression that cannot be classified or defined. The way one skater uses his board is unrepeatable and the feeling we get from skating is ineffable. The way Danny Way skates vert, the skills Daewon shows on street, and the way Chris Senn tears it all up is unmistakably their own, and unlike other more popular sports, a skater can excel, even if his team doesn't. Unlike basketball, football, etc., skaters can wear and be any style they want. But most importantly, skateboarding is a way to express yourself.

Skateboarding has always been about individuality, and in my opinion, always will. The way one person skates a line can be imitated, but never repeated. When you think about the millions of factors, facial expressions, distribution of weight, foot placement, compression, rotation, and on and on, it's easy to realize that skateboarding is not like a computer file that can be exactly copied a thousand times over. Skateboarding is your own. So is art. I believe it's this nature that spawned great skateboarding artists like Mark Gonzales, Neil Blender, Tommy Guerrero, Natas Kaupas, Ed Templeton, and so on.

In this chapter, we bring you some of these creative individuals. Ed Templeton is known for going on skate tours to six weeks: that's two weeks to skate and four weeks to visit art galleries. His work is seen in galleries as well as in magazine ads for his company, Toy Machine. Chris Senn started out simply drawing and has evolved into an incredible painter. He keeps a regular column in *Heckler* called SENNterpretations where he features a skater/artist, as well as one of his pieces. Mike Vallely does poetry and drawings and keeps an approachable profile in the skateboarding world. Mark Gonzales does performance art and his work can be seen in galleries throughout America and Europe. In the last ten years, we have been lucky enough to see these and more skaters unleashing the intrinsic nature that drove them to skate in the first place, and they are expressing themselves through art.

I had always been a fan of the Reverend Howard Finster's (he did the cover pictured at right) artwork since seeing the album covers he did for R.E.M. and the Talking Heads. After reading his autobiography (Stranger From Another World, Abbeville Press) I decided I'd try and contact him about doing a cover for us. I thought that some of skateboarding's artists that I really liked such as Mark Gonzales and Ed Templeton, had a style similar to Finster's, and that it would be fitting to put him on the cover.

I found his number and talked with his daughter Beverly, who acted as his agent. I explained who I was and asked if Howard would be interested in doing a magazine cover, and if so how much would he charge. I was pretty sure we wouldn't be able to afford whatever he wanted, but I figured it couldn't hurt to ask. Beverly asked me how big the magazine was, and I told her our circulation was 60,000.

"No, no, I meant what size is it?" she replied.

"Oh, OK, it's ten by twelve inches," I said.

After a short pause she told me that would cost $175.

It turns out that after being represented by some pretty expensive New York galleries, Howard decided to take control of his own business and drop his prices in order to reach as many people as possible. I should explain that Howard paints in order to preach the gospel and every piece has some kind of verse on the back or as part of the painting. The piece he did for our cover is his 42,937th painting.

Anyway, I sent off a check and a few mags, along with a rough draft of what I wanted. "Just draw a skateboarder," I put in the note.

"I don't think Howard's ever done a skateboarder before," said Beverly.

A few weeks later, I got a voice-mail message from Beverly. There was a problem with the painting and I needed to call her before Howard could work on it. Uh oh, I thought, this was where the problems were gonna start. Either Howard had actually read the magazines I sent and was offended by them, or else he saw the spread ads up front and was gonna ask for more money to be on the cover of a national magazine. If it was the first, I figured that was cool. I had sent him the mags because I didn't want him to work on something he didn't feel OK about.

When I got Beverly on the phone, she told me that the painting was a little more involved than she had thought and that they would have to charge me more money. OK, here it comes, I thought, and asked her how much more.

"Well, we're gonna have to charge you an extra $35, and I wanted to make sure that was OK before Howard started on the painting."

"Oh, OK. So it'll be $210 total then, right? Do you need me to FedEx a check for the balance?" I asked.

"Oh no, that's alright, you just pop it in the mail. I just wanted to make sure that was OK."

A year or so later, I stopped by Finster's Paradise Gardens in Georgia, while traveling, and met Howard. Although he was in his late 80s, he still seemed pretty sharp. I introduced myself, and he remembered drawing the skateboarder for the cover.

"Ain't too much call for skateboarder paintings," he said.

MARK GONZALES
BY BRYCE KANIGHTS

Opposite: San Francisco, California hills, 1998.
Right and page 175: Setting up for European show.
Below: Lipslide, San Francisco schoolyard, 1998.
Following Page: Five-O crail grab at Max Schaff's ramp
with one of Mark's paintings in the background.

If you've been involved with skateboarding and the related culture for any length of time, then you've undoubtedly heard of Mark Gonzales. For the past fifteen years, he has had a huge influence on countless skateboarders all over the world with his phenomenal talents both on and off his board. But, what he possesses goes so much deeper than that. Mark is like a free-spirited performance artist and he flows to the rhythm of his own actions. His talents express themselves through his drawings and paintings, writings, and skateboarding and reflect on an individual who is independent of modern society's trappings. Mark is blissfully unaware of daily stock tradings, frequent-flyer miles, the dot-com world, and "keeping up with the Joneses." To put it bluntly, Gonz is an original and thankfully, nobody can come close to duplicating his supernatural style.

I had a book published in dual languages [English and German] so I went over for a few book readings and this museum wanted me to do a skateboard demo. So I thought it would be good and different to choreograph a routine to music to show skateboarding like moving art with grace and elegance.

WHAT DO YOU DEFINE AS ART?

Beauty is art and much of art is ugly. But the tables turn and then turn again.

IS SKATEBOARDING AN ART FORM TO YOU?

Skateboarding is an art form because its possibilities are endless.

WHO ARE SOME OF YOUR FAVORITE ARTISTS AND WHY?

Raymond Pettibon. I can't give a clear definition why. I just feel his work touches all people in a personal way because he leaves it open to interpretations. A lot of the text is biblical, at least that's how I see it. Also, Sabato, Sam Rodia, the man who built the Watts towers in L.A. I think his towers are awesome. Most of the old seashells are gone, but I heard stories that he'd be traveling on a ship from Europe with stones in his suitcase to use for his towers. That's dedication. They didn't know why he was traveling with a suitcase full of rocks. They were for his towers.

HOW DOES YOUR ARTWORK RELATE TO YOUR SKATING AND VICE VERSA?

Mainly I'd say no relation. Mark Gonzales the skateboarder has nothing to do with Mark Gonzales the artist.

WHAT INSPIRES YOU TO DRAW OR SKATE?

My mood to feel free is what inspires me to skate and if I want to express something visually, this is an inspiration to draw.

MANY SKATERS POINT OUT THAT YOU ARE A BIG INFLUENCE UPON THEIR ABILITIES. ARE THERE ANY SKATERS IN PARTICULAR THAT HAVE MADE AN IMPACT ON YOU PAST OR PRESENT?

I like Neil Blender a lot. Lee Ralph taught me how to become more relaxed and not so uptight. I liked Stacy Peralta and I used to want his G&S Wraptail 2 model. I liked Mickey and Steve Alba, Tony Alva, Ray "Bones" Rodriguez, Doug Saladino, Christian Hosoi, and Tony Hawk. Really, I like all skateboarding. Eric Koston, Daewon Song, and a lot of the new guys are so incredible. Kareem Campbell, Cairo Foster, Danny Gonzalez, and Rick McCrank.

IF THERE WAS TO BE A SKATEBOARDER'S HALL OF FAME, WHICH FIVE RIDERS WOULD YOU VOTE TO HAVE INDUCTED?

Torger Johnson, Larry Bertleman, and Jay Adams for sure. I can't name them all. They're all good.

HOW DID YOU GROW UP AND BECOME INVOLVED WITH ROLLING ON A PIECE OF WOOD WITH FOUR URETHANE WHEELS? HOW DID IT START FOR YOU?

I was always observing the older crowd. My Uncle Tom was a surfer, stoner, skateboarder. I used to like the craftsmanship my grandpa put into his boards that he'd make for my uncle. Mostly, I'd say I was in my own world watching people around me. My best friend, David Chin, was into skateboarding and I hung out with him and we used to draw Z-pig skates and Powerflex riders. We were into Foghat and Foreigner. We were too young to be liking that stuff, but we were pretty hip.

DO YOU FEEL THAT EDUCATION BY MEANS OF FORMAL SCHOOLING IS IMPORTANT AS A CONDUIT FOR SUCCESS?

I think success can be achieved by means of an informal education. It's not what you're taught, it's how you apply it to everyday life. To me, success means being happy with who you are and where you're at. Sometimes the most simple achievement can be the most gratifying, like holding a door open for someone and being appreciated. Small things are important. The Unabomber taught at UC-Berkeley and graduated from Harvard; whether he was successful depends on your definition of success.

ARE YOU MUCH OF A FAMILY MAN?

Family is important. I think it was the breakdown of my family that pissed me off and made me struggle so hard. I think it's every man's dream to make a nice home and have plenty of kids to run wild. America's beautiful because we have the right to bring our kids up however we choose, or at least we used to. Now they have child protection laws, so you have to be careful in disciplining your children. You can just take away their toys when they misbehave.

ARE YOU A WASTEFUL OR RESOURCEFUL PERSON?

I try to be resourceful but it's hard. So many times I see stuff getting thrown out. I'm like, "Wait, hold it. Don't do that. I can usually make something out of that." But, usually I don't have much time so stuff that I'd like to salvage gets tossed. I know a lot of scavengers go through the garbage, though, so when I throw out shoes, I tie the strings together so someone can find them and sell them or use them. I'm resourceful when I'm wasteful.

HOW DID THE GALLERY INSTALLATION OF YOUR ARTWORK IN GERMANY GO?

WHAT WAS THE BIGGEST SLAM OR INJURY IN YOUR SKATING CAREER?

When I was fifteen, I was skating in the street through this bad area of town. It was too scary to be riding on the sidewalks. Anyway, this black figure with a baseball bat emerged out from between two parked cars and was swinging for me, I pushed like crazy to get away and got hit by a police car. The front bumper, you know how beefed up they are, well that jacked my right thigh and I ended up beneath the cop car. I was dragged for twelve blocks and it wore down my Schmitt Stix rails. I couldn't skate for like two months (joking). When I was in England and Pat Duffy and I collided in midair off two jump ramps over a car, that hurt and I hit my head. Things got fuzzy. That was probably my worst fall.

DO YOU WATCH MUCH TELEVISION?

I used to. Not so much anymore. I like the local news. I miss the Popeye channel.

DO YOU SNOWBOARD?

Yeah, I like zooming through the trees and clipping branches.

WHAT TYPES OF MUSIC HAVE YOU BEEN LISTENING TO AND WHO ARE SOME OF YOUR FAVORITE ARTISTS?

I like Thelonius Monk's "Underground." Prince, Morris Day and the Time. I like Morrissey and Jim Morrison. I like all kinds of music. I used to listen to a punk group called Double 0. I like this Oi! compilation with The Jam, The Clash, and The Kinks. I just saw a good documentary on Robert Johnson *Hear the Wind Howl*. Music is universal; it reveals feelings and true emotions. It's what makes movies good. A soundtrack is important. Try turning the volume off and watching your favorite movie, you'll start humming the parts that you like.

WHAT ARE YOUR FAVORITE THREE THINGS INVOLVED WITH SKATEBOARDING?

Timing, turning, and pushing.

WHAT ARE YOUR LEAST FAVORITE THREE THINGS INVOLVED WITH SKATEBOARDING?

Being hurt, bunk equipment, and being told when to do it.

WHAT IS YOUR VIEW AND OPINION ON THE MAINSTREAM MEDIA COVERAGE OF SKATEBOARDING SUCH AS ITS INCLUSION WITH ESPN'S X-GAMES?

I don't have much of an opinion. It's good though because now some kids that might not have had the chance to see skateboarding can see it and maybe they'll enjoy it and their parents will allow them to do it.

FAVORITE TRICKS PAST AND PRESENT?

A nosewheelie for the past and a nosewheelie kickflip out for the present.

WHAT'S THE BEST FEELING TO YOU WHEN YOU'RE SKATEBOARDING?

Getting close to falling and then not falling.

OF ALL THE PLACES YOU'VE TRAVELED TO THROUGHOUT THE WORLD, WHICH LOCATION WOULD YOU LIKE TO RETURN TO AND WHY?

Brazil because of the people. There are so many. Czechoslovakia when it was still Communist because I like government-owned everything. I don't like independent companies. I like when the government protects its people from ad campaigns and buying frenzies.

WHAT'S YOUR FAVORITE ANIMAL?

I like night animals. Birds, sharks, ostriches. Zebras are cool. The African badger. Bats are flying carnivores.

HOW DID YOU GET HOOKED UP TO PLAY A ROLE IN HARMONY KORINE'S FILM *GUMMO*?

I was skating inside Aaron Rose's art gallery on this chair. I was ollieing up to nose stall and goofing off and Harmony was there. He kept telling me about this guy, Andy Kaufman, who would fight chairs and things. So I ended up fighting the chair and he thought it was funny and wanted me to do it in his movie. Isn't life silly?

WERE YOU PLEASED WITH THE FILM?

I thought the movie was good. I would have liked it if the cats had come back from the dead and wreaked havoc on all the children.

DO YOU ENJOY ACTING?

It depends on who I'm acting with.

WHAT DO YOU ENVISION YOURSELF DOING TWENTY YEARS FROM NOW?

Harvesting crops on the moon.

HOW LONG DO FEEL YOU WILL CONTINUE TO SKATEBOARD?

I'll stop when all the cars are gone.

ANY LAST WORDS OR IDEALS THAT YOU ADHERE YOUR LIFE TOWARDS?

Embrace all things. Have compassion. See things from as many different perspectives as possible, and keep your feet firmly planted when dropping bombs.

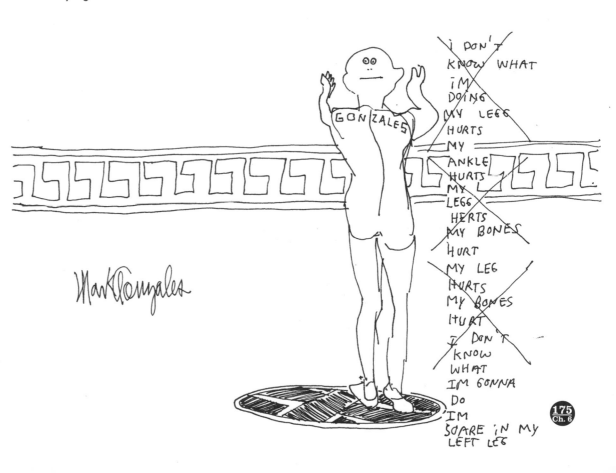

175
Ch. 6

PARKING BLOCKS AS OBJECTS OF ART AND FUNCTION

BY JOHN REED

"Be conspicuous, stand around and drink coffee...like someone is paying you to work," I was told. While rollin' with Robert Stone on Sunset Blvd. in his not-inconspicuous slammed '56 Ford, he explains that there's no risk involved in the crime we are about to commit: "It is illegal...something between vandalism, trespassing, and littering...but it's so fucked up an activity that it doesn't even register with most people." What he's talking about is permanently installing his art piece "Altered Parking Block" in place of a normal parking block in the lot of the trashy-futuristic Cinerama movie theater in Hollywood. This functional sculpture is a redesigned concrete parking block that looks normal enough to be invisible to property owners and cops. But its smooth launch transition, steel pipe edge, and careful placement next to a wall with a good slider lip makes it instantly recognizable to skaters.

Robert describes the project half like a skater and half like an artist: "If you listen to the way Steve Alba talks about searching for pools, he's analyzing architecture, landscape, and culture for clues to find the best backyard pools to skate. It's this fully developed system. **Skaters scan the environment of handrails, walls, platforms...everything, looking at texture, scale, form, and compositional relationships between parts.** I am trying to fit this thing into that formal language to attract skaters and at the same time make it look normal enough to not attract other attention."

The normal parking block is removed in a few seconds with a crowbar, and then I realize why I am here...the new concrete block weighs over two hundred pounds. We lift it into place over the bolts that held to normal block, Robert mixes some anchoring cement in a paper coffee cup and pours it over the bolts and we're done.

A few weeks later I drive by and the block is almost black with a pattern of wheel marks. It looks good.

Robert talks about his work as open-ended, with a life of its own: "The art project is more than this object. It includes the performance of skaters using the object and this do-it-yourself design strategy for customizing the urban environment that throws all public and private space up for grabs." Imagine the world that could slowly evolve if more skaters had this attitude and started replacing everything with a skateable version of itself.

Ron Cameron tests out the altered blocks.

CONFESSIONS OF A TEENAGE SKATEBOARD ARTIST

BY DONALD BELL

Streetskating is one of the last indigenous performance arts of urban America. Like breakdancers and graffiti artists, streetskaters use the surrounding concrete-covered modern landscape as a canvas for personal artistic expression. The art of streetskating lies in its ability to incorporate objects of architectural utility (curbs, benches, driveways, handrails) into a high-speed dance that critiques the significance of the object and shows to those with open minds the beauty that can be found in the everyday. This crucial artistic element is what distinguishes streetskating from the world of sports and separates it from seemingly comparable activities like snowboarding, surfing, and vert skating. Streetskating's natural environment is the unnatural, the manmade concrete structures of our cities and suburbs, built with finite purpose and human utility in mind. I spent my youth destroying people's confidence in the absolute meaning of these objects.

Skateboards change things. Skateboarding allowed me to revision the wasteland of my suburban hometown into a playground of pavement. Parking lots turned into asphalt planes of possibility. Concrete benches spoke to me in a private language only I could understand. Curbs, sidewalks, handrails, and staircases lay scattered and static across my city, yet only I and a handful of like-minded friends took the time to lend these objects a fresh identity as our momentary playthings.

We are all harbingers of concrete chaos. It's all we have left. The baggy pants and punk rock that once defined us as a threatening teenage subculture can now be found in the discount bin at your nearest Wal-Mart. Yet after all these years the skateboard itself, just a board on wheels, still retains its power to disturb. I've seen people use a park bench to change their kid's diaper, tie up their dog, shoot heroin, breast-feed, fuck, puke, and pass out. But despite all of the odd ways a public bench can be used without comment, skating on it will always cause someone's fist to clench. Take pride in the unease you create in people: it is your gift. We are suburban subversion on four wheels.

We need to once again revel in the knowledge that the objects we are grinding, sliding, and launching over are being spitefully misused for our own personal pleasure. Like a child who is given coal for Christmas and uses it to write Santa a death threat, it is the power of the artist, the rush of empowerment in a world that makes every effort to diminish you. It is the power of saying:

**This is not a curb.
This is not a bench.
This is not a dead-end suburb or a
thriving metropolis.**

This is my playground.

Artist Mike Rafter in Modesto, California, 1997.

CHRIS SENN

When I think of Chris Senn, I get filled with inspiration. To understand why, you must understand Chris. He is an average guy of epic proportions. Born and raised in the small Northern California town of Nevada City, Chris is a public-spirited, altruistic, blue-collar skateboarder. His interests are in painting, art, snowboarding, and sucking the nectar out of life.

Family plays a huge role in his life and his son, Anakin, is blessed with Chris's everlasting dedication. **Fashion never meant anything to Chris, who is a guy that shows up to a skate session not decked in the latest high-tech gear, but rather wearing an overly worn-out white T-shirt embossed with the logo of a favorite Mexican restaurant in faded black ink.** In skateboarding, these characteristics usually garner underground respect, but curses with obscurity and ill fame. Chris Senn defies all stereotypes because he is not only a humane, compassionate, and creative skateboarder, but he is a champion with incredible technique and a super smooth flow.

After winning multiple skateboarding titles worldwide, his international fame was sealed forever when he won Best Street Skater at the summer X-Games in 1999. Chris has been a regular contributor to Heckler, where he founded a column called SENN-terpretations. There, he features skateboarders who are also artists. He represents a part of me, a part of you, and a part of all skateboarders everywhere. He represents the potential we all have within us, the potential to fulfill all the talent within, to be an average guy, to live life our own way, and still be a champion. —SM

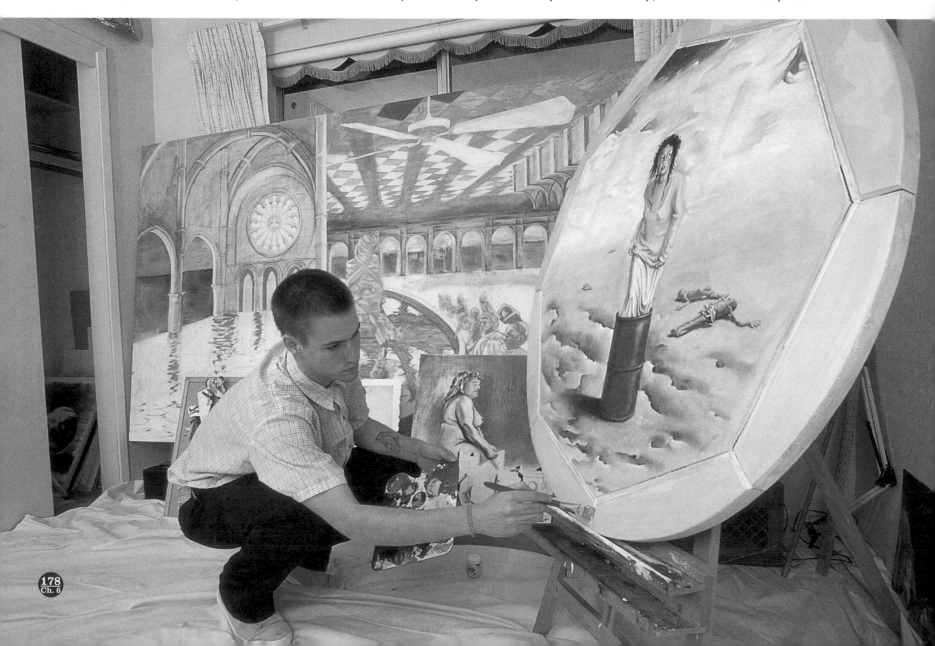

Opposite: Chris in his studio.
Left: Berkeley, California, 1999.
Below: Chris going over the steps for the first time in 1999 at the 99 Bowl, Sacramento, California.
Bottom: In 1993, Chris and his good friend Emile Janicot moved into a new rental in Grass Valley, California. "There's a pool, but it won't hold water and it's empty," the landlord informed them.
"Oh that's O.K., we're not that big on swimming," they told their new landlord. They were later evicted for skating in their own backyard.

It seems to me that it's fair to understand an activity in terms of its essentiality. In this way, I have some aesthetical interpretations of the board sports in which I examine styles as essentially deeds, as significant actions, as gestures vis-a-vis a world. I'm thinking of just what it is that an athlete does when she/he moves across, over, through a terrain. Just what is the movement? Just what is the terrain? Perceivable differences and similarities give rise to style. At the heart of a style is a confrontation between the athlete and a portion of the world—wave, pave, powder, etc. The meaning of the style is to be found in the way the athlete confronts the terrain—the attitude, the love, the hate, etc.

On Style & Meaning
by Roman de Salvo

Surfing, skating, and snowboarding are various styles of essentially the same activity— a traversal of multiplanar terrain aboard a single plank-like vehicle. Of course the differences are significant enough to warrant that these be classified as different sports. But in seeing them as basically the same activity, for starters, we see that at bottom the deed is one of confrontation or contact with terrain aboard an enabling stick. However, not all styles follow this paradigm, but more about that later.

Surfing is about confrontation with a wave. It's about contact with the water. You can dip your head in it as the curl gently folds over on you or you can slash back at the lip with utter violence. Each is a different attitude, a different approach to nature. I found that I didn't care for the amount of equipment and preparation that so many surfers involve themselves with, so I tried it with just a stick and myself. I ended up burning off my nipples by constantly rubbing them on the sandy wax of my stick by endlessly paddling out. I found the ocean to be a reluctant hostess. Surfing is for those who can take her on. The deeper meaning is in how.

I've skated everything. Some terrain is made for skating; some terrain is made for something else—it's all rippable. The fact that the original terrain was not made for skating and thus tended to be forbidden gave rise to customized skate terrain in the image of the original. Skateparks learned from ditches and pools, ramps learned from pipes and skateparks; now skateparks learn from ramps and the common street fixtures of the urban environment. Skateboarding has evolved into its own terrain. But the original terrain still exists and is still an option. Choice of terrain is a meaningful decision. One is a sort of inbred activity; the other engages with the world. In any case, one's deeds are akin to those of surfing: skateboarding, too, is about contact. **One makes contact with terrain in the most precarious of ways and extends it via the dynamics of traversal.** One contacts an edge with hand, foot, or tool. One contacts on various altitudes. Contortion maximizes contact with as many cubic inches of air as possible. The hand can make contact with all parts of the tool as well as the terrain.

Roman de Salvo in 1986.

Jay Smith, when he laid down on a surface such as Upland's three feet of vert in a movement called the "layback," was trying to contact burly regions with as much of his body as possible. In the built environment, nothing is exempt from contact by the athlete with skate underfoot. Unlikely original choices such as handrails and transitionless vert attest to this. The constant question for the skater is "What can I contact next, and how?" It is an attitude. To carry it out is a meaningful deed. In a world that resists contact, or at least mediates it through an endless variety of insulating representations, the skater usurps contact at the concrete of its foundations or relishes contact with the designed regions of his own utopian terrain.

I've always thought of snowboarding as skateboarding to be done when there's snow on the ground. Living in Reno, it was often a viable alternative, although certainly not as simple as stepping outside with a skate. But when traversing the terrain, the attitude remains the same: "What can I contact and how?" We see the importance of contact in snowboarding exemplified by the compulsion to grab what is already attached to the feet by bindings. We see the same interest in bonking some object or dragging a hand. We also see in snowboarding the options of natural or cultural terrain: powdery cliffs or hard-packed halfpipes. Again, the choices are meaningful.

Does one explore the gnarly, chancy regions of the wilderness or does one say "hello" to the custom-installed steel pipe? These are the sorts of profound choices one makes in the contact paradigm, choices that are made with an endless variety of idiosyncratic attitudes. But as previously mentioned, there are other styles, independent of the contact paradigm. I want to address a major one in particular which, as far as I can tell, doesn't have its roots in surfing as does the contact paradigm, but rather seems to be in a family with yo-yos and pogs. It seems to be a sensibility that developed in freestyle skating and then contaminated streetskating, in which the skate shifts from vehicle to toy.

The skate is no longer a vehicle with which to contact the world, but rather an object to lose contact with and somehow regain it underfoot. The less contact, the better. The skate is now akin to a remote control plane or a kite: something to be controlled at a distance from the body. The essential deed is remote control. Like a yo-yo, it is an object that one does tricks with. But no one is impressed with a yo-yo that stays in the hand. The tricks must occur away from the body. The athlete's focus is on the object, the toy, not the body, not the contact. With its pog-like wheels that are too small to traverse 99 percent of the terrain offered by the paved world, the skate is often walked across streets, carried here and there to the special place where it can be played with, flipped, flung, spun, and with any luck, landed on, right-side up.

It is said that the difference between men and boys is the price of their toys. I say the difference is in what one does with them.

Pink Motel drop-in, 1998.

MIKE VALLELY

BY JESSE PARK

Mike Vallely was immortalized as one of the skaters in the Powell-Peralta Bones Brigade videos directed by Stacy Peralta and C.R. Stecyk. Although he later expressed doubts about its relevance in the Etnies documentary, Sponsored, his part in Public Domain forever cemented his name into skating's consciousness as it opened with him running through a graveyard. Mike is one of skating's all-time greats and a true original. Still skating hard as fuck in the year 2000, Mike is also a father, a husband, and a poet and lives a healthy vegan life.

WHERE ARE YOU LIVING NOW?

In Long Beach. I've been there for a year and a half, and I live in a really nice, suburban community. It's really quiet, it's perfect for us. We're sorta like tucked right next to Lakewood, sorta on the Long Beach/Orange County border. Most people don't know about the area, they associate Long Beach with other areas, but we're not far away from problem areas.

DOES THE QUIET AREA HELP YOU WITH YOUR WRITING? HAVE YOU TAKEN A BREAK?

No, I'm always writing, it doesn't really matter where I am, you know, most of the inspiration, most of the writing, most of the stuff I'm doing now is really auto-biographical—it's just about where I'm at in my life, you know, the lessons I'm learning, and trying to figure out what's important to me, where my energy needs to go. So it's really sort of therapeutic. The last book that I put out and the last bunch of writing that I did was stuff that I was talking about when I went out on a spoken word tour and stuff was more focused, not just about me. I actually felt like I was bringing up issues and different things that I had learned about and felt the need to try and communicate. But now my writing's gone back to more...

MORE STORIES OR MORE POEMS?

Most of the poems that I wrote for my last book, called *Grand Canyon* was a lot of story-oriented, storytelling-type poems, where there were characters, and a story unfolded in several verses. I was really intrigued with trying to tell that kind of a story like a folk song.

SO YOU WERE TRYING TO BRING YOUR POEMS MORE TO LIFE?

Yeah, whereas it could have been short stories, but I like the idea of trying to sum up a character in a couple lines. Say key words that say something about that person that everyone could get a sense of what this person's about by just a couple lines. So I played around with that and I still write a little bit of stuff like that, but right now most of my stuff is what's going on with my head and my heart.

YOU EVER READ BUKOWSKI?

Yeah, I had a real big Bukowski period around '89, '90...I still have all the books. I haven't read the stuff since then, but one thing always sorta leads to another. I found his stuff then, and I've wanted to go back and read a couple of his stories, like *Post Office* and things like that. It's real simple. It gets right at you from the first line, you're right in the story, you know?

Father

You work your whole life
Just to get by
You work your whole damn life
'Til the day you die
Four mouths to feed besides your own
But you always brought dinner home
And when I saw that distance in your eyes
I felt your compromise deep beneath my bones

Some good deals turned bad
And from under you the rug is pulled
I saw you hit the ground, I saw you taken down
I watched you unfold
And man this world don't stop
It wouldn't for you and it wont for me
I watched you pick yourself back up
And do what you had to do
And that meant everything to me

Dad, you've made me a proud son
I respect you immensely
They stole away our time
They slaved you for every dime
And still you always walked a straight line
Now, you've got the roughest hands
I believe I've ever felt
And physically your heart is bad
But with all the love it has
It has loved me well

Now, I've got a family of my own
And there's so many miles in-between
But they're bridged by this gift
You have given to me
And I promise to do my best
And keep my priorities straight
You showed me how to be a man
A father and a husband
And dad, I just want to say thanks

DO YOU HAVE A FAVORITE AUTHOR THESE DAYS? OR ANYTHING THAT YOU'VE BEEN READING THAT STANDS OUT?

I haven't been reading so much maybe the last year and a half, but before that I was pounding through books like mad and it was mostly a lot of Steinbeck. Steinbeck is really where my mentality has been, and I've found a lot of myself in his writing, and things that I didn't have words for before I found them in his stuff, so I'm a big fan and a big pusher of a lot of the ideas that he brought to life.

IT'S FUNNY THAT IT'S REQUIRED IN HIGH SCHOOL AND THEN WHEN YOU GET OUT YOU ACTUALLY GO BACK AND YOU REALIZE THAT...

I don't know, there's something just about the education system that doesn't...for some people it works but for most of us it just doesn't seem to happen. That stuff just wouldn't go over with me when I was in high school, I couldn't relate to it, it wasn't presented properly to me, or whatever the case was. When I was twenty-five, I started reading Steinbeck, and I pounded through all his books in a matter of a year and a half. I wish I'd got turned on to them earlier. I've also found that I probably would have found out a lot of the stuff that I'm finding out now a lot earlier in my life, but skateboarding consumed me so much that as far as the stuff that I was interested in and different things that I've written and read I feel like I probably would have found him earlier in my journeys but I was always touring about.

IT'S EASY TO GET SIDETRACKED BY ONE THING WHEN YOU'RE SO HEAVILY INTO IT.

It was good though, I lived up in Santa Barbara for a year and a half and the whole time I lived up there I skated a little bit. Actually what happened is that I injured my shoulder really bad and it basically took me out of skating for a year and a half and its funny 'cause I still got coverage, I still attended enough events that the general public didn't realize that I was out of commission, but I was definitely out of commission for a long time. And during that time I did a lot of reading and very little writing, and now I still feel like I'm coming in on that wave, like all the material that I'm putting out now was all inspired by that time a couple of years back.

SO YOU FELT THE NEED TO BRING IT BACK IN?

Yeah, I really hated being injured, and I really wish I never had that injury in a lot of ways—my skating suffered, and it's still affecting my skating, but in other ways, it was a great time for me because I was able to get down a lot of knowledge and information that I'm thankful for.

The billboards flash me signals
And in the rearview I see signs
And on the horizon I see the picture
That I've pictured in my mind
And though the highway bends and turns
The picture does not shift
And even from this canyon's floor
I'm driving right towards it

Now to you it might sound silly
But to me it's everything
'Cause from out here on this highway
It's hard to believe in anything
So to this family picture
I pledge my allegiance
And I do solemnly swear
To protect and guard against

Now I'll reveal my vision
It's of my little girl
She's sitting in the back seat of a car
With her hair of curls
Me and her Mom are in the front seat
As we drive hand in hand along the road
And we're going on a vacation
Where the journey together is the goal

Someplace

In a town where young men inherit their fathers seat at the bar
And their one prized possession is a flexed muscle car
In a place where churches line the streets
And on Sunday they serve as a sinner's retreat
In a town where the roads don't go anywhere
And people drive in circles and don't seem to care
In a place where children are forbidden to dream
And once a week their parents take them out for ice cream
In a town where the cops referee domestic disputes
And firefighters start fires to have something to do
In a place where the stars don't shine at night
And no one's looking anyway

Christmas 1993
(South River, New Jersey)

The snow settles in on these streets
It's a "White Christmas" after all
I walk up the porch of my parents house
and feel secure again like when I was small
Into the rooms I unwind
I sit down at the kitchen table
Everything's fine

Dad, I'm a father too, just like you
If I can be half the man you are I'll be all right
My girls are all that matter in my world
I want to do right by them
When I set out on my own
I never thought I'd come crawling home
But here I am
Mom, please hold me again

Tonight in this room we're calling our own
Under the roof of my parents home
My girls are asleep, I listen to their gentle breath
and know I'll never be alone
And I can hear my dad snoring through the walls
and the heater clanking in the halls
And I know everything's all right
And I know it's a good night

In a town where cancer is passed like the flu
And kids sit on the interstate watching the cars pass through
In a place where suicide's the leading cause of death
And the cops will shoot you for some petty theft
In a town where Bingo is the only God
And people kill each other over parking spots
In a place where the television is always on
And kids and video games have a special bond
In a town where dogs sit at home waiting to get kicked
And broken homes means broken kids
In a place where the sun doesn't shine, it burns
And no one seems concerned

In a town where you live until you die
And all the houses are for sale but nobody buys
In a place where kids start smoking in the third grade
And growing up, the only rite of passage is getting laid
In a town where the lottery jackpot grows
And nobody wins that nobody knows
In a place where generations plant but don't sow
And children play under the refineries glow
In a town where the streets are alphabetized
And strip malls line the highway on both sides
In a place where the wind screams as it passes through
And no one hears it's cry

In Hot Pursuit of a Dude Called Donger

by Roman de Salvo

Part of the artistic side of skateboarding is this playful activity with names that goes on. Perhaps skating is as pleasurable for the accompanying language dorking as it is for the actual rolling activity. I've always liked some of the names of skate moves—slappies, wallies, stinkbugs, stale fish. Think, if you will, of the words, "feeble grind." Quite poetic, if you ask me—especially given the nature of the move. This sort of poetic playfulness also gets carried over to the names of skaters. A lot of skaters I've known have had names that my parents thought were peculiar: Grub, Hospital, Rat's Ass, Lamey, Fullslam. Usually the names were improvised by someone else as a gurn, and then somehow the names would stick and even become embraced by the bearer. But they weren't always embraced. I know Jamie Linker never really liked being called "Lamey."

"Donger" is an unmistakable name. Likewise, the skater. I had seen him skating around town a couple of times. He was always flying over things, unlike any skater I had ever seen, with two long, braided ponytails gesturing in his wake. But not being a close friend, I wasn't sure if it was appropriate for me to call him Donger or his birth name, Kien. So I asked him about the name. I thought it might have been an onomatopoetic analog to his propensity to ollie as if he were equipped with springs. But as it turns out, he was called Donger prior to his getting into skating.

The name came about as a reference to a character named Long Duk Dong in the movie, *Sixteen Candles*. Long Duk Dong was an Asian exchange student taken in to do the chores, who gets blasted, falls out of a tree, and kicked in the balls—a peripheral character who was the subject of ridicule in a decidedly slanted representation. Kien's friends used to cap on him by likening him to Long Duk Dong. I asked him which name he preferred me to use. "Kien," he said. Given the origins of "Donger," I wasn't surprised.

Still, when I called him on the phone, his roommate answered and I asked for Kien. I then heard his roommate call, "Hey, Donger, it's for you." Kien likes to park his car up on Fifth and Maple Street and skate down the hill into downtown San Diego. It was easy for Carnage and me to remember Maple Street because, coincidentally, that happened to be the type of wood that our skate decks were made of. Not only that, we came to find out, Donger's board was made of maple, too, and "Maple" is even the name of his skate company. Anyway, that's where we met up with him, at Fifth and Maple, to tag along on his session.

The route is chock-full of fun lines: lots of bumps, rails, ledges, banks, and such, scattered along a downhill cruise leading into the civic and financial fortresses of downtown with its smooth plazas, handrails, and rent-a-cops. Because much of the terrain is downhill, he hits a lot of the lines at sick speeds. And given that a portion of the terrain is a bust, it helps to be swift in one's onslaught. We liked the idea of just following along, documenting the typical, casual Donger session without being the intrusive media with a bunch of questions, or constantly asking him for a move to be repeated for a better shot. We wanted to just tag along on our skates, try to keep up with his natural pace, and get some photos that would hopefully represent something of the larger experience.

My role was that of a caddie for Carnage the photographer, who I handed a different camera or lens whenever he felt circumstances dictated. Unlike Carnage, I didn't have to look through a 200-millimeter lens while skating downhill in an obstacle-infested environment, so I was able to have some fun of my own on the skate. But generally, I was more interested in seeing what Donger was lofting. This being his stomping grounds, he knew his lines well. Yet he is still vitally spontaneous. Some of the elements that came into play at Mach 12, no less—were not part of the usual routine, but rather obstacles that happened to be there at the moment to be casually flown over and played with: a backhoe shovel here, a waist-high boundary of yellow caution tape there.

Pages 184—186, downtown San Diego, California, 1995.

We stopped for a short session at an asphalt hip bank that was partially soaked in old piss. Donger floated a fat frontside ollie high above the hip, appropriately grabbing stale. We continued on into the core of downtown where things got a bit more precarious due to matters of legality.

As soon as Donger passed through a plaza it became a bust for the rest of us on the tour. So sometimes, Carnage and I had to take different routes than Donger while still trying to keep a camera on him. Once a passing pedestrian caused him to bail on a line that he wanted bad, so he chanced to give it another try. But as soon as he went back security closed in on him. A conflict of words and postures ensued. The skating was over and we were on our way, but the security geeks wanted to press the issue and laid hands on. That's when things looked like they might get ugly.

Fortunately, security came to their senses and realized that their jobs didn't require them to get their heads busted by Kien's friend John who quickly responded to the call to arms. As we continued our exit, a cool, formidable Kien said to them that they ought to relax and not stress out every time we come around. One of the security chumps condescendingly replied, "We get paid for it." Kien laughed, "So do we." And that was about the end of our pursuit, nothing to do with the security encounter, though.

We had worked our way to the bottom of the hill, to the center of the city, to an all-around natural closure. Carnage was even about out of film. And it was an easy place to catch a cab, which we did, and headed back up to Maple Street. Along the way, Kien told us about his recent skate gig at a kid's birthday party in Oregon. He spoke kindly of the kid's folks, some enlightened rich people that had several pet tigers that they rescued from abuse at the hands of the Las Vegas entertainment industry. Clearly, he has a fondness for tigers.

The Egg-Throwing Parallel

by Brion Burkett

Imagine you are a security guard. You've got a kick-back job, nine bucks an hour, cool benefits, and all you have to do is walk around your building and make sure it doesn't fall apart or burn up or anything. You have to wear a stupid-looking cop suit and take shit from all your friends for being a rent-a-cop, but overall, you've got it pretty good.

Now imagine this group of kids showing up at your building one day and for no apparent reason, they're throwing eggs at one of the walls. You see them on your security camera and it's like, "What the fuck?!?" You walk out there and these kids are still at it, throwing eggs at one little part of the wall. Over and over. Each one taking turns. You notice each kid is totally into it. Their eyes are lit up like they've never been so thrilled. You eventually get over trying to understand why they are so into it and start focusing on whether or not your boss is going to tear you a new asshole for letting a bunch of kids mark up his wall with eggs.

The closest kid makes eye contact with you and you yell at him and all his friends to stop whatever the hell it is they're doing. They all stop and look at each other. They actually look surprised that you are out there in the first place.

"What the hell do you think you're doing?!?" you yell, more out of confusion than actual anger. One of the older ones replies, "Throwing eggs at your wall. What does it look like?"

His tone is so relaxed and nonchalant you almost forget why throwing eggs is such a big deal. Now you are even more perplexed and getting a little angry.

"Look at what you're doing to this wall!" You walk up to the egg-splattered wall and point to it. "How would you like it if I came over to your house and threw eggs at your wall?" you ask angrily, trying to talk some sense into them.

A kid with egg logos on his shirt and hat steps up and says, "I would be stoked. We just got back from my house. Been throwin' eggs all day."

By this time, you are fully pissed off. The only logical conclusion that your confused brain can come up with is that these kids, for whatever reason, are fucking with you. They all got together and created a gang. A gang of egg-throwers. They all dress funny because that's what gangs do, right?

They all just stand there waiting for your next move. You think about calling the cops but instead decide to just threaten them with a warning: "Get the hell out of here or I'll call the cops! And if I see you around here again, I'm taking your eggs!" At that, they gather up all their unused eggs in their cartons, get in their car, and drive off.

Wow. What a day, huh? The next day you tell your boss what happened and he eventually hires somebody to come in and clean the egg off the wall. Whatever. At least it was an isolated incident, right? Wrong. A week later and they're back, throwing eggs at the same exact spot as before. You walk out to kick them out, but this time they all run as soon as they see you. This happens again and again over the next couple months. Sometimes only one or two kids show up. Other times one of them actually has a video camera to record the egg-throwing. And always at the same specific spot on the wall.

About a month ago your boss stopped cleaning all the egg off his wall. The wall looks so nasty to you, but it's an everyday thing nowadays. In fact, you've heard of this same thing happening all over town. Kids throwing eggs at a specific part of a wall over and over again. You still don't understand it, but you now realize that it has nothing to do with you. "What could they be doing?" You are so curious.

One day you are getting off work and you see some kids throwing eggs at your wall again. This time you just sit and watch. It seems a little crazy, but the way these kids throw eggs actually looks thought out and calculated. You start to notice patterns. It seems like they have different ways of throwing their eggs. Sometimes one of the kids throws it in such a way you never thought possible. The whole thing is just one big mystery to you. You aren't in uniform so when you call one of them over, he smiles and walks up to you. Here is your chance to get in on what's really going on.

"Hey man, why do you guys always come here to throw eggs at only that one spot of the wall? What's the difference between that wall and any other wall?"

"Well," he casually replies, "It's not just a wall that we are looking for, but more so the actual texture of the wall itself."

Whoah! You would have never imagined it like that.

"Well, doesn't it get expensive buying eggs every day? I mean, do your parents buy them for you?" You are so intrigued.

"Hell no, man! I'm twenty-three years old! I haven't bought an egg for like five years! When an egg-thrower gets good enough, he gets a company to send him crates of eggs in the mail with their logo on them. So we help advertise for the egg companies and they give us free eggs."

You are completely blown away. You now realize that an entirely separate culture surrounds and exists within egg-throwing. What a strangely cool thing.

In case, dear reader, you haven't figured it out yet, this is how security guards see skateboarding. We show up at their building or shopping center and tax that ledge or bank or handrail for a purpose. But how do they know? You'd be surprised how many people really don't know. Skateboarding is so subversive. It can never be mainstream because it is so opposite to the mainstream's way of thinking. Some get it, but most don't.

If egg-throwing was on ESPN, would you get it? Probably not. The reason is that we are skateboarders, not egg-throwers. The common ground is doing what you love and getting something positive and fulfilling out of it. All other aspects, like fashion and the industry, are irrelevant. Keep pushing....

ED TEMPLETON

BY RON CAMERON

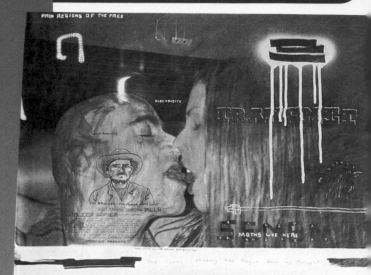

Out of the middle of the schizophrenetic Orange County grid comes a real human being named Ed Templeton. Knowing no conventional fear, he is more interested in impressing himself rather than impressing others around him. It may be his ninja-recluse roots that propel him toward anything of genuine interest in a bulldozer-type fashion, and lets his naïveté push the purity of anything he does to the foreground. The outcome is raw.

His interest in drawing and painting has been the true vehicle for unleashing the real Ed. His reality-driven portraits of people are his way of reporting modern man back to a sometimes unwilling audience (nudity never sits well with the inhabitants behind the Orange Curtain). He has recently published a book called Teenage Smokers that, well, you guessed it, simply has photos of teenagers sucking the smoke in!

Ed has also been skateboarding for well over ten years and has become one of the top professional streetskaters of the time. His skating, like everything he does, is pure, raw, and simple in an explosive and memorable way. If that wasn't enough, Ed founded and runs Toy Machine Skateboards, one of the most popular and certainly unique skateboard companies that continues to generate new superstars like Jamie Thomas, Elissa Steamer, and Brian Anderson. Lucky for us, Ed seems to have ignored the common social and peer conditioning that keeps most of us from attempting our true goals. Sit back and watch him go.

My name is Ed. I am a professional skateboarder. I live in Huntington Beach, California. I'm twenty-three years old. I'm married to Deanna. I have a cat.

The Extreme Games are pretty tweaked. Some people have this theory that ESPN is trying to take over skateboarding. At the games they have wakeboarding, skydiving, rollerblading, biking, all these "extreme" sports. ESPN's feeling 'em all out and the sports that survive will obviously be skateboarding and maybe rollerblading. But those other industries have their shit together; the skateboard industry is a just bunch of people who are dorks basically. Some people theorize they are just gonna come in with money and steal all the good riders by making their own companies offer them like two hundred thousand dollars a year.

The thing I believe is that skateboarding is just raw. It's supposed to be what it is. It's illegal. Streetskating is illegal. ESPN could do that if it was like vert only. But they can't because street is illegal. They wouldn't be able to make as much money as they would like to on something that is basically "outlawed."

I go to the Extreme Games and it's pretty fun to skate in it. But at the same time, I gotta go there at a certain time, check in, get my photo taken for the little TV graphic. Some guy is constantly asking me what is my strategy for winning the contest so the commentator can talk about it during my run: "Yeah, Ed Templeton here has told me earlier today when I caught up with him in his dressing room that his strategy is to try and get the Hawkster. He figures if he takes down the Hawkster he'll do ok." That's what they want to hear. It's just 100 percent processed Cheese Whiz, you know, and you just kind of deal with it. The main thing is that it's just a fun contest. It's an interesting and retarded course. It's huge and it's built for rollerbladers, it's different so it's challenging I guess. Plus Newport, Rhode Island, is a nice area. There's a boat taxi that goes from the contest site to the dormitories. You just ride boats and have fun.

Mike Mills, a graphic designer from New York (who did Sonic Youth's *Washing Machine* cover) and the Jon Spencer Blues Explosion is doing a documentary with me. He came down to Huntington to visit me and was just fascinated with how tweaked it is here. The skatepark, the architecture, the people. He thought it was weird how someone like me lives here. You know, I'm an artist, my paintings are of naked people, the opposite of what Huntington Beach is supposed to be like. He got this idea to make a film about that subject. So he came and filmed nonstop for four days, which is hard to go through. I had to work on a painting all night because part of the film was me completing a painting. So I go to bed at 3 am and wake up at 11 am with him at my door ready to film me in the shower, or sittin' around in my underwear in the morning like I normally would. Then, all day long we'd go from spot to spot filming and interviewing people and skating. It's gonna be called "Deformer."

Anyway, after traveling, I clicked over and went whoa, look at this place I live in, it's rad! I mean it's fucked, but it's rad! The weather's nice of course and it's nice to live here, but Orange County is just tweaked! Just like I think a lot of suburbs are tweaked. In the city everyone's raw. No one's hiding anything at all. Like "Here's what I am," I walk to my house, I see you in the street, I steal people's stuff or I don't steal people's stuff, but either way I'm in poverty. That's just what it is. The farther you get from the city's center the more tweaked it gets, from the people trying to hide their problems. The suburbs are the epitome of that. It's supposed to be this nice row of houses with lawns, a two-car garage, a family, a kid, and a puppy, and it's supposed to be just great, it's "The Suburbs." You know, planned living, wealthy people. Here's the thing though, it's not like that—people are just tweaked everywhere.

So you go around and see these nice neighborhoods, but look a little closer in the windows and see some kid getting beat up by his parents, or some teenager smoking crack or something. That's what I think is interesting about Orange County, the plainness of the architecture, the staleness, the retardedness, the awkwardness of some of the spots you go to. You walk down some street with all these perfect houses, and there's like nothing going on. You feel like your on Mars. It's like, "What's going on here, there's no life on this block!" Like a

big movie set, but behind that movie set there's just tweaked stuff going on. But it's all hidden, it's supposed to be normal suburban families. The psychologists are just abounding because that's how it is. People have problems, people are tweaked, but they try to hide it.

There's also a lot of underground stuff here in a way, but it's all kind of cheesy in my opinion. Like "alternative." That Electric Chair store bothers me to no end every time I go by it, you know, "Body piercing, cool records, and bondage pants." It's like, "Come here to be alternative," your one-stop shop to be cool. I could walk in looking like a businessman and get a tattoo, a fuckin' nosering, buy a Dead Kennedys album, dye my hair green and spike it and now I'm "crazy." I'm not against people doing what they want to do, but I would venture to say that 95 percent of the people who look that way (modern primitive piercing), aren't even into it for the reasons the original guys did it. You know, the whole body mutilation and the pain, etc., and all the ideas behind it. They're just into looking like a "tattooed-love-machine-guy." I think times are getting worse and worse for teenagers. Every couple years they get a tad more grown-up but without actually growing up. TV and information. That's what it is: information moves too quickly now. Your average kid is getting information that he wouldn't have normally gotten 'til a couple of years later.

I don't know what happened with skateboarding. I know when I started, being an artist was part of being a skateboarder. You know, the best guys you were stoked on were artists. Neil Blender, Mark Gonzales, and Chris Miller were pros I looked up to and were artist guys. Somewhere it changed and turned into this "jock" thing. There's a bigger "anti" side to the skateboard artist now. I get a lot of stuff because I paint naked people, male or female, so people think I'm a fag. Like "Ed's a fag, he's into painting guys' dicks!" I get that a lot but whatever. People that know what's up, know what I'm into.

Now skating's back to where it was when I started. It was just for fun and it was rad, you know? Just go out and try to attack stuff and do whatever you wanted to do on new and different stuff. Then skating went through that change into pressure flips and stuff, technical stuff. I was one of the top pros at that time and felt like I had to keep up with what the current trend was or else I was gonna be "cut." So I got fully into that stuff and skateboarding became trying to practice my flat ground and get it down. It was like I had to do this, I had to do that. But now, with Toy Machine doing well, I've gotten to this point where I'm like a "respected old guy" in the industry, even though people don't think of me as an old guy. Kind of like Ray Barbee or Mike Vallely, people that have been around and haven't slowed down in any way. The pressure's off for some reason. I'm having more fun than I ever have. And I feel like I'm skating better.

Every day I get stacks of mail at Toy Machine from kids saying we like your riders, we like your ads. It's not really about making money. Toy Machine's always been first about just doing something cool, having cool ads, a cool image, and good riders. The advertising seems like we're out for money, 'cuz it's all like fake consumerism type stuff. Like "Buy our product now" and "We're bent on world domination" and stuff. Kids know it's sarcastic. We're not out there like saying we're the coolest, check us out—you can't even begin to comprehend how cool we are. We're just like: look, we're a dorky company, fuck you, eat my shit, don't look here, go away, you know? Just fun stupid stuff. But at least there's something there for kids to look at. It's not just like a photo and a logo.

Do what you want and tell everyone to suck your ass! Do all the

things you want to do and don't take shit from people. Don't listen to 'em. Just do what you think is good. If you're a retard it'll suck, and if you're rad it'll be rad. I've found that when I have listened to people it has been disastrous. Like I've done a painting or something and people come and criticize it and wrecked it, and I realize that, fuck, that was a good thing that I liked and this person that didn't like it doesn't mean shit. You just gotta do what you want to do. I'm not telling you what to do, I'm just saying look at my life as an example. I honestly believe that anyone else that follows what they want to and just sticks with it will also be successful.

I was speaking with designer Rudy Vanderlans of Emigre *once about how much I liked zines and the handwritten text in them. "You should do an issue that is all handwritten," he suggested. The seed was planted and a few years later, I finally went through with it. Besides Rudy and his wife and partner, Zuzanna Licko, I enlisted lots of designers, artists, musicians, skaters, and zinesters whose work I admired. The entire issue was handwritten except for ads, and no fonts were used at all. It was really unique and one of the funnest issues we ever did.*

Rudy Vanderlans, Emigre.

Zuzanna Licko, Emigre.

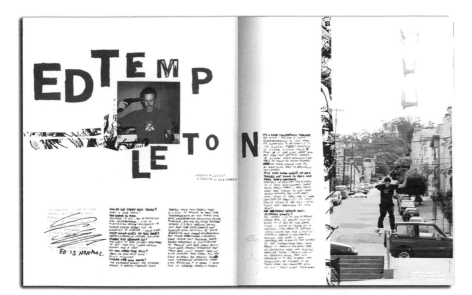

Ron Cameron, Designer for Blockhead and ACME Skateboards.

Jason Lytle, singer–songwriter for the band Grandaddy.

Judd Hertzler, skateboarder.

Tom Flowers, Oleander vocalist.

Elliott Earls, The Apollo Program.

All the music reviewers had to handwrite their own reviews.

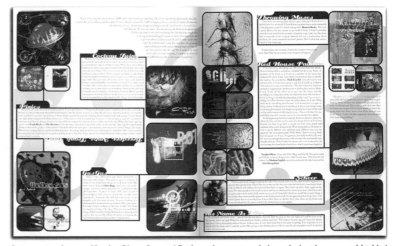

We only ran letters from people with nice handwriting.

Interviewing designer Vaughn Oliver from 4AD about the musicans he's worked with was a real highlight.

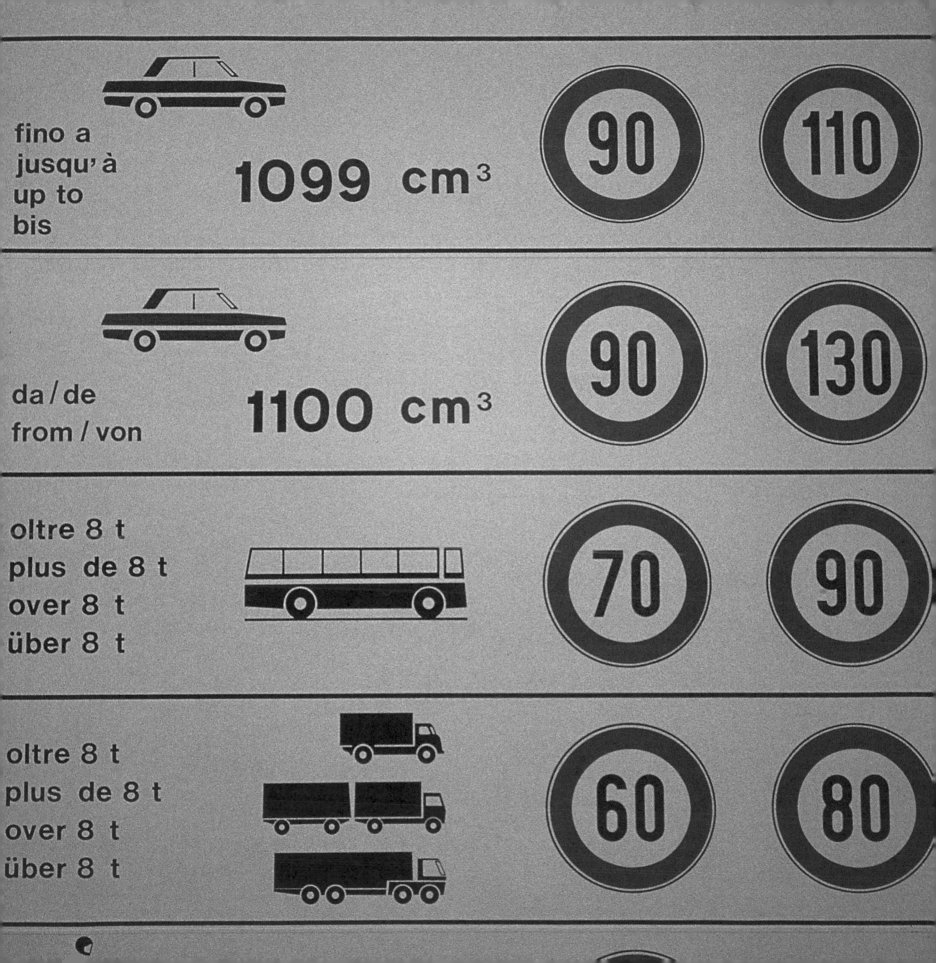

CHAPTER 7. HIT THE ROAD

Hit the Road

by John Baccigaluppi

After our first year of publishing the newsprint zine version of *Heckler*, we decided to take a few weeks off and go on a road trip. It was the summer of 1994 and the Yo Yo Festival was happening in Olympia, WA. It was a three-day festival at the Capitol Theater downtown, with over forty bands playing including Beck, Rancid, Yo La Tengo, and lots more in a homegrown DIY atmosphere. As the big festivals were becoming increasingly more corporate, Yo Yo was a welcome oasis. On the way there, we spent a few days snowboarding on Mt. Hood, where ski racers train and the offspring of the wealthy go to snowboard camps. We slummed it, camping in the woods and barging the plywood paradise of the skate ramps thanks to the ever-gracious Windell's Snowboard Camp. And then we skated Burnside in Portland, OR.

There are lots of skateparks now, but when Burnside was first built it had a mystique that was undeniable. It was a mecca for real skateboarders. The first time I skated there, I had three days off. Two were spent driving there and back and one skating all day. It was totally worth the long drive. It's hard to explain if you've never been there, but skating Burnside somehow cleanses your soul. It's like surfing the North Shore, or snowboarding Alaska. There are lots of skateparks, but there's still only one Burnside.

We began a tradition that summer that's only growing stronger.

Snowboarding, skating, and playing music cannot be done standing still. They all involve movement—from the movements involved in the activity itself to movements to other places. Hitting the road in pursuit of new terrain or new audiences is one of the best things in the world. Why? Well, for instance, in the spring of 1999 *Heckler* went to Spain with thirteen people to skateboard. Spain has more concrete skateparks than just about any country in the world. Any country, that is, except for the U.S. There are at least a dozen really good skateparks within a few hours from our home base in Sacramento, CA. I've skated most of them and they're all a lot of fun. But they're not in Spain, where very few people speak English and you will either love or despise the food.

Pablo Picasso and Antonio Gaudí lived in Spain, as do our new friends Jaime, Ruben, and David. You can visit Spain someday and wander around looking at the amazing architecture, drink till dawn in the bars, and visit the famous museums and churches. We did all that. But why wait till you're older and part of some tour group? Why not go right now and take your snowboard and skateboard? If you let your board guide your travels, you'll see plenty of the "sights" the tourists see and a lot they won't. But more important, you won't just be a tourist; you'll be a skater and you'll see things and meet people in the way that only a skater can. The opportunity, or more bluntly, the excuse to travel is one of the best reasons to ride a board of any kind. When you let your board be your guide, let it plan and shape your destiny, you'll always stumble across something new, and you'll always be pleasantly surprised.

In the following chapter are some photos and words gathered from trips that we've done as well as some our friends have done. We hope they inspire you to leave home.

"I had no reason to go before I left, but when I came home I had every reason to have gone. I am a better person because of this journey. There is comfort in flying to the other side of the world and finding people who feel and think the same way you do.

Before going to Brazil, I was not doing a very good job of enjoying the life I had. I was stressing out on things that didn't matter: school, work, et cetera. It was bad news. This trip and the people I met on my way reminded me of what is good and what is worth believing in."

—Amanda Marsalis on an impromptu trip to Brazil in search of skateboarding and graffiti art

Right: Mark "Red" Scott, one of Burnside's founders, 1992.
Below: Toad at Burnside, Portland, Oregon, 2000.

This page: Tom Gilles at Windell's giant ramp and an unidentified jibber on a giant Mt. Hood handrail.

MT. LASSEN

By our third year of publishing, we had grown weary of the media overkill at Mt. Hood yet we were still jonesin' for some summer snow. It had dumped that year, and the road to Mt. Lassen in Northern California didn't open until late July. So along with snowboarders Dave Rogers and Tracey Latzen, we decided to go camp and hike the snow at Lassen in lieu of Mt. Hood. We were very pleasantly surprised to find almost twenty feet of snow. In August!

GREEN TORTOISE

There are many ways to get to your snowboarding destination, but sometimes the journey is the destination. Such was the case when *Heckler*, along with snowboarders Dave Rogers, Tim Manning, and I.J. Valenzuela, used the bus known as the Green Tortoise to get from Sacramento, California, to Seattle, Washington, and ultimately rode Crystal Mountain Resort. With three levels of beds, tables, chairs, music, and room to spread out, relax, and meet someone if you wish, these huge tour buses are converted to fit the comfort of the human body and spirit; it is a complete departure from the well-known Greyhound. This typically thirteen-hour trip took twenty-two hours. However, along the way, we skateboarded, ate at various restaurants, cooked a full-course vegan meal on beautiful Oregon private property, steamed in a redwood sauna, swam in a clean river, and met a cast of characters. When asked to describe the Green Tortoise, our bus driver Larry said it best: "The Green Tortoise is alternate travel, which is refreshing in this day and age of ultra-conservatism. It's a refreshing way to travel where people can be themselves. We get all kinds of people. We get straight people, gay people, freaks, squares, and everything. There are all kinds of people that ride the Green Tortoise and the thing they all have in common is they tolerate each other. It's kind of a freedom, a freedom trip."

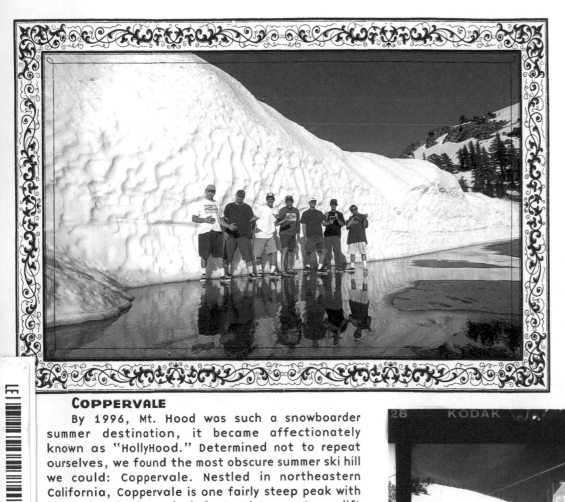

Opposite: Dave Rogers at Mt. Lassen.
Left: Mt. Lassen parking lot, August 1995.
(Left to right: Joey Washburn, Chad Lyons, Sonny,
John, Dave Rogers, Tracey Latzen, and Carnel.)
Below: Scenes from Coppervale.

COPPERVALE

By 1996, Mt. Hood was such a snowboarder summer destination, it became affectionately known as "HollyHood." Determined not to repeat ourselves, we found the most obscure summer ski hill we could: Coppervale. Nestled in northeastern California, Coppervale is one fairly steep peak with seven hundred vertical feet. The one Poma lift handed down from Lake Tahoe's behemoth Alpine Meadows originally ran on the rear drive of an old Chevy engine. The first rider of the day had to hike up with a gas can and get her started. The nearest town, Westwood, was put in *The Guinness Book of World Records* for the most dogs per capita. The locals we also found out were some of the friendliest and most hospitable folks we've ever met. We went with snowboarder Jon North and had one of the most fun and unique snowboarding trips ever.

GRAND TARGHEE, WYOMING
BY ARLIE JOHN CARSTENS

Through seeing the world and having new people and experiences in our lives, we can continue to grow and learn and have the confidence and support to take our hard times a little more in stride. I can't tell y'all enough about how important it is to rebel and defy expectations without succumbing to despair and violence against yourself and others. You may not think so now, but you can leave every asshole you ever hated behind and go see the world and live your life however you want to. Just keep playing at anything: music, skateboarding, hopscotch, cooking, zines, basketball, bike riding...anything! Never stop learning or doing. Know the power for good you possess inside. **Then one day, get the hell out of Dodge.** Travel and get to know how other people live and what their passions and struggles are.

As the lone voice of reason, my sweet but very worried father would often lament over faraway phone lines: "Why do all this running around?" I'd toss him the simple cool-guy answer borrowed on such occasions from a friend of mine: "There's no such thing as being bored, there's only boring people." Had I been within two feet of him, he'd forever roll his eyes and give me a hug and a peck on the cheek as he'd kick my ass out the door. But what can I say that wouldn't sound obnoxious? Could I tell him that I don't want to die oblivious to all the freaks, saints, and funny people who inspire me to take the next step into the unknown? Or that I want to live with visions of wonderful, beautiful places dancing in my head to remind myself that there is more to life than pouring concrete or the pain of papercuts? Personally, I am totally blown away by how fortunate I am to be able to come so far with my friends, doing something as silly as snowboarding in a place this sublime and graceful.

YAHMOS 1994 TOUR
BY SCOTT TORGUSON

Being on the road in a small band is a travel experience that just can't be beat. Being crammed into a small van and having no idea where you'll sleep is half the fun. In the summer of 1994, Heckler contributor Scott Torguson booked a tour for the punk band, The Yahmos, and then went along with them. The Yahmos consist of Nic, vocals, scabies; Tristan, guitar; James, bass; Mike, drums; and Aragorn, van.

Here are some of the highlights.

DAY 5: LOS ANGELES, CA. The Yahmos had a new record that had just come out, only we didn't have any yet. The guy that put it out was supposed to come to one of the L.A. shows and give us the records. He never showed up. So we went off in search of his house. The directions we had were kind of fucked. So we basically drove around pointlessly through a lot of Los Angeles at midnight. Aragorn was getting annoyed. The Yahmos came up with a new game that consisted of seeing who could piss off Aragorn the most. We finally found the house, got the records, and took off for San Diego, where we spent the night.

DAY 6/7: JACUMBA, CA. After the show in San Diego we decided to drive at night to Tucson, AZ, so we wouldn't have to drive through the desert midday. So I'm sleeping on the loft, and we stop. We had gotten about thirty minutes out of S.D. and broke down. I was half asleep and realizing we were spending the night on the side of the road. I kept half dreaming, and every time a car came by, I thought it was going to smash into us because I thought we were still in the middle of the road. We got the van towed the next morning to the vacation resort of Jacumba, CA, population 400. The van needed a new transmission, so we were stuck for two days. I had the flu to top things off. But luckily we were there the same night as the weekly dart tournament. This is where all the locals drink and throw darts. Alcohol and small pointy projectiles sound like a bad combination to me, but what do I know? I found a pinball game with low replay and played for one-and-a-half hours on one quarter. As we were hanging out in town, a British TV movie called *Shawnengate* was being filmed so everywhere we sat down we'd be quickly pushed away.

DAY 11: MEMPHIS, TN. The only thing notable about this show was the fact that the soundman heckled the Yahmos with things like, "Get a real amp," and "Play a fucking song."

DAY 13: ATLANTA, GA. There was a cool show in someone's basement. The guitar amp liked it so much that it stayed the next day when we left.

DAY 14: CHARLESTON, SC. As we unload, we realize there is no guitar amp, which means that Tristan must be nice to other bands he doesn't like in order to borrow amps. After the show, we and some locals went down to the ocean for a 3 A.M. nude swimming session.

DAY 15: WINSTON-SALEM, NC. We show up at 7 P.M. for a 3 P.M. show. In other words, we missed it.

DAY 17: HARRISBURG, PA. The show got cancelled because the hall double-booked a wedding and for some reason they gave the wedding priority over our punk rock show. So we went to the Hershey's Chocolate Factory, got to see how candy was made, and stole some candy bars.

DAY 18: WASHINGTON, DC. Due to my great planning, we got to spend one hour visiting museums. The show was at one in the afternoon, which was wonderful because it was about one hundred degrees and *really* humid. To top it off, the floor we slept on had fleas.

DAY 19/20: NORTH WINDHAM/MANCHESTER, CT. Nothing interests me here besides good shows and cool kids. Played with a Hare Krishna band called Shelter who were pretty laughable.

DAY 22: NEW YORK, NY. Wandered around NYC all day and all night. If you've never been there, I recommend checking it out. Cheap vegan food, and lots of rad things to see.

DAY 26: MOONESTOWN, NJ. Destroyed Car vs. Driver, a band from Atlanta, in Wiffle ball, even after they brought us the amp from Atlanta. No mercy for the weak.

DAY 32: LANSING, MI. First drunk party show of the tour. Kids moshing it up with forty ouncers in hand. Beer spitting on the ceiling and general tomfoolery.

DAY 36: CHICAGO, IL. Got to have legendary chef Kim Nolan cook for us. She does an awesome vegan cookbook called *Bark and Grass*. You should write her and get it: P.O. Box 447496, Chicago, IL 60647.

DAY 38: MILWAUKEE, WI. After the show we gathered up about fifteen locals, a boombox, and took over the streets. We blasted tunes and went dancing throughout Milwaukee until the sun came up. Then we went to a diner to get some breakfast. Two guys with their girlfriends were there and decided to call us "faggots." Since there were about fifteen of us, we winked and made faces at them. So one yells at Nic: "Let's take it outside." Nic yells back, "No thanks, I don't want to fuck you." This gets him steaming and grunting and turning red. Someone else at our table says, "Don't worry, man, you're just not his type." So he gets up like he's going to attack the fifteen of us, but luckily for us, his girlfriend holds him back.

DAY 40: RAPID CITY, SD. We get to stop at the world famous Wall Drug! What a load of shit. It's not even a decent tourist attraction. A couple of cowboy stores and that's it. We were going to graffiti Mt. Rushmore, but the van blew a tire and we had to get new ones.

DAY 43: GRAND JUNCTION, CO. We show up at this kid's house who is doing the show and he says, "I didn't know you guys were coming, there's no show." I guess me saying, "We will be there on the fourteenth for sure" wasn't enough confirmation for him.

DAY 44: PROVO, UT. Everyone in Provo is white, and all the women are pregnant. We were scared.

DAY 45: RENO, NV. I gamble for the first time in my life, and win over $200 in quarter slots.

DAY 46: SACRAMENTO, CA. We come home to a sign saying, "Welcome home, fuckers" and the Yahmos play to a packed house.
Everything is OK.

Opposite: Paul Laca, J.P. Martin, Arlie and Nate Mendel in Wyoming. Arlie's flying off the rock as well. 1998.
Above: The Yahmos in Sacramento, 1994.

EUROPE

It's every snowboarder's dream to ride big mountains in foreign countries. As *Heckler* progressed, so did our travel budget. In March of 1998, we, along with snowboarders Shawn Sterken, Tucker Fransen, Travis Yamada, and Marisa Stoler, did our first trip to Europe. There, we were blessed with fresh powder all over the Chamonix Valley in France and some of the best riding known to man. But in true *Heckler* travel fashion, we did not only snowboard. We skated and partied in Amsterdam, saw the art of the mentally institutionalized in Lausanne, Switzerland, traveled by train through Italy, snowboarded an incredible resort there called Courmayeur, and even skated on ancient ledges in Rome.

N.1.A.
LA SPEZIA
HARDCORE

Opposite, top: Travis Yamada dropping in at Chamonix, France.
Opposite, bottom: Marisa Stoler snowboarding in Courmeyer, Italy.
Clockwise from left:
Shawn Sterken skating in Rome;
Manarola, Italy, one of the "Cinque Terre";
Venice, Italy;
Ancient Rome, Italy.

SPAIN

On our second trip to Europe, we chose Spain as our destination. Spain has more concrete skateparks than any other country in Europe, and you can snowboard in the Pyrenees. It was also cheap, and our budgets had gotten smaller because we were independent again. Along with skaters Tim Brauch, Judd Hertzler, Mike Rafter, and Jeff Landi, and snowboarders Temple Cummins and Greg Goulet, we had one of the best trips ever.

Right: Greg Goulet in the air above the Pyrenees.
Below: Temple at Gaudi's Parc Guell.

Clockwise from top left:
Greg Goulet at the Bilbao skatepark with
the Guggenheim in the background.
Gaudí's Temple de la Sagrada Familia.
Greg again, this time at a cement
mini-ramp on the beach in Barcelona.
Judd Hertzler fingerflipping lien to tail at a
skatepark on the outskirts of Bilbao that was built in
the ruins of an old stone building overlooking the
Bilbao river mouth and the Atlantic Ocean.
Everyone agreed that it was the most scenic
skatepark they'd ever ridden.

Clockwise from top:
The late & great
Tim "Beans" Brauch ollies
some very stoked kids at the
Alcobendas skatepark in the
suburbs of Madrid.
Our Spanish friend
Jaime Fontecilla tailsides at
"The Bridge" in
downtown Madrid.
Temple Cummins very close
to the sun in the Pyrenees.
Sonny and a Barcelonian
trade notes on wheeled devices.
Picasso's Guernica.

"That feeling of hitting the highway is such that if you know it, you
can't explain it and if you don't know it, you're missing out."
—Sonny, on driving from Barcelona to the Pyrenees

Alaska

Alaska University has become the place where you take your final exam for your PhD of snowboarding. **"As a teacher, the school that is Alaska has taught many a lesson,"** wrote *Heckler* senior contributor I.J. Valenzuela. In April of 1999, he, along with Sky Rondonet, Sam Shields, Greg Manning, and Colby Leonard used a twenty-seven-foot motorhome to get to their riding destination. "Even saying the name immediately transcends your mind to a place where few rules exist and less are followed," said I.J. He completed an Alaskan travel story that would outshine all before it. Heli-skiing the Chugach mountains, this crew encountered attitude-adjusting terrain including five thousand-foot vertical runs. One of their friends was flushed out of a chute by an avalanche: "As an example, there are cliffs that dot the landscape that are as big as the biggest ski resort in Tahoe and they are merely part of the terrain," said I.J. "This year, Alaska had given everyone experiences that they either would not live to remember or will never forget."

Left to right: Johan Olofsson, Nate Cole, and Noah Salasnek, all in Valdez, Alaska.

CHINA

As a contrast to our first trip to the Northwest, in August of 1999 we were invited by the Chinese government to put on a skateboarding demo on the Great Wall of China. Skateboarders Antonious "Toad" Dintcho, Steve Bailey, and Jessie van Rouchoudt were with us to make history and experience a trip that consisted of showing skateboarding to people who had never even seen a Westerner, let alone a skateboard. The people of China loved skateboarding and embraced our presence. We did thirteen demos in three different cities over the course of sixteen days. However, we still had time to see things such as the Forbidden City and the Ming Tombs. Chinese skaters were very scarce, though we did get to meet and skate with a few.

The Great Wall demo was set in two parts: a vert ramp session below the Wall and a set of four quarterpipes on the Wall. The crowd was very energetic, but when the Chinese got on the P.A. system and announced, **"Let's go to the Wall!"** there was a frenzy.

Actually skating on the ancient divide, feeling our wheels roll over the cupped, yet smooth stones was a thrill like no other. Though short-lived (the demo only lasted about forty minutes), we impressed the people. Once warmed up, Toad started into a series of aggressive airs from ramp to ramp that had the crowd in an uproar. The Chinese organizers actually had to dismantle the ramps with hammers and steel bars to make us stop skating. It was beautiful. There are monumental moments throughout our lives. Skateboarding the Great Wall of China was one of the greatest.

Opposite: Toad does the first-ever crail air on the Great Wall of China while Steve Bailey snaps a frontside ollie at a sold-out Shanghai demo.
This page: Toad and Sonny on the Wall; Toad tailslides the Great Wall handrail; Sonny and very excited yet mystifed kids in Huzhou.

Above and right: Steve Bailey in China.

QUESTION: WHERE AM I?

I'm rocking hard at the Hard Rock Cafe. Everything I could ever want is here on the walls at Wal-Mart. I get nice and wired at Starbucks. I fill my gut with chicken and mashed potatoes at Boston Market. When I'm ready for a tomato-basil schmear, I go to Noah's Bagels. When I'm in the mood for a sandwich, you'll find me under the warm, yellow glow of Subway. And to wash it all down, I go to 7-Eleven and buy a Snapple.

I fill up my car with petrol at Chevron. I buy my hardware at Home Depot. When I'm in need of new tunes, I go to Sam Goody; or, for the safe, censored version of that new Beck record, again, I'm in the lovely aisles of Wal-Mart. When I need a new stereo to play my circumcised CD, I go to Fry's Electronics. When I'm feeling real crazy, I go see the latest rock, country, alternative, and comedy acts at America Live! When I wanna chill out and watch a movie, it's off to Blockbuster. Or if I don't feel like going out, I'll just pump some juicy cable!

So...where am I?

From the book Radical Modernism *by Dan Friedman.*

ANSWER: ANYWHERE, USA.

America is becoming homogenized like milk and it blows me away more and more every time I travel. I remember a time when traveling meant leaving a place called home to go to a place that looked, felt, smelled, and was totally different. Be it a small town in Oregon or a city on the East Coast, everything was different. You couldn't find familiar restaurants to save your life. If you wanted to fill up with gas, it was Bubba's Service Station or bust. Need a little something? There was a small- to medium-sized grocery/hardware/pharmacy that was locally owned and operated. Good coffee? Hah, good luck. Every place had its own character and was unique.

Part of the reason to travel is to see different cultures, experience new ways of life, and soak up local culture. With franchising, many cities and towns are starting to look the same, and it's having a much more harmful effect than fast-food chains had on the restaurant industry. Most restaurants have a niche a fast-food joint can't fulfill and vice versa. However, with these goods-oriented franchises, it's putting local guys out of business due to convenience, more selection, and price. I remember seeing small storefronts with cool, hand-and-machine-crafted signs that read "Bill's Bait Shop" or "Ed & Shirley's Grocery" or "Newbert's Hardware." Now, they are boarded up while two miles away, casting a dominant shadow, is a Wal-Mart, Price Club, or Home Depot. Everything changes, but the strip-mall culture is creating a uniform, changeless, boring, dreary society that limits the character and uniqueness of geographical regions. Already, there are people who don't have to leave their neighborhood. They sit at the end of their suburban cul-de-sac and have everything they need, including medical care, within a 2.4-mile radius of their living room couch.

One could say it's the government's way of controlling overpopulation. I say it is making for weak minds, weak hearts; a class of sheep. One of the most important parts of snowboarding, skateboarding, and playing music is traveling to new terrain, going on tour. I can imagine a life without travel and that deepens my gratitude for the trips I take. Whether they be by plane or jumping a train or road-tripping in a van, I am thankful for the enrichment it has added to my life. But, it kinda sucks to go to other places and see the same shit I left two thousand miles ago. It's way more fun and exciting to check out weird shops in foreign places, eat crappy food that makes you sick, and drink bad coffee served by a waitress whose father owns the diner.

I don't know what we can do to stop the homogenization of America except maybe think globally, act locally. Go to that local record store. Get your Twinkies at that little cool corner market. Take your business to that small hardware store some of the time. Take a chance on a hole-in-the-wall grub spot. Meet the locals in other weird towns and cities and on the hill. And whatever you do, do not shop at Wal-Mart! —SM

THE MOUNTAINS ARE BIGGER THAN YOU ARE

"Tired, nerve-shaken, over-civilized people are beginning to find out that going to the mountains is going home; that wilderness is a necessity; and that mountain parks and reservations are useful not only as fountains of timber and irrigating rivers, but as fountains of life."
—John Muir, founder of the Sierra Club

The Chamonix Valley and the French Alps.

This past winter, I made an observation: A vast majority of people who visit Lake Tahoe for its winter sports come from the coastal Bay Area as well as the Sacramento/San Joaquin Valley. If you are from the West and ride Tahoe as much as I do then you know the drive like the back of your hand: Interstate 80, Roseville, Foresthill exit, Highway 49, Rollins Lake, Emigrant Gap, Cisco Grove, Soda Springs, Boreal, Highway 89, Incline, Homewood, Squaw, etc., etc. Just rambling those off and thinking of snowboarding gives me a stoked feeling of excitement and bliss.

My feelings, though, are not as universal as I had so naively believed. On the contrary, many riders and commuters feel a sense of burden while on the mountain. For example, a skier at Boreal Ski Resort complained that in order to have a good day, he needed to get at least twenty-seven runs in. But that looked doubtful considering the Accelerator Quad lift kept stopping, so he left unhappy. Then, a friend of mine was driving to Tahoe during a mild storm and was told to put chains on his pickup truck. His complaining within his heated cab was incessant, saying it was such a drag to drive a car in chains and that storms sucked.

Yet another example is the people I hear all season who constantly complain of lift prices, lift lines, amateurs on the mountain, stalled chairlifts, traffic, and closed roads. **It seems as though these visitors to the Sierra Nevada mountains take the whole experience of riding for granted and even feel cheated by nature's elements.**

I believe that this feeling exists in part because too many people don't know the history of the mountains and the pains taken by the pioneers that enable you to slalom a run or jib a tree. In this modern age of cybertravel, private jets, instant coffee, and cable television, people forget the history behind the mountains. Let's compare the soul of the pioneers with that of snowboarders and take a look at the many things we take for granted. I live near the Sierra Nevada, so I am writing about their history, but I am sure that the mountains you ride share a similar background.

Right: Randy Walter.
Opposite: Alagna, Italy,
and Grand Montet, Chamonix, France.

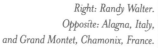

Spanish settlers named the range after the Sierra Nevada in southern Spain. The name means "snowy range." It is one of the highest mountain ranges in the United States. Along the jagged, snowy crest of the Sierra Nevada, a dozen peaks rise more than 14,000 feet. The highest of these peaks is Mount Whitney at 14,495 feet. It is 400 miles long and between 50 and 80 miles wide, and composed mostly of granite. Forests of pine and fir cover the western slopes to an elevation of 9,000 feet, where groves of giant sequoias, some of the largest trees in the world, exist.

The Sierra Nevada's eastern side rises abruptly from the desert plains. The longer, gentler western slopes have deep canyons and valleys carved by ancient glaciers and rushing streams. In great gorges are the Merced, Kern, Tuolumne, and Mokelumne rivers. High on the north face lies Lake Tahoe. At the northern end of the Sierra Nevada, the north fork of the Feather River flows through a gap making the separation from the Cascade Range. The Sierra Nevada ends at Tehachapi Pass in Kern County, in the south.

The migration increased when James Marshall, a superintendent at a saw mill, saw a shining rock in the waters of Coloma, California. The Gold Rush was on. In 1848, California had a mere 400 settlers. By 1849, after Marshall's discovery, California saw 90,000 settlers. But, it was the early pioneers that changed the path of history forever. The names are too many to list, but include William Swain, James M. Hutchings, John Carr, and Dave Young. As everyday people of the Plains states, these farm owners and cattlemen spoke of lush, green valleys and crystal waters. In 1510, a Spanish romantic novel wrote of "an island called California very close to the Terrestrial Paradise. Ruled by an Amazon queen named Calafia, the island everywhere abounds with gold and precious stones and upon it no other metal is found." [1]

Lansford Hastings wrote *The Emigrants Guide to Oregon and California*, which described the "California Trail." The Trail begins in Independence, Missouri, winds across to and along the Humboldt River, through the Sierra Nevadas and down to the Sacramento Valley. Hasting's book inspired

tent to escape them. The bugs covered the animals like sheets and the poison caused bloating and swelling. (Remember, they did not have OFF! insect repellent and there was no control over insect growth.)

To reach the base of the Sierra Nevadas, they first had to travel over miles of sand and salt deserts in covered wagons, not 4WD Toyotas. Alkali, a hydroxide chemical compound found in the dust of the salt deserts, ate the skin of the pioneers and caused dreadful itching and scratching. Try pouring the acid from your car battery all over yourself, don't wash it off for three days, and then go hike a bit. Are you still gonna go big brah?

The path through the Sierras, if there was one, may have been one- to two-feet deep with dust and full of ruts that caused broken legs and broken wagons. There were no roads; just towering rocks and cliffs surrounded by desolate dust and sage and greasewood. But this did not break the pioneers' spirits. Julia Cooley Altrocchi, author of *Snow Covered Wagons—A Pioneer Epic* wrote, "And now the earth begins to climb against the knees of

Visualize the magnificence of this uncharted terrain. Beautiful by the hand of God, callous to the desires of man. Why did the first pioneers feel the need to cross such a godforsaken place?

They were searching for better economic status, escaping cold prairie winters. More important, it was frontier restlessness that sent the pioneer fathers to load up their covered wagons and head west.

many early settlers to trade all their belongings for oxen- and horse-drawn covered wagons, in order to move west.

Along this troubled and grave-staked trail traveled William Swain. He kept a journal filled with hopes and dreams, despite the seemingly endless snags, drawbacks, hindrances, and delays. Some of the many obstacles on the trail were mosquitoes and gnats. Swain said that the bugs were so bad that the travelers had to enter a smoke-filled

heaven, slowly at first and gently do the great earth ripples rise against the sky's incline, along the slopes of yellow pine with here and there sharp rocks upthrust like warning fingers." [2]

The travelers also had to set up guard duty when they slept because thieves called the Digger Banditti would shoot their animals and raid campsites. It was kill or be killed. There were no laws, Motel 6s, or police; no highway rest stops or Chevron AM/PMs with bathrooms and drinking water. When the desperate search for water was successful, that did not mean it was safe. The water was often contaminated with cholera, sulfur, or dead carcasses that caused the pioneers to become violently ill and sometimes die. Cholera, a disease whose symptoms include cramps, vomiting, and diarrhea; and scurvy, which is caused by a lack of vitamin C, killed many people during the passage.

On the California Trail, there were two ways to go: Lassen's Cut-off to the north, or the Sink to the south by the Truckee and Carson Rivers. The Truckee/Carson route had the worst reputation for death according to William Swain: "The sides of the trail were lined with swollen carcasses, equipment piled and scattered, skeletons of burned wagons, wagons pushed off the trail and toppled over, wagons left in line where they had been unhitched from teams driven ahead for water. 'A man can get used to anything' is an old saying, the truth of which is pretty clearly demonstrated on this journey...We have seen a man eating his lunch gravely sitting on the carcass of a dead horse. And we frequently take our meals amidst the odor of a hundred rotting carcasses. Well, they say misery loves company, so we can have some enjoyment after all, for there is plenty of that kind of company here." [3]

These men on the trail were swollen, bitten, dry, sick, hungry, and desolate. How far was a good day of travel? Twelve miles was average, sixteen miles was good, and twenty was a great day. They were up at four in the morning and traveled well into dark. Today, we travel sixteen miles in ten minutes without breaking a sweat.

If a pioneer was unlucky enough to chance the Sierra Nevada during the snowy winter, it always meant misery and death. In the winter of 1846–47 the infamous Donner Party tried to cross the Sierra Nevadas at Donner Summit. The snow was twenty-two feet deep. Of the ninety people in the Donner Party, forty-three of them died, and the survivors resorted to eating the dead to stay alive. Patrick Breen, a survivor, kept a diary during their expedition. He tells of how the snow fell three to four feet each night, freezing everything. A random entry reads, "Froze hard last night, today clear and warm. Wind SE blowing briskly. Martha's jaw swelled with a toothache. Hungry times in camp, plenty hides but the folks will not eat them. We eat them with a tolerable good appetite. Mrs. Murphy said here yesterday that she thought she would commence on Milt Elliot and eat him. I don't believe she was done here yet. It is disheartening. The Donners told the California folks they would commence to eat the dead people four days ago if they did not succeed in finding their cattle under ten or twelve feet of snow and did not know where the spot or near it. I suppose they have done so ere this time." [4]

There were no freeways, no Ford Broncos, no AAA Road Service, no lifts, no resorts, nothing except harsh conditions and jagged peaks with no regard for the comfort or convenience of those who had to travel them. Many were sick, most died, and those that didn't resorted to cannibalism. Still, the pioneers moved on. They paved the way so we can now park in the parking lot, dress, and go play in the snow.

Opposite: Jason Beaton, Alaska.
Left: Switzerland.
Below: Marcus Egge, Crater Lake, Oregon.

"Look at my breasts. They are drying up!
The food you have brought is not enough," said a weary Harriett Pike as malnutrition and the harsh elements of Northern California's newly famed and dreaded Sierras began to not only affect her physique, but also her dying baby. [5]

Catherine Pike, an infant who would never know the historical significance of her existence, lay crying for milk while the rest of the Donner Party contemplated their next move on their trek west. It was late January of 1847 and as the wagon trains sat broken and the oxen moved through the deep snow, the pioneers planned to set out on foot toward California and baby Catherine Pike was dead.

The next time you drive your car on Interstate 80 over the Donner Summit and you are grumbling about chain controls, remember the Donner Party. We don't have to face disease, starvation, dehydration, and death to go snowboarding because those roads have already been paved with the lives of the pioneers. They put their hearts and souls into crossing the mountains. Shouldn't you?

How many of you stand at the peak of your favorite mountain and take notice of the grand view of Sierra Nevada? Examine the soul of the pioneers. They did all they could do to leave a legacy of history at the price of life itself. To us, the native sons and daughters of the Sierra Nevada, they have given us a strong state and precious heritage. We must appreciate it and guard it well.

Take note of the steps taken before your measly fifteen steps towards a quad chairlift.

Take note of the majestic beauty surrounding you that was tamed by the lives of your forebears.

Take note of the people who could hike no more and are buried in the ground under your feet after you wait in the ninety-second lift line and take the two-minute ride to the peak. Their souls are still there within the rock, dirt, air, and snow. Become one with the mountain, ride with the soul of a pioneer, and absorb all the Sierra Nevadas have to offer. See that she receives no ill treatment at your hands and pass it on to your children as you received it from your pioneer fathers. —SM

Marisa Stoller, Sonora Pass.

"Since they had no way of knowing that it would later be regarded as one of the truly difficult peaks of North America, they simply went ahead and climbed it. That, in my mind, is the way to climb a mountain."
—William Henry Jackson, photographer, 1872

FOOTNOTES
1 Murphy, Virgina Reed. *Across the Plains in the Donner Party*, 1996 pg. 52
2 Altrochi, Julia. *Snow Covered Wagons—A Pioneer Epic*, 1936 pg. 52
3 Murphy, Virgina Reed. *Across the Plains in the Donner Party*, 1996 pg. 52
4 Murphy, Virgina Reed. *Across the Plains in the Donner Party*, 1996 pg. 54
5 Murphy, Virgina Reed. *Across the Plains in the Donner Party*, 1996 pg. 55

PHOTO CREDITS

ACKNOWLEDGMENTS

A huge thanks to our wives and families—**Maria Baccigaluppi, Lynn & Violet Mayugba**—and our parents.

Patty West for getting the ball rolling and especially **Alan Rapp** for keeping it rolling. Thanks to everyone who ever contributed to *Heckler* and thanks to all of our office staff over the years: **Allison, Kate, Tommy, Brian, Jeaneane, Allegra, Carla, Aaron, Monica, Mitch, Big Chuck, Melanie,** and **Isac,** and especially **Lee Madison** and **Faye Moss** for being on their game while we worked on this book.

A big thanks to **Peggy, Brian,** and **Larry,** and everyone at TransWorld.

Thanks to all of our interns over the years: **Chad Lyon, Kent Snow, Alan Galbraith, Tracy Lee, Patrick Speckman, Kevin Burns, Brad Oates, Susie Granucci, Seth Forester, Darin Keatley, Heather Graham, Jen Vogelman, Lisa Ryan, Jeff Kriege, Lisa Gunter, Justin Finsley, Hiram Chu, Anne Ichikawa, Sean Schroeder, Rodrigo Gomez & Michael Heintz, Kevin Shelton, Steve Kline, Miles Smythe, Mike Rafter, Jeff Landi, Dawn Peiper, Donald Bell, Phong Ung, Marco Montesclaros, David Fung, Lindsay Guenther, Jean Phillippe Audin, Aline Sogorb, Jackson Lynn, Emmery Lee, Nelson Wong, Josh Simpson, Andrew Trinidad, Dawn Angelica, Elaine Fok, Melissa Tafoya, Leslie Payne, Steve Huebner, Ed Rayner, Leslie Payne, Jesse Bennett, Kyle Van Auker, Carrieanne Kowalczyk, Jessie Cohen, Jocelyn Dunn, Chris Sprouls, Don Clark, Brandy Faucette, Amy Johnson, Akemi Hong, David Fung, Jen Rofe, Ian Williams, Kisha Guyton, Jula Pereira, Katie Lind, Loni James, Ben Croft, Jacquelyn Walter, Zarpana Kabir, Lush Perera, Dustin Klein,** and **Maria Anderiasian.**

Special thanks to **Hal Hammond, Frank Washington, Steve Orlando,** and **Rudy VanderLans.**

And finally, thanks to all our readers—you're the ones we do this for.

PRIMARY CONTRIBUTORS:

CYNTHIA CONNOLLY is a photographer who published *Banned in DC*, a book on the D.C. punk scene in the early '80s. She also Letterpressed artwork that opens each chapter of this book. She can be reached at Cynthia@dischord.com.

DAVID CARSON is a surfer and a graphic designer. One of his first design jobs in 1983 was *TransWorld Skateboarding* magazine. Since then he's gone on to design *Raygun* magazine and ad campaigns for Nike.

AARON SEDWAY is a Senior Photographer at *Snowboarder* magazine.

BUD FAWCETT was a photographer for the world's first snowboarding magazine, *International Snowboard Magazine*. His photos have been published in *Snowboarder, TransWorld Snowboarding*, and countless foreign magazines. He now lives in Switzerland with his wife Elaine and daughter Lila and works for Palmer Snowboards. He can be reached at info@PalmerUSA.com.

GLEN E. FRIEDMAN is a self-taught photographer who has been shooting photos since the 1970s. Aside from doing gallery shows worldwide, he has self-published three coffee table books. *Fuck You Heroes, Fuck You Too*, and *The Idealist* were published under his company Burning Flags Press. His work can be found at www.burningflags.com.

MIKE BLANCHARD shot for *Thrasher* in the '80s.

RUBEN SANCHEZ is a contributing photographer for *Snowboarder* and *TransWorld Snowboarding*. He has been shooting photos for over a decade and self-published his work in a coffee table book called *Through The Rings*. www.throughtherings.com

MATT "HECKLER" KENNEDY was a co-founder of *Heckler* and named the magazine. He has been snowboarding for nearly two decades and shooting photos for over half that time. He resides in Sacramento with his wife Nicole and son Max.

CHRIS ORTIZ is a Senior Photographer at *TransWorld Skateboarding* magazine and is an integral creative force for *411 Video Magazine*.

BOB CONRAD played drums in Zoinks! and writes for *Punk Planet* magazine.

JAMIE MOSBERG has been shooting photos for over a decade for *Snowboarder, TransWorld Skateboarding* and *Snowboarding*, and others. He is also a filmmaker. He has made such classics as the Birdhouse skateboarding film *The End* and the Billabong surf movie *Pickled*, under his company High Voltage Productions.

IAN RUHTER is a pro snowboarder turned pro photographer.

DAWN KISH was a co-founder of *W.I.G.* magazine.

QUINN SHIELDS is a senior photographer for *Snowboarder* magazine.

JIMMY CLARKE was an early contributor to *Heckler*. He is a senior photographer for *Snowboarder* magazine.

ISAC WALTER sold advertising for *Heckler* magazine.

JOEY WASHBURN worked at The Wave snow/skate shop.

MIKE CHANTRY was a snowboarding pioneer and built the world's first snowboard halfpipe in Tahoe City, California.

RICK KOSICK is a photographer for *Big Brother* skateboarding magazine.

BRYCE KANIGHTS was a professional skateboarder in the '80s for Schmitt Stix and went on to be the photo editor for *Thrasher* skateboard magazine for 13 years. He was the team manager at Switch snowboard bindings and freelances for *Heckler, Big Brother*, and various other publications and web sites.

ROMAN DE SALVO is an artist whose work was published in *Fun Follows Function*, a book about him.

I.J. VALENZUELA was a sponsored snowboarder who appeared in the pages of the early *Heckler*. He became one of our best contributors. He is a staff photographer for Santa Cruz Snowboards.

DON BOSTICK opened Skateboards Etc. skateshop in 1976. Since then he's worked as Donner Ski Ranch's Marketing head and currently runs World Cup Skateboarding with his wife, Danielle.

RON CAMERON is a graphic designer and skateboarder. He created the graphic identity for Blockhead Skateboards and has also worked for ACME and G & S Skateboards.

STEVE ALBINI is a recording engineer who has recorded Nirvana, The Pixies, PJ Harvey, and thousands of other bands.

SILJA J. A. TALVI, SCOTT TORGUSON, AMANDA MARSALIS, JEFF GROS, ERIC STENMAN and **ANGIE SILVY** are all steady contributors to *Heckler*.

ARLIE JOHN CARSTENS plays in a band called Juno and has contributed to *Heckler* since the early days.

GENE SUNG and **DONALD BELL** were two of *Heckler*'s best interns.

JUSTIN HOSTYNEK is a Senior Photographer at *Snowboarder* magazine and a filmmaker.

JAKE BURTON CARPENTER founded the largest (and still independent) snowboard company in the world, Burton Snowboards.

DAVE SYPNIEWSKI was a professional snowboarder in the glory days. He then went on to be the editor of *TransWorld Snowboarding*, the world's largest snowboard magazine. He now works with the Burton team.

BOB KLEIN has been snowboarding for over two decades and was one of the first snowboarders in the Lake Tahoe region. He is an agent to athletes such as Shaun Palmer and Terry Kidwell and also works for Palmer Snowboards.

ADDITIONAL HELP

Sharon Harrison – additional copy editing
Dustin Klein & John Bateman – photo interns
The Electric Page – additional scanning (pages 171, 191, 213)
Rebecca Zellmer – additional editing
Brian Shevlin – design assistance
Allison Johnson – photoshop assistance

For more information on the individuals profiled in this book and many more who we would have liked to include but couldn't due to space limitations, visit our web site: **WWW.HECKLER.COM**

"If you pursue any one thing, like skateboarding, in this world and you really get into it, you're going to find the universe there. You find that in religious thinking, and you'll find that in philosophical thinking, and it's true. Whatever you pursue, if you really begin to pursue it thoroughly, and you really get into many, many aspects of it instead of dealing with one simple thing, it flowers out and blooms and begins to get into areas you never would have imagined were possible to get into."

—Steve Reich, composer and one of the founders of minimalism